Democracy at Work

A VOLUME IN THE SERIES

Cornell Studies in Political Economy
EDITED BY PETER J. KATZENSTEIN

A full list of titles in the series appears at the end of the book.

Democracy at Work

CHANGING WORLD MARKETS AND
THE FUTURE OF LABOR UNIONS

Lowell Turner

Cornell University Press

ITHACA AND LONDON

THIS BOOK HAS BEEN PUBLISHED WITH THE
AID OF A GRANT FROM THE HULL MEMORIAL
PUBLICATION FUND OF CORNELL UNIVERSITY.

First published 1991 by Cornell University Press.

International Standard Book Number 0-8014-2627-8
Library of Congress Catalog Card Number 91-55049
Printed in the United States of America
*Librarians: Library of Congress cataloging information
appears on the last page of the book.*

⊗ The paper in this book meets the minimum requirements
of the American National Standard for Information Sciences—
Permanence of Paper for Printed Library Materials, ANSI Z39.48-1984.

For Kate

Contents

Preface

*T*his book examines the comparative political economy of advanced industrial societies, with a focus on comparative industrial relations, an increasingly important area of concern in the contemporary period of intensified world market competition and industrial restructuring. As governments seek simultaneously to facilitate adjustment and stimulate growth, and as firms pursue production and work reorganization including rapid technological change, they pay increasing attention to the apparent competitive advantage afforded by industrial relations systems in countries such as Germany and Japan. In other countries, however, such as the United States, Britain, France, and Italy, processes of adjustment have given rise to new instability in industrial relations, major challenges to union influence, and decline of unions. My main concerns are to cast light on contrasting cross-national outcomes for industrial adjustment, for industrial relations, and above all for the changing role and position of contemporary unions.

Unions in the modern world present a paradox. On one hand, we have heard the growing demands for free trade unions in Poland, South Korea, and other countries that are less economically developed and where free unions have not been allowed; on the other hand, we hear of widespread union decline among the advanced industrial countries, where free unions have played substantial roles in industrialization and political democracy. These two contradictory trends were brought together dramatically in the fall of 1989, when Lech Walesa appeared on TV screens in the United States in prime-time commercials for the AFL-CIO, thanking the American people for supporting Solidarity and urging workers in the United States to join and support their own free trade unions.

I wonder whether Walesa is fighting a winning battle at home but supporting a lost cause abroad? Are unions important and appropriate in early stages of industrial development but increasingly inappropriate and counterproductive later on so that in advanced societies today, as some have suggested, they are a spent force?

This question has motivated my research. It is a question with considerable economic, social, and political implications, ranging from the prospects for successful industrial adjustment, to the prospects for industrial democracy, to the possibilities for domestic political coalitions and the fate of labor-linked political parties, as well as to the future of social legislation for which labor has often played an important advocacy role. The empirical answer, demonstrated through comparative analysis, is that unions are not necessarily a spent force in industrial societies; there is a wide diversity of outcomes for workers' interest representation. Although the influence of unions declined seriously after 1980 in Britain, France, Italy, and the United States, it did not in other countries such as West Germany and Sweden. And in Japan, where unions are weak, they nonetheless play a critical and stable role, as enterprise unions, at the heart of Japanese industry.

The central purpose of this book is to examine and explain these contrasting contemporary outcomes. To get at the differences, I have focused on the politics of new work organization at the firm and plant levels. Although work reorganization is not the only important issue managers and unionists face, it is an increasingly important locus of negotiation that provides a useful lens through which to view the contemporary fate and prospects for unions and for established patterns of industrial relations. Because the extensive reorganization of work challenges established office and shop-floor orders, new relationships are carved out among management, work force, and union; the ways unions and industrial relations systems adapt to and shape the new circumstances says a great deal about the prospects for the stability of industrial relations and union influence. And I contend that a stable industrial relations settlement is a prerequisite for sustained industrial adjustment and competitiveness in the modern world economy.

A buzzword in contemporary discussions of new work organization is "teamwork." Although the concept means different things to different people, the shift toward team or group forms of work organization represents, for better or worse, a potentially major change in the nature of work, the employment relationship, and the politics of the workplace.

Thus, in the largest empirical portions of this book, chapters on the U.S. and West German auto industries, I have emphasized the shift toward teams or "group work" (as the Germans call it). Although there are problems and dangers inherent both in the concept and in the processes of transition, I think that current moves toward enhanced responsibility for groups of workers offer the possibility of an opening up of the work-place, of expanded voice for the work force, and even of a partial resolution of the tension between a democratic society and an all-too-often author-itarian workplace. Union-promoted group work concepts in Germany, discussed in Chapter 2, offer particularly appealing prospects in this regard.

It is humbling these days to write about West Germany, not only because West Germany as a political entity has ceased to exist, but because the opening up of the East and the rapid unification of Germany cast new uncertainty on future institutional and political configurations. For aca-demic, journalistic, political, and everyday observers alike, events move so fast that Monday's concepts often end up in the wastebasket by Friday. Although highly successful West German institutions are spreading to the East to dominate a unified Germany, political balances within the insti-tutions along with ways of functioning in the new environment have become newly contingent. This is certainly true for industrial relations, as (West) German firms and unions confront a new and differently so-cialized work force in the East. How these processes play themselves out in labor-management relations and the politics of work reorganization in a unified Germany will be exciting and probably unpredictable for both observers and participants. In the portion of this book that considers West Germany, I have charted aspects of the politics of new work organization up to 1989, just before the tumbling of the Berlin Wall. Although the institutions and processes portrayed here will most likely provide the basis for continuing negotiations in a unified Germany, the future has suddenly become much more uncertain.

For all the countries and industries considered, this is a study of estab-lished "core" work forces. I focus on a declining segment of the overall work force and neglect two other groups that are growing in size and importance: "peripheral" workers (part time, temporary, unskilled, largely nonunion, and to a significant extent composed of women and members of national minorities) and mobile, highly skilled workers, who use their skills as leverage to move across workplaces and firms. While industrial relations practitioners from labor and management grapple with organizational problems posed by the growth of these two groups, core work forces remain critical both for the stable production of goods and services and for the future of industrial relations. Unions will no doubt need to retain a strong base here at the core if they hope to maintain broader influence and reverse declining fortunes; and organizational innovations among established unionized work forces could possibly lay the groundwork for union influence to expand in new areas.

Although I have interviewed managers both extensively and intensively as part of my research, the emphasis of the analysis is decidedly on the fate and prospects of contemporary unions. My hope, however, is that the book will find a broader audience beyond those primarily interested in unions. Even at their weakest, unions remain important actors in the political economies of industrialized societies; and, as I have suggested, the prospects for successful industrial adjustment may in important ways hinge on a stable industrial relations settlement that incorporates unions.

The emphasis on unions reflects both my background and my own bias. Although I grew up in an academic family, the war in Vietnam and the activism of the 1960s took me away from a normal professional career path. I held several jobs while participating in various antiwar and countercultural projects until the war ended in 1975. In need of steady employment, I then went to work for the U.S. Postal Service. As a letter carrier and parcel post driver in San Francisco, I became active in the union and served for several years as shop steward, chief steward, and branch editor for the National Association of Letter Carriers Branch 214. Though I thrived on union work, I often felt that both labor and management were trapped in a system of relations, partly adversarial, partly cooperative, that in many ways was counterproductive. By the early 1980s, I had developed an interest in stepping back from the day-to-day conflict and negotiation to gain perspective on the problems facing labor in the United States. In 1983, I enrolled for a year of night classes in labor studies at San Francisco State University, and in 1984, I left the union and the Postal Service for a fellowship at the University of California at Berkeley as a graduate student in political science.

The opportunity to combine the resources and insights of academia with the practical knowledge from my own experience was exhilarating. I soon discovered that the study of comparative political economy and industrial relations afforded a useful window through which to look at the questions that interested me and to gain perspective on the problems facing labor in the United States. The idea for this book first took shape during the years I was fortunate enough to spend as a graduate student studying and pondering these questions.

Miriam Golden, in the preface to her 1988 book *Labor Divided*, mentions the often unacknowledged quality of empathy as a research method for fieldwork in studies such as this one. I have also had the opportunity to try out this approach, thanks to the many practitioners of industrial relations in the United States and West Germany who opened their doors to me for intensive interviews and plant visits and who generously shared documents and data with me. Most of these people will go unnamed, for reasons of organizational politics and confidentiality; but I was consistently amazed by the willingness of overworked individuals to give an hour or two (and sometimes more) of their time to tell me their stories and answer my questions. Without the generosity of these many unionists and managers, this book would have been impossible.

I owe a special debt to friends and contacts in the U.S. labor movement. In cross-national comparison, labor in the United States today is in an unfortunate overall state. My purpose here is neither to dwell on this obvious reality nor to prove it, but to explain it, and to point toward the conditions for union success. There are, it turns out, potential remedies for unionism that are compatible with successful industrial restructuring and renewed competitive strength. If this book makes a small contribution toward uncovering such remedies, it does so thanks to the many dedicated union representatives who have educated and inspired me and who have aided my research along the way.

For reading and commenting on earlier versions or sections, for pointing out fruitful directions of inquiry, and for opening valuable doors for me, I extend my sincere thanks to Roy Adams, Paul Adler, Chris Allen, Barbara Baran, Michael Borrus, Clair Brown, Gloria Busman, Haldor Byrkjeflot, Stephen Cohen, Tony Daley, Owen Darbishire, Don Ephlin, Elizabeth Farnsworth, Sheldon Friedman, John Gerring, Jana Gold, Michael Gorges, Andy Gould, Walter Graze, Mark Hardesty, Chris Howell, Candace Howes, Rick Hurd, Harry Katz, Peter Katzenstein, Martin Kenney, Richard Locke, Dan Luria, Andy Markovits, Ruth Milkman, Larry Mishel, Leslie Nay, Hikari Nohara, Mike Parker, Jonas Pontusson, Dennis Quinn, Greg Saltzman, Annalee Saxenian, Lee Schore, Tim Scully, Hiro Shibata, Jim Shoch, Steve Silvia, Jane Slaughter, Sven Steinmo, Jay Stowsky, George Strauss, Kim Su-Jin, Gudrun Trautwein-Kalms, Lloyd Ulman, Peter Unterweger, Daniel Verdier, Paula Voos, and John Windmuller. Michael Belzer provided excellent research assistance in the final stages of revision. Invaluable technical and personal assistance in the United States was provided by Gordon Adams, Anne Bishop, Ellen Borrowman, Lynn Buckman, Ann Mine, Brad Palmquist, Ben Schneider, Genie Scott, and Jay Tharpe.

I spent a year in West Germany, during 1988–89, gathering data, conducting interviews, and visiting auto plants and telecommunications facilities. I was tremendously impressed by the openness, generosity, and goodwill of German unionists and works councillors, who invited me in, endured my bumbling German, patiently repeated their answers when I did not understand, and sent me along to further contacts. Part of the beauty of comparative work is that in West Germany I had something to offer; in the auto industry, for example, people were eager to hear of NUMMI and other developments in the U.S. auto industry. I was invited repeatedly to speak to works councils or shop stewards' meetings; I thank these work force representatives for their curiosity about the world beyond their own borders, which in turn gave me the opportunity to stay a while and ask my questions. Although I mention few names (again for organizational reasons), I owe special thanks to my friends and sources at the IG Metall and the Deutsche Postgewerkschaft (DPG), and in particular Hans-Jürgen Uhl and colleagues at the VW General Works Council, Wilfred Kuckelkorn, Jürgen Aigner and colleagues at the Ford-Werke General Works Council, Wilhelm Gröber and colleagues at the IG Metall office in Bochum, Siegfried Roth, Horst Neumann, and Karl Pitz at the IG Metall headquarters in Frankfurt, Albert Stegmüller at the DPG headquarters (also in Frankfurt), and Alfred Dahmen and colleagues of the Cologne area Bundespost personnel council.

The numerous researchers who helped me with my work in West Germany include Jens Alber, Norbert Altmann, Peter Auer, Eva Brumlop, Christoph Deutschmann, Egon Endres, Klaus Franz, Jürgen Hausler, Eckhardt Hildebrandt, Hans-Willy Hohn, Christoph Köhler, Lothar Krempel, Renate Mayntz, Fritz Scharpf, Ronald Schettkat, Brigitte Schenkluhn, Volker Schneider, Rainer Schultz-Wild, Arndt Sorge, Douglas Webber, Raymond Werle, and Paul Windolf.

On the technical side, Gisela Bastelberger, Ernst Braun, Jürgen Lautwein, Pia Schaefer, and Susanne Schwartz provided me with useful and consistent assistance. Cynthia Lehmann advised me on everything from German customs and proper communication channels to the use of a word processor and available resources—without her I would have been lost. Marie Haltod-Hilgers helped also in numerous ways.

I could not begin to thank the many Germans who made it possible for my family and me not only to survive a year in Germany but to thrive. In particular, Jürgen and Susan Häusler helped with both work- and family-related concerns; and Josef and Edith Nagelschmidt welcomed us into a comfortable apartment in their home and filled as well the role of substitute grandparents for our children.

Four institutions offered indispensable and extensive resources as well as places of work: the Berkeley Roundtable on the International Economy

(BRIE), at the University of California at Berkeley; the Institute of Industrial Relations, also at Berkeley; the Max-Planck-Institut für Gesellschaftsforschung in Cologne, which subsidized my stay in Germany; and, during the final stages of revision, the School of Industrial and Labor Relations at Cornell University. Funding for this study was provided by the Social Science Research Council in conjunction with the American Council of Learned Societies, BRIE, the Max-Planck-Institut, the Economic Policy Institute, the Carnegie Forum on Education and the Economy, and the University of California at Berkeley.

I also owe special thanks to several people: Mina Silberberg, whose friendship and support helped me through this project; John Elder, whose example inspired me to move to academia; Helen Wickes, who frequently discussed with me the rigors of research, writing, and manuscript preparation; Manfred Muster, who opened doors for me in auto plants all over Germany and gave me a valuable education in both the politics of work reorganization and the relationship between union and works council; Ulrich Jürgens, who invited me to the Wissenschaftszentrum in Berlin and shared numerous insights and contacts; Kathy Thelen, who commented extensively on early proto-chapters and advised on doing research in Germany; and Wolfgang Streeck, who sent me numerous working papers and to whom I owe a substantial intellectual debt.

John Zysman pushed me at key moments to reconsider concepts and rewrite chapters; he also inspired me with original and persuasive insights into the meaning of changing world markets and contrasting domestic responses. Harold Wilensky provided my basic education on concepts of democratic corporatism as well as labor politics and gave extensive feedback ranging from the general argument to specific sentence construction. Michael Reich encouraged the direction of my research, discussed plant and industry stories with me, and on several occasions saved me from embarrassment by pointing out critical problems in my work. The late Gregory Luebbert taught me a great deal of what I know about comparative methodology and urged me to pursue an ambitious comparative study. Peter Swenson entered into the argument and proposed revisions that have strengthened the analysis considerably. Jonathan Zeitlin also gave the manuscript a close reading and suggested numerous useful revisions, especially for the background country cases in Chapter 5.

At Cornell University Press, Roger Haydon gave this project strong support and has been a pleasure to work with as well; the copyediting and production work of Trudie Calvert and Carol Betsch has significantly improved the clarity of the text.

I also thank my parents, Ralph and Christine Turner, who worked extremely hard to give me a head start in life and who, years later, when I arrived reincarnated as a late-starting scholar, gave me their consistent encouragement and support.

I owe a great debt to my wonderful children, Eric and Jennifer Turner, who in the course of this project kept me sane and playful and prevented me either from succumbing to my own native workaholism or from taking myself too seriously.

Finally, I thank my wife, Kathleen Eveland Turner, who, as she puts it, married a letter carrier and ended up with a college professor. We have shared fifteen roller-coaster years, during which she has provided extraordinary support and tolerance for my aberrant behavior, including giving up lifetime employment security to begin graduate school at the age of thirty-seven. Although she has always had her own work life, she gave it up for a year to accompany me to Germany (''why not comparative restaurants in the south of France?'' she still asks) and serve as a somewhat isolated hausfrau in a foreign land, for which she promises she will one day get even. This work is dedicated to her.

LOWELL TURNER

Ithaca, New York

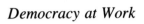

Democracy at Work

The Politics of Work Reorganization: Pervasive Union Decline?

*T*hese are hard times for unions. There is currently a broad cross-national trend toward the decentralization of bargaining in industrial relations, which challenges established bases of union influence everywhere. The combined effects of intensified world market competition, new microelectronic technologies, managerial strategies to reorganize production, and the success and influence of Japanese production models are exerting great pressure on systems of industrial relations in Western Europe and North America; in many societies, unions are among the major losers in political realignments and industrial adjustment. Alongside wide-ranging discussions of competitiveness and the causes and consequences of trade and other economic problems, heated debate is heard in both public and academic arenas within every industrial society concerning the contemporary position of major interest groups, including (often most prominently) organized labor.

This book addresses critical questions arising from these debates. Why have Western industrial relations systems experienced widespread destabilization since the late 1970s? What accounts for the prolonged decline of unions in the turbulent markets and changed political circumstances of the past decade? Are contemporary unions, once critical bastions in the historical development of political and industrial democracy, now a spent force, increasingly irrelevant in highly differentiated modern societies (playing important roles only in countries in earlier stages of development such as Poland and South Korea)? If not, what constructive role can unions play in a period of market turbulence and rapid, continuous industrial adjustment? What, if any, conditions are necessary for contemporary unions to succeed in advanced industrial democracies?

The argument advanced here recognizes both pervasive contemporary changes in industrial relations and contrasting outcomes in different countries. The starting point is recognition that dramatically changing world markets have transformed the tasks facing companies and unions. Intensified market competition, new technologies, and path-breaking Japanese production models have created managerial imperatives to reorganize production and work, confronting unions with unexpected challenges. Labor leaders schooled in the politics of wage negotiation and contract enforcement suddenly find themselves confronted with the politics of work reorganization: conflicts and negotiations that precede or accompany managerial attempts to reorganize work. Since the late 1970s, these market-driven changes have destabilized systems of industrial relations and in many cases undermined the traditional bases of union influence, setting the stage for further union decline. The effects of the new market-driven imperatives, however, vary substantially from country to country, depending on the institutions of industrial relations in place. For explaining national variations in the stability and extent of workers' interest representation, two variables are critical: integration into processes of managerial decision making versus adversarial, arm's-length unionism; and the presence or absence of laws or corporatist bargaining arrangements that encourage and regulate firm-level union participation from outside the firm. Where union integration and appropriate laws or corporatist bargaining arrangements prevail, unions have adapted well to challenges posed by the reorganization of work. Where the opposite institutional attributes prevail, unions have declined substantially in influence since the late 1970s. In the United States at least, this argument runs counter to received industrial relations and union wisdom, which favors arm's-length unionism (viewing integration as the path to co-optation and weakness), a decentralized labor movement (in which competitive organizing spurs the expansion of union influence), and a minimum of government intrusion into collective bargaining and plant-level labor-management relations.

In short, I emphasize the general driving force of world market changes and new technologies and the particular national institutions that represent workers' interests, shape domestic response, and account for contrasting national outcomes. This perspective differs from most analyses of the fate of unions and industrial relations systems, both traditional and contemporary.

The dominant quest in the recent literature is to account for the decline of unions. The studies fall into two broad groupings: general explanations for widespread cross-national decline that invoke pervasive social, economic, or political forces;[1] and country-specific explanations that emphasize the behavior of the major national actors in industrial relations—firms, unions, and governments. The difficulty with the first group is that union decline is *not* pervasive; the second category is flawed because country-specific analyses fail to explain why union decline and destabilization in industrial relations are occurring in many advanced industrial societies, which indicates that more general processes are at work. Although both sets of explanations may be theoretically weak, they can provide useful insights toward developing a theoretical argument that accounts for differentiated outcomes.

Several recent comparative analyses grapple with similar questions. Michael Wallerstein (1989) offers a far-reaching explanation for contrasting cross-national levels of union density (the key variables are size of the labor market and cumulative left-party participation in government); but his data end in 1979 and in any case could not account for the dynamic changes under way since then. Other analyses, such as those developed by Alan Altshuler et al. (1984), Harry Katz and Charles F. Sabel (1985), and Richard B. Freeman (1989), offer comparative, institutional perspectives that fall into the same arena with this one, although differing in important details; in Chapter 3 and in the Conclusion, I examine these arguments in relation to my own and to the evidence considered.

The argument developed here builds on two sets of literature. First is the recent innovative work in international and comparative political economy. Researchers have identified dynamic changes in the international political economy and effects on domestic outcomes such as the organization of production (Piore and Sabel 1984; Cohen and Zysman 1987; Gilpin 1987; the French "regulation" school).[2] Comparative political economists with a particular interest in unions have tied this work to analyses of changing industrial relations and the prospects for union influence (Lange, Ross, and Vannicelli 1982; Gourevitch et al. 1984; Streeck 1984a; Sorge and Streeck 1988). Related studies over the past fifteen years

---

[1] See Ross and Fishman 1989 for a brief but useful survey of the general arguments; and Goldfield 1987, pp. 94–104, for a clear presentation of how some of these arguments are applied to the U.S. case.

[2] Included in or closely related to this literature is the growing body of work that identifies a broad shift from Fordism to new models of "post-Fordist" production organization. Since the contours of this shift are contingent and remain unclear, I will speak here of rapid production and work reorganization but will avoid debatable characterizations such as "flexible specialization," "flexible automation," "neo-Fordism," and "lean production."

on "democratic corporatism" have revealed persistent institutional differences in national political economies and their profound consequences (Schmitter 1974, 1981; Wilensky 1976, 1983; Schmitter and Lehmbruch 1979; Berger 1981; Goldthorpe 1984a; Katzenstein 1985). Second, the traditional industrial relations systems model, though theoretically weak, offers a useful conceptual map, pointing to the critical variables that shape industrial relations outcomes: markets, technologies, and power relations in society (Dunlop 1958). This model becomes more useful as modified and expanded by Thomas A. Kochan, Harry Katz, and Robert B. McKersie (1986) to become dynamic and to broaden the conceptual map to include the behavior of strategic actors. In the study of comparative industrial relations, my work builds in part on an earlier tradition that emphasizes the importance of national institutions (Commons 1934; Kassalow 1969).[3]

Although the main focus here is on the place of unions in rapidly changing contemporary circumstances, the book is also a study of both labor and management, with implications for both (and much of the primary research consists of intensive interviews with managers as well as union representatives). Industrial adjustment, perhaps the critical economic task of our time in advanced industrial societies, appears to require a stable industrial relations settlement, whether this includes strong or weak, integrated or excluded unions. As a study of industrial relations in transition, this analysis aims to offer a lens through which to assess the prospects of industrial adjustment and the effectiveness of managerial initiatives to reorganize work as well as the preconditions of union success.

Most important, this is also a broader political study, analyzing the relative success or failure of contrasting modes of interest representation. The arbitrary distinction between industrial relations on one hand and the role of labor and business in politics on the other prevents us, I think, from looking clearly at either. Shop-floor battles spill over into national politics, and the policies pursued by dominant political coalitions shape labor-management relations at the firm and plant levels. The effects of market forces and institutional arrangements at work in the contemporary politics of work reorganization have profound implications for broader

---

[3] It is clear, however, from the contemporary literature in international and comparative political economy that the world has changed tremendously in the past two decades. Traditional institutional perspectives appear narrow and static in the current context. The perspective offered here is thus a "new institutionalist" one (see Reshef and Murray 1988; Steinmo 1989), emphasizing both dynamic changes in the world economy and in national patterns of industrial relations and the continuing importance of particular institutions. This new institutionalism, however, should not be confused with the similarly named contemporary variant of neoclassical economics (see critique by Dugger 1990).

interest group representation, for national politics, for the success of industrial adjustment, and for the prospects of economic and political democracy.

From Harmony to Disarray: Dynamic Postwar Industrial Relations

In the preceding section, I asked what, if any, conditions are necessary for contemporary unions to succeed. A decade ago, different questions were being asked. Unions almost everywhere in Western Europe and North America were viewed as major actors in the political economy, benefactors of a long and respectable development paralleling the history of industrialization; if questions were raised, they more likely pointed to excessive union power. In the aftermath of World War II, unions cashed in on their antifascist and anticonservative traditions, grew rapidly, and helped labor-friendly governments hold or regain power in many Western democracies. If the Cold War undercut labor's plans for socialism and in many cases returned conservative governments to power in the 1950s, unions nonetheless dug in at the core of industrial structures and grew in numbers and influence in the years of rapid postwar economic growth. Theorists of industrial relations pointed to the integrative effects of (tamed) unions in industrial society and predicted harmonious economic development based on balancing interest group representation and stable labor-management relations (Dahrendorf 1959; Kerr et al. 1960; Slichter, Healy, and Livernash 1960; Ross and Hartman 1960).

But just as the ink dried on optimistic predictions of stability, labor flexed its muscles in new and unpredictable ways. In some countries, such as West Germany, Great Britain, and the United States, labor-linked political parties returned to power, expanded the welfare state, and grappled with labor's rising expectations in periods of inflation and stagflation. Elsewhere labor "exploded," rocking the country from end to end in France in 1968 before spending itself (and still contributing to "the long march of the French Left"; Johnson 1982); transforming an ineffective, fragmented labor movement in Italy in 1969 into an entrenched power within the factories (Salvati 1981). Wildcat strikes plagued industry everywhere from 1969 to 1973, even in such famously pacific countries with low strike rates as Sweden and West Germany.

Criticizing the earlier theorists of harmony and integration, scholars in the 1970s wrote volumes on the "resurgence of class conflict" in Western Europe and North America (Aronowitz 1973; Crouch and Pizzorno 1978).

Industrialists in Italy, Britain, and elsewhere denounced labor's "excessive" factory and political power. At the same time, a new body of academic literature on "corporatism" emerged, to question liberal/pluralist assumptions and point to the entrenched power of organized labor as well as business at the core of many Western political economies (Schmitter 1974; Wilensky 1976; Schmitter and Lehmbruch 1979).

The corporatist literature itself was often critical of the rigidity of hierarchical interest group structures and peak bargaining among elites far from labor's rank and file and capital's small and medium-sized business sectors (Schmitter 1981, 1982). Although democratic corporatism in its various definitional incarnations was generally associated with good past economic performance (Schmidt 1982; Cameron 1984), powerful interest groups such as labor were often viewed as internally undemocratic and too unwieldy for the tasks of industrial adjustment in newly competitive world markets. By the mid–1980s, "Eurosclerosis" had become a catchword for industrial stagnation; Western Europe's social democracies, in this view, were too burdened by welfare state spending and interest group demands (especially from labor, the main promoter of both rising wages and state welfare spending) to shift resources rapidly toward research and development, new investment, and the reorganization of production, as world markets required (Olson 1982; Scott 1985).

President Ronald Reagan and Prime Minister Margaret Thatcher led a resurgence of conservative economic policy that included cutbacks in the welfare state as well as direct and indirect challenges to the power and influence of organized labor. This time labor proved vulnerable. Instead of conflict, "explosions," growing strength, and the high-level bargaining of the previous two decades, unions braced themselves defensively. In several countries, such as Italy, Britain, and the United States, the decline of unions turned into a rout. Even after the deep recession of 1980–82 passed and economic growth was reestablished, the decline of union influence continued in most societies and the terms of growth included a weaker role for organized labor in both the political arena and industrial relations. And even where labor appeared strongest and where union membership levels did not decline, serious challenges to labor's position were evident: in Sweden, centralized collective bargaining broke down and scholars wrote of the demise of the Swedish model; in West Germany, labor faced a new conservative regime committed to rolling back labor's conflict potential, and academicians developed their own theories of domestic union decline or the breakdown of "neocorporatism" (Streeck 1984b; Hoffman 1988; Hohn 1988). Studies of unions *and* crisis (Lange, Ross, and Vannicelli 1982; Gourevitch et al. 1984) were replaced by studies of unions *in* crisis (Marshall 1987; Hohn 1988; Müller-Jentsch 1988a).

Why do unions now appear to face long-term secular decline in many industrial societies? Most of the answers offered fall into two broad groupings: explanations that emphasize general economic, industrial, and social change; and country-specific explanations, most often focusing on the behavior of managers and union leaders themselves or emphasizing changing domestic political relations and coalitions.

In the simplest version of the general explanations, a shift in the locus of employment from manufacturing to services has undercut the traditional industrial bases of union strength (Freeman and Medoff 1984, pp. 221–28). A related view has it that recent generations of young workers (many of them in service sectors) are more oriented toward individual than collective concerns; in this view, unions are in part victims of their own success, and even the well-educated children of unionists perceive less of a need for unions today. Another argument emphasizes the rise of the new social movements: activist students and younger workers in industrial societies are more interested in peace, the environment, and gender and racial equality than they are in unions and traditional labor concerns, and the new social movements have everywhere cut into both the political influence of unions (by disrupting old coalitions) and the ability to organize on the shop floor (Dalton et al. 1984; Inglehart 1984; Heckscher 1988; Halfmann 1989).

Important contributions to an understanding of broad, general trends have come from Michael J. Piore and Charles F. Sabel (1984) in the United States and Horst Kern and Michael Schumann (1984) in West Germany. In these analyses, changes in world markets and new technologies are driving the reorganization of production and the introduction of "new production concepts," which increasingly decentralize labor-management negotiations and undermine traditional national bases of union strength. In the United States, Piore and Sabel view "job-control unionism" as increasingly inappropriate, while Kern and Schumann see the decentralization of responsibility for production accompanied by a problematic shift of influence from unions to firm-identified works councils in West Germany.

In every advanced industrial society, there are contemporary theorists who advance country-specific explanations for the decline of unions. In Italy, unions overstepped their power, lost touch with the rank and file, and were vulnerable to a management counterattack in economic recession; in France, François Mitterrand and the socialists cleverly united with and drained off strength from the communists and their dominant labor federation, and the competing unions continue to fight among themselves; in Britain, unions discredited themselves under a Labour government in the 1978–79 "Winter of Discontent," and Thatcher's subsequent firm grip on political power squashed labor's strength; and even in Sweden, centralized bargaining and "wage solidarity" have proven inappropriate institutional responses to new market challenges and the demands of young workers, leading to the breakdown of traditional bargaining with a still uncertain effect on the future influence of unions.

In West Germany, a perceived decline of union influence is explained by the "dual system" (in which unions and works councils are legally distinct) and by the actions of unions themselves in transferring power to firm-oriented works councils (Hohn 1988; Hoffmann 1988). In the United States, union decline predates the contemporary period and is explained from the left as caused by offensives conducted by employers, "business unionism," and the fear on the part of entrenched union leaders of rank-and-file mobilization (Goldfield 1987; Moody 1988; Parker and Slaughter 1988); and from the right by excessive and obstructive union power (Reynolds 1984). In the two most comprehensive and influential recent studies of industrial relations in the United States, greatest weight in explaining union decline is given to the anti-union behavior and ideology of American management, with insufficient union organizing effort or adaptation to new circumstances as a secondary cause (Freeman and Medoff 1984; Kochan, Katz and McKersie 1986).[4]

At the subnational level, there have been, in addition to broad and country-specific explanations, numerous studies in recent years of the decline of specific unions; these studies, rich in empirical data, generally produce explanations rooted in changing market circumstances in particular sectors, firms' strategies (ranging from product-segment decisions to union-avoidance strategies), and the behavior and structure of specific unions. But as with country-specific explanations, we are left with specific causes for what look like very general processes in modern advanced industrial society.

There is some truth, of course, to all of these arguments, and a good deal of truth to many of them. But how do we sort through the vast patchwork of causal analysis? If broad, general causes are at work, are the country-specific accounts useful only as *description* of the workings of general economic and social forces within national contexts but invalid

---

[4] See also Goldfield 1987, both for evidence supporting this interpretation and for a thorough discussion of various explanations for the decline of unions in the United States (pp. 94–112).

in themselves as *explanation*? If country-specific arguments are valid, are the broader forces at work only a backdrop, a set of background "contextual variables"?

The obvious answer is that a full explanation for the fate of contemporary unions requires reference to both sets of factors. But it is easy to get lost in the rich tapestry. It is possible, I think, to construct a parsimonious explanation for cross-national outcomes in industrial relations, one that both acknowledges the driving force of international economic and social changes and identifies the critical domestic institutions that shape contrasting national responses and outcomes.

The Argument: Markets Matter but So Do Institutions

The starting point for an analysis of the fate of unions in the current period is recognition that workers' interest representation has faced new challenges in the 1980s. Drawing on the work of Kern and Schumann (1984), Piore and Sabel (1984), Stephen S. Cohen and John Zysman (1987), Robert Gilpin (1987), and others such as the French "regulation" school, I begin with the perspective that in the past fifteen years, world markets and economic relationships have experienced a new dynamism. Markets have changed for a number of reasons, but perhaps the single most important factor has been the rise of Japan as a world-class industrial and exporting nation. Not only have Japanese products gained rapidly rising market shares across a whole range of industries throughout the advanced industrial world, but Japanese firms have developed innovative models for organizing production that are perhaps unrivaled in their ability to bring low-cost, high-quality products to market and to change product offerings rapidly in response to market changes. In addition, the rise of the newly industrializing countries (NICs, especially South Korea, Taiwan, Hong Kong, Singapore, Mexico, and Brazil), the successful export strategies of firms in West Germany, Scandinavia, and northern Italy, and the "multinationalization" of American, European, and Japanese firms have put new pressure on world markets.

Capitalist markets, of course, are never static: firms compete and many fail, new technologies require new skills while making old skills obsolete, workers are displaced. But in the past fifteen years, as Japanese, European, and NIC-based competitors have caught up with once dominant U.S. firms, and as the pace of microelectronic technological change has escalated, world markets have become increasingly interdependent and competitive. With the Japanese leading the way, the principal characteristic of the current world economy is intensified market competition, in response to which firms everywhere have been forced to move at a pace unprecedented in the postwar period to introduce new technologies and reorganize production.

A critical part of the reorganization of production and technological change is the reorganization of work;[5] and this, for workers and their unions, is "where the rubber meets the road." Managerial strategies for reorganizing work in the recent period have presented unions with major new challenges at precisely the time when changing world markets and high unemployment in many countries have undercut the ability of unions to bargain for the steadily rising real wages that characterized most of the postwar period. To the politics of wage bargaining have been added the politics of work reorganization. Whereas in the past, unions (and their members) could be content to bargain for wages and benefits while "letting management manage," the new pace and content of work reorganization have challenged established shop-floor orders in ways that divide the work force (into the winners and losers of reorganization) and threaten established bases of union influence.[6] Developing responses to managerial reorganization strategies, to protect workers' interests and defend union institutional security, has become a major preoccupation for unions everywhere in Western Europe and North America.

Country-specific as well as comparative studies of unions in the 1980s make it clear that these broad changes in markets and the organization of production are forcing unions to adapt to similar new tasks and are driving change in industrial relations across a range of countries (Kochan 1985; Thelen 1987b; Golden and Pontusson 1991). Even where unions retain effectively centralized structures, as in Sweden and Germany, there is a

[5] Reorganization of production here refers to firms' strategies to change what is produced and how (this includes sourcing decisions, supplier networks, product and process decisions, personnel policy, and so on). Reorganization of work (changes in job design, content, or technology) is one part of the reorganization of production. Although technological change is often an important part of work reorganization, work can be extensively reorganized without changes in technology. Technological change almost always requires changes in job content; when work is reorganized without changes in technology, new work organization often lays the groundwork for technological innovation. Thus although the focus here is on reorganization of work rather than technological change per se, there is a close relationship between the two.

[6] Work reorganization in earlier periods has also upset shop-floor orders, creating winners and losers among the work force; note, for example, the 1960s "automation scare" in the United States. But whereas in the past unions generally faced incremental technological change that affected particular groups of workers (Slichter, Healy, and Livernash 1960), unions and workers today face much more extensive and rapid reorganization, as we will see in the case studies beginning in Chapter 1.

broad trend toward the decentralization of bargaining. Managerial initiatives have forced unions to scramble for negotiations on pay protection, employment security, and retraining rights as trade-offs against the new shop-floor flexibility, and often the enhanced responsibility given workers, that management seeks. Because the specifics of work reorganization take place at the plant, local bargaining assumes critical new importance. And as the torch passes to local negotiators, national unions grapple with problems of their own identity and strength (Locke 1990a).

In many, but not all, countries, these changes appear to be closely linked with problems of widespread union decline. Reorganization of work aims at higher productivity, which often means a work force reduced in size. Quality circles or problem-solving groups often accompany the reorganization of work because one managerial goal in reorganization is to increase workers' input and commitment; but such groups provide a new forum for the expression of workers' interests outside established industrial relations channels. The increased importance of plant-level bargaining has enabled managers to extract new concessions by playing one plant off against another (both domestically and internationally). And in many cases, managerial initiatives to reorganize work have been accompanied by direct challenges to union influence, as firms find it necessary to push aside old restrictive union power on the shop floor. Analysts in countries such as Italy, France, Great Britain, and the United States have linked all these processes to the decline of unions.

Given these general processes at work, country-specific analyses that emphasize, for example, managerial ideology or particular union strategies within a particular nation become less convincing, at least as full causal explanations. It stretches the imagination to believe that unions have declined in numbers and influence across a whole range of industrial societies in the past decade but for quite different reasons within each country. It makes more sense to argue that general economic changes, including intensified market competition and managerial imperatives to reorganize production, have driven widespread processes of change in industrial relations, which in many cases have included union decline.

In many cases, but not all. There have been, in fact, substantial, empirical, cross-national differences in the performance of unions since the early 1980s. Theorists of union decline in Germany and Sweden, for example, are quite wrong when their arguments are looked at from a cross-national perspective. By almost any measure—union membership levels or density, bargaining gains, institutional stability—unions have not declined in these countries. They have had to grapple with new problems, develop new strategies, and make organizational adaptations, but they have not seriously declined in influence as unions in France, Italy, Britain, and the United States have done. So the question becomes, why not? Why have unions in some countries declined precipitously in the face of new external and shop-floor circumstances, while unions in other countries have held their own and adapted?

The answer offered here, and the argument that will be tested with evidence, is that the key to an explanation for contrasting, cross-national union outcomes in the present period lies in the way interest representation is institutionalized, or more precisely, the structures that represent workers' interests.

In particular, two critical variables account for relative union success or decline and the stability of industrial relations systems in the contemporary period: first, the extent to which unions, as a broad national pattern, are integrated into processes of managerial decision making, especially concerning work reorganization; and second, the existence of laws or corporatist bargaining arrangements that regulate firm-level union participation from outside the firm.

Where unions enter the current period of work reorganization already integrated into processes of managerial decision making, as in West Germany and Japan, union influence remains stable, as do patterns of industrial relations in general.[7] This is true because agreement is required before change can be implemented, and agreement between labor and management ensures labor's stable place, even if work reorganization is far-reaching. Because labor is integrated at the level of the firm, union representatives or works councillors participate in decision making that considers both market imperatives to reorganize work and the viability of the representation of workers' interests.

But it also makes a big difference whether labor's integration into managerial decision making is backed up by law or corporatist bargaining arrangements, which include a cohesive labor movement. When this is true (as in West Germany), labor participates in firms' decision making from a base that is independent of management; unions are in a position to assess the needs of the work force and market requirements indepen-

[7] Stability in Japanese industrial relations includes a modest decline in union membership density, from 32% of the nonagricultural work force in 1979 to 28% in 1986 (Freeman 1989, p. 130). But the essential labor-management relationship (enterprise unions, management-led integration) remains unchanged. Japan fits into this analysis somewhat awkwardly because the success of Japanese production models, including teamwork and enterprise unionism, is a driving force destabilizing industrial relations systems in the other countries examined. But Japanese industrial relations are nonetheless included among the cases to be explained because Japanese unions must cope, as is true in all other advanced industrial societies, with ongoing and intense work reorganization.

dently and to bring a new perspective to the discussions and perhaps even an independent, worker-oriented vision of the shape of new work organization. Most important, statutory or corporatist regulation narrows managerial discretion concerning both work reorganization and union integration, which allows for a more stable and extensive union role. Both management and labor, at the firm and plant levels, are pushed from without toward collaboration on issues such as new ways of organizing work.

By contrast, where no such statutory or bargaining arrangements exist and the labor movement is fragmented (as in Japan), the union has little independent basis from which to develop its own information and analysis. Because statutory or corporatist regulation is not present, managerial discretion is wider; collaboration that occurs does so on management's terms (Japan, numerous plant-level cases in the United States, Britain, and Italy). Weak labor is integrated into managerial decision making in a decidedly subordinate way.

Where unions are not integrated into firms' decision making, usually because of adversarial or arm's-length labor-management traditions, worker representatives have no solid position from which to influence the shape of work reorganization (except indirectly through threats to file grievances, fail to cooperate, and strike). Consideration of the institutional interests of unions tend to be left out of the discussion in these cases, and often work reorganization aims explicitly at the reduction of union influence.

But where corporatist bargaining arrangements exist, unions can use broad political and economic influence to gain new integration into decision making at the firm level, in a period when such integration appears critical for continued union success. This is exactly what happened in Sweden beginning in the mid-1970s.

The real problems come for unions in countries where labor is not integrated into managerial decision making and there are no appropriate laws or corporatist bargaining structures. In these cases, labor has little political leverage to push for a new national pattern of engagement; integration that occurs does so on the basis of a single firm or plant, often as a result of management prodding and major union concessions, thus raising the specter of weak enterprise unionism. Where managers perceive unions to be standing in the way of work reorganization, unions have no societywide base to prevent either direct challenges to their influence or strategies to move around unions and marginalize their influence. Thus in France, Italy, Britain, and the United States, unions have declined seriously in influence in the past decade; and this is true whether they were relatively strong at the end of the 1970s (Italy and Britain) or already in decline (France and the United States).

At first glance, there is an apparent tautology in this argument, with the representation of workers' interests on both sides of the equation. Looked at more carefully, however, the tautology disappears. There are different ways in which such representation can be institutionalized; since the economic crisis years of the mid- to late 1970s, some of these ways have proven more conducive than others to the persistence of stable industrial relations and union influence. Structures are on one side of the equation, stability and influence on the other side. As noted at the beginning of this chapter, this argument runs counter to received wisdom in the United States, which held that both adversarial, arm's-length unionism and decentralized, competitive organizing were most conducive to the expansion of union influence (and this may well have been true in the early postwar period).

Linked to this argument is the fact that industrial relations systems in countries such as Germany and Japan appear highly compatible with economic and competitive success (Streeck 1987a). Although it is beyond the scope of this study to test such a linkage (because there are so many factors that contribute to market success), plant- and firm-level industrial relations that integrate unions into managerial decision making appear to contribute to the micro-foundations of economic success. The case studies will strengthen this speculation. In a sense, then, this argument includes an "intervening variable": particular structures of interest representation, in part because they contribute to favorable production outcomes, ensure stable industrial relations and union influence in the contemporary period.

The advantage of this argument is that it allows us to move from the driving economic changes at work in the world economy to work reorganization at the levels of the firm and shop floor, which is necessary to compete in today's markets, by way of the institutions of industrial relations that shape country-specific options for reorganization and determine the relative stability and influence of unions in the new era. This analysis links the fate of unions and industrial relations systems directly to world economic changes, through the prism of country-specific institutional mechanisms. From the perspective of comparative union success or decline, these linkages make sense of broad economic trends affecting all contemporary unions: the impact varies substantially depending on how interest representation is structured.

Another advantage of this argument is that, if true, it shows what unions must do to reverse widespread decline: they must abandon or overcome arm's-length traditions and get integrated into processes of managerial decision making. But it also shows the risks: where unions are not backed up by appropriate laws or corporatist bargaining, there is a clear danger that they will be subordinated to management.

Definitions and Hypotheses

A useful way to gauge relative union success as well as the stability of industrial relations is to examine cross-nationally the stability and extent of workers' interest representation. In some countries, unions alone represent workers' interests; in other countries, both unions and works councils are present. The proper subject for cross-national analysis is thus workers' interest representation rather than unions, although the latter term along with phrases such as "relative union success" will be used here, as it is elsewhere in the literature, as shorthand in cross-national discussions.

The stability and extent of workers' interest representation in an era of ongoing work reorganization can be measured along three dimensions: first, stability or change in the density of union membership in the time period examined (1982–89); second, the pay, employment, and protection of status afforded union members against the effects of technological change and work reorganization; and third, the credible promotion of an independent union perspective on the content or shape of new work organization.

The first dimension is an important quantitative measure of the relative ability of unions to hold on to rates of membership; and membership rates have a great deal to do with union influence. The second dimension reflects the reactive capacities of unions: the ability to respond to managerial initiative and effectively defend workers' interests. The third dimension reflects unions' proactive capacities: the ability to formulate and bargain for alternative worker-oriented forms of organization. This last dimension is fairly new in the history of postwar unionism, but it is a capacity that unions throughout North America and Western Europe are seeking to develop in the face of rapid technological change and work reorganization.

The stability and extent of workers' interest representation, as indicated along these three dimensions, can best be examined within particular industry sectors (which is where work reorganization takes place). The first dimension is a quantitative measure that can be taken from available data. The second and third dimensions can be assessed in part on the basis of contracts, agreements, and documents; but to a significant extent these dimensions can be fully understood only by means of case studies that demonstrate the extent *in practice* of protections afforded and alternatives promoted. Ideally, a range of representative case studies demonstrates the stability and extent of workers' interest representation at the sectoral level; sectoral outcomes can then be compared cross-nationally.

What is critical for this argument, of course, is that cross-national sectoral comparisons translate into general cross-national comparisons. It is necessary, therefore, to look at more than one sector. If it turns out that there are no general national patterns, then the argument advanced here, based on national structures of interest representation, is wrong.

As for the structures themselves, integration into managerial decision making is defined here as substantial participation on the part of unions or works councils in discussions with management regarding plans to reorganize work before actual decisions are made on the shape of new organization and the pace of implementation. Integration into managerial decision making is juxtaposed to arm's-length unionism, in which unions receive little advance information or opportunities for input; in these latter cases, "advance information" usually means after the final decision but before implementation, and the union role is to react to independent managerial decisions.

Laws that regulate union participation are products of national legislation that establishes a legal framework to encourage and regulate, from outside the firm, union integration into managerial decision making. Germany's Works Constitution Act passed in 1952 and strengthened in 1972 is an example (although the original intent of the legislation was to encourage participation by workers rather than unions). The point here concerns not just any legislation but laws that give workers and unions substantial rights to participate. As we will see, it is also important that a labor movement make use of the laws in proactive ways (the weak participation legislation adopted in France in 1945, for example, withered on the vine because of union hostility or neglect; Lorwin 1954; Stephens and Stephens 1982, p. 230).

Corporatist bargaining is here defined as regularized peak or subpeak negotiation between relatively cohesive units of business and labor, with the formal or informal backing of the state. This concept builds on the work, over the past fifteen years, of a variety of theorists of "corporatism," "neocorporatism," and "democratic corporatism." The central insight of this literature is that there are, among industrial democracies, different types of political economies, ranging from the more pluralist (the United States, Britain) to the more corporatist (Sweden, Austria, and Norway), and that these different structures greatly influence political and economic outcomes.[8]

---

[8] There are about as many definitions of democratic corporatism as there are theorists

For the encouragement and regulation of union and worker participation in management, a cohesive labor movement is the dynamic element within a structure of corporatist bargaining. A cohesive labor movement is one that includes a relatively small number of national unions and is effectively, if not formally, centralized, either through a dominant central labor federation or through the centralizing influence of one dominant union. A formally centralized labor federation has the power to make binding decisions for national unions; this is not necessarily the case for a cohesive labor movement, in which central authority may be less well defined. A cohesive labor movement is a broader category, including but not limited to centralized labor movements.[9] A cohesive labor movement is juxtaposed to a fragmented one, in which either labor is divided into contending, plural union federations, or authority is highly decentralized within a single federation.[10]

Summarized, the above discussion offers the following hypotheses, suitable for cross-national comparative analysis (applicable to advanced industrial societies in the contemporary period of work reorganization):

1. Where unions or works councils, as a broad national pattern, are integrated into managerial decision making, representation of workers' interests remains stable in the recent period of major work reorganization.

2. Everywhere else, where unions have arm's-length traditions of various kinds, organized labor experiences declining influence with the onset of major

---

of the subject, and indeed conceptual confusion has undermined some of the value of the literature. It is beyond the scope of this book to enter into specifics of the definitional debate; nor is it my purpose to make this another study of corporatism. What I do is to draw on some of the insights of this literature to formulate definitions and to argue that differences in the structure of political economy matter for union outcomes in the contemporary period. For those interested in the recent literature on corporatism, some of the most important works are Schmitter 1974; Wilensky 1976 and 1983; Schmitter and Lehmbruch 1979; Lehmbruch and Schmitter 1982; Berger 1981; Goldthorpe 1984a; and Katzenstein 1985.

[9] A cohesive labor movement is a comparative category that is not inconsistent with intraclass or intra-labor-movement conflict and division. There is conflict between unions just as there are relative winners and losers within any labor movement (see Markovits 1986 on the "activists" and "accommodationists" within the West German labor movement; and Swenson 1989 and 1990 on labor divisions in the early processes of corporatist labor inclusion).

[10] There are thus two types of cohesive labor movements, those that are formally centralized (Sweden) and those that are not (Germany). There are also two types of fragmented labor movements, plural unionist (France and Italy) and highly decentralized (the United States, Britain, and Japan). Although Japan has both contending federations *and* extreme decentralization, the latter is the most salient defining characteristic. For a useful comparative discussion of centralized labor movements in West Germany and Sweden, see Swenson 1989, pp. 31–34. Swenson contrasts these labor movements to the more fragmented ones found in the United States and Britain (pp. 20–21).

work reorganization, unless unions participate in regularized arrangements of corporatist bargaining. In the latter cases, a cohesive labor movement can use its broad political and economic clout to organize a new integration of labor into managerial decision making.

There are two important corollaries to the first hypothesis:

1a. Where unions are integrated into management decision-making processes *and* where such participation is backed by statutory and corporatist regulation (as in West Germany), union or works council influence remains significant from a base that is substantially independent of management.

1b. Where union integration into firms' decision-making processes lacks the backing of statutory or corporatist regulation (as in Japan), union voice has no platform from which to be substantially independent of management.

And the second hypothesis also has a corollary:

2a. Where organized workers are neither integrated into managerial decision making to begin with nor part of corporatist bargaining arrangements (including a cohesive labor movement), unions have no societywide leverage from which to negotiate for integration into management decision making—as Swedish unions did in the 1970s and 1980s. Union integration that does occur at the plant and firm levels is usually a result of managerial prodding and often includes major union concessions of traditional bases of influence, thus presenting the danger of subordinate enterprise unionism and making unions suspicious of further collaboration.

The Evidence Required

Managerial initiatives and union responses in the politics of work reorganization have developed and increased in importance in the past ten to fifteen years. Testing the argument presented here, therefore, requires above all getting inside firm- and plant-level negotiations and conflict over work reorganization, to examine the interactions between management and labor, the role of unions, the stability and extent of workers' interest representation, and the causes for contrasting outcomes.

Overall union decline, of course, is based only in part on the weakening of union influence in its established bases. It is here that I concentrate in this analysis. But union decline is also a product of the inability to organize the unorganized in growing sectors (which in turn is related to a shift in employment and investment away from traditional unionized sectors). That is not where this research is focused; but I think the argument would in any case apply. In the contemporary period, union organizing efforts are arguably facilitated both by corporatist bargaining arrangements and by legal frameworks to regulate and encourage union participation in management decision making.

But if unions are in decline everywhere in contemporary industrial societies, as much of the country-specific as well as the general literature implies, then an argument based on cross-national contrasts and country-specific institutions of interest representation is misplaced. The first task is thus one of discovery: to find out whether in fact substantial cross-national differences exist in the stability and extent of the representation of workers interests. This can be accomplished by a study of contemporary industrial relations in one key sector of two national economies, backed up by secondary studies of other sectors in each of the two countries.[11]

The first task dovetails nicely with the second and third tasks. The second task is to examine in depth the substance of labor-management relations and negotiations concerning work reorganization in the selected sector of the two countries to assess contrasting outcomes and determine whether the argument presented here is consistent with the facts.

As core cases, I have chosen to look at the U.S. and West German auto industries in the postrecession years 1982–89. In the United States, by all accounts, unions in general have experienced seriously declining membership and influence in the past decade; in West Germany, unions appear, at least from the outside, to be much stronger by comparison. The automobile industry in both countries remains a critical sector at the center of the respective national economies; and autoworkers' unions in both countries have traditionally played pattern-setting roles within their respective national labor movements.

Examining the politics of work reorganization in the U.S. and West German auto industries requires looking at a range of representative plant-level cases within each country. Cases can then be compared cross-nationally, but most important, the range of outcomes (and the general national pattern, if there is one) can be compared. In this book, the focus is on the auto assembly plants of high-volume, mass-market producers: in West Germany, Volkswagen (VW), Opel, and Ford (with a background look at Daimler-Benz); in the United States, the dominant firm, General Motors (GM) (with a background look at Ford and Chrysler). In West

[11] Ideally, to test an argument of this scope, numerous sectors in several countries should be studied; both the sectors and the general national patterns should then be compared cross-nationally. But this would require the work of a team of researchers for several years. The present study has thus focused empirical research on one critical sector in two countries, and the findings of this research are broadened by way of background studies both of other sectors within the two countries and the critical sector in several other countries. In recent literature, many have argued in favor of industry studies (rather than broad studies of the economy or of national labor federations), since the sector or firm is generally the locus both of industrial development and of national union power (see Zysman and Tyson 1983; Bean 1985, pp. 13–15).

Germany, where plants are larger in size and smaller in number, I look at both Opel assembly plants, both Ford assembly plants, and the dominant VW assembly plant at Wolfsburg. In the United States, I examine five GM plants, chosen to represent a range of contrasting outcomes. The empirical presentations and analysis of the politics of work reorganization in the U.S. and West German auto industries, in Chapters 1 and 2 respectively and in Chapter 3, where the two national cases are systematically compared, together make up the largest portion of this book.

The third task is to broaden the sample beyond the auto industry in both the United States and West Germany, to determine whether more general national patterns exist and whether the argument is generalizable beyond one sector. This is done in Chapter 4, with a study of contemporary industrial relations in telecommunications (and specifically, telephone services) in both countries, based on primary research and secondary material, and a study of industrial relations in the apparel industries of each country, based on secondary material. These industries are chosen to provide useful counterpoints to the auto industry, given very different market circumstances and industry and union structures. And as James Kurth (1979) has argued, apparel was historically a key component of the first stage of industrialization (the "textiles" stage); the automobile industry has been the critical sector since about World War I; and telecommunications is the most logical candidate to lead the next major stage of industrial development. If general national patterns of industrial relations can be discovered that apply to all three of these very different sectors in the contemporary era, we can perhaps be reasonably confident of the general nature of the findings.[12]

The fourth task is to move the analysis beyond two countries, to see if a more general argument is supported. In Chapter 5, the politics of work reorganization in the auto industries of Sweden, Italy, Great Britain, and Japan is considered, based on available secondary material. In addition, I assess general trends in industrial relations in these four countries. Looking at developments in additional countries is a critical step in broadening the evidence to assess the relative merits of various arguments, including this one.[13]

---

[12] I am grateful to Peter Katzenstein for pointing out to me that the three industrial sectors I had selected fit nicely into Kurth's product cycle framework, thereby strengthening the plausibility and general applicability of this argument.

[13] Bean (1985) and Dogan and Pelassy (1990) both argue that two-country ("bipolar") analyses are useful for the depth of comparison they allow, but that a broader framework is necessary to isolate explanatory variables and avoid false generalizations (Bean 1985, p. 13; Dogan and Pelassy 1990, pp. 126–30).

The final task is to assemble the evidence and draw out conclusions. In the final chapter, the hypotheses presented here are tested against the combined evidence from the previous five chapters; in both Chapter 3 and the Conclusion, other country-specific and general arguments are considered in light of the evidence produced.

The concluding chapter presents a discussion of the implications of this argument: for the literature; for theory-building; for unions, firms, and governments and their respective policy choices; for the comparative prospects of industrial adjustment; and for industrial and political democracy.

Preview: The Evidence Discovered

The core research for this book consists of case studies of work reorganization and industrial relations in the U.S. and West German auto industries from 1982 to 1989. Findings of these case studies, generalized into sector-level patterns, can be summarized as follows.

The period since 1982 has been characterized by major managerial initiatives at reorganizing work in the U.S. auto industry in the face of persistent and successful Japanese competition. Most evident and perhaps most important as well have been conflicts and negotiations around the introduction of various forms of teamwork in many large U.S. auto plants. Managerial initiatives and union and work-force responses have resulted in a wide range of outcomes, from new nonunion plants, to plants with conflictual and still traditional industrial relations, to plants with traditional but more cooperative industrial relations, and finally to plants in which team organization is accompanied by an integration of the union into new levels of managerial decision making. The latter cases offer variants on a new model for the U.S. auto industry, in which more cooperative labor-management relations are combined with a more flexible deployment of labor in teams or groups and a union actively engaged in processes of managerial decision making. Although there are plant-level cases of success for such a model (at GM's Plant #1 in Lansing, Michigan, and at the GM-Toyota NUMMI plant in Fremont, California, for example, which are examined in Chapter 1) a common pattern includes heavy (and often counterproductive) managerial challenges to union influence, accompanied by labor-management and intraunion/work-force conflict and a very rocky, uneven road to work reorganization. Because the United Auto Workers (UAW) entered this period with no entrenched position within processes of managerial decision making, managers in the auto industry have had wide discretion in their strategies for the implementation of new work organization; and it is precisely this wide discretion that best accounts for the remarkably wide range of current industrial relations and work reorganization outcomes in the U.S. auto industry.[14] Although market circumstances cry out for a new plant-level model of organization, the successful spread of such a model is undermined by persistent old-fashioned managerial thinking and practice (including authoritarian shop-floor approaches and a broader pattern of adversarial management).[15] The UAW, in 1984, 1987, and 1990 contract negotiations, broke new ground in protecting autoworkers against the effects of reorganization, but these gains remained modest in comparison to parallel protections for unions in West Germany. Union membership in the auto industry declined after 1979 both absolutely and as a percentage of the industry organized.[16] Not coincidentally, I would suggest, the U.S. auto industry taken as a whole (and this is especially true for the dominant firm, GM) has adapted only slowly to the major competitive challenges from Japan and elsewhere.

In the West German auto industry, work reorganization has proceeded steadily in the past decade, and although management initiative has dominated, the shape of reorganization has resulted from a process of negotiation between company drives for "rationalization" and demands from unions and works councils for "humanization of work." Labor-management relations have been stable; the influence of unions and works councils is strong and steady in the plants (as indicated by the three dimensions of workers' interest representation); works councils have a voice at various levels of management decision making and engage in a daily process of negotiation regarding the allocation of labor. Union membership in the industry is high and stable, both absolutely and as a percentage of the industry work force, and nonunionism is not an option in the German auto industry. New forms of team and group work are now looming rapidly on the horizon, over groundwork laid by the gradual

---

[14] The UAW itself remains rather centralized, engaging in pattern-setting collective bargaining at the national level with GM, Ford, and Chrysler. But because the U.S. labor movement as a whole is organizationally fragmented, unions in many industries have proven vulnerable to attack or exclusion in the 1980s. Labor's decline has emboldened managers even where unions are strongest, as in the auto industry, and this is reflected in the wide range of plant-level strategies and outcomes.

[15] The main problem, the evidence here suggests, is not job-control unionism, as Katz and Sabel (1985) and others have implied. At plant after plant, workers (usually under pressure) have proven willing to give up job classifications in return for promises of new participation—only to return from training programs to the shop floor, where their raised expectations are dashed by old-fashioned managerial ways (Milkman and Pullman 1988; Turner 1988b).

[16] The decline in the organization rate has two sources: the nonunion Japanese transplants and the declining rate of organization in the parts-supplier branch of the industry.

introduction of quality circles and group work (*Gruppenarbeit*) pilot projects in several plants. The entrenched position of works council and union in the plants and the projection of an independent union vision of the nature of group work means that teamwork is coming to the German auto industry in a very different way from in the United States. Here it is primarily the Metalworkers Union (IG Metall),[17] with its own independently developed, detailed concepts and strategies for new work organization, that has promoted group work, and only since about 1985 has management begun to press for its own new concept, a more Japanese-style team approach. Teamwork is coming to the German auto industry in the negotiations between these two strong and contending views. Variations within the relatively narrow range of outcomes can best be accounted for by variations in firms' strategies (based on differing firm characteristics, such as the position of Ford-Werke and Opel as part of worldwide Ford and GM, and the unique history of VW) and in works council strategies (a product, for example, of *Geschlossenheit* or unity at VW, compared to the existence of contending factions at Opel-Bochum); but the differences across plants and firms are small compared to the United States. Both the smallness of the range and the stable influence of union and works councils are best explained by the entrenched position of works councils within the plants, backed by the Works Constitution Act, and the inclusion of a relatively cohesive labor movement (in which the IG Metall retains a central position) within a broader framework of unique, West German corporatist bargaining. Within this institutional framework, the West German auto industry adapted very well to increasingly competitive market circumstances at home and abroad in the 1980s.

This analysis should not be interpreted either as belittling the recent accomplishments of the UAW (such as the creation of job banks and expanded employment security) or as overlooking the difficult and growing problems faced by the IG Metall. The UAW has remained a pattern setter and innovator for the U.S. labor movement, and if a new U.S. model of industrial relations emerges that promotes both market success and new union vitality it may well come out of the many labor-management experiments currently under way in the auto industry. At the same time, the IG Metall faced high and enduring unemployment in West Germany as well as new managerial aggressiveness in issues such as flexibility of working hours and work reorganization. A shift in the locus of influence

[17] The full name is Industriegewerkschaft Metall, which translates literally as "industrial union for the metal industries." In Germany, the union is known simply as IG Metall, and it will be referred to as such here as well. The IG Metall organizes several industries, including autos.

to the works councils arguably contributed to a new "plant syndicalism" (Hohn 1988), which has made it possible for German managers to begin to learn the art (well developed at U.S. auto firms) of playing one plant's work force (and works council) off against another. The strength of employers in this regard may well increase with the opening up of East Germany. Both German unification and the coming of the single European market pose new and potentially serious problems for German unions.

But the cross-national outcomes in the 1980s did contrast rather sharply, and these differences make clear the very real constraints faced by the UAW—regardless of leadership decisions or strategy. In the contemporary U.S. industrial relations climate, the UAW's efforts may in fact be a best-case scenario. This is clear from a brief look at the telephone services and apparel industries, which together bring out well the broad (as opposed to industry- or firm-specific) nature of the U.S.-West German contrast. In both cases, the patterns are similar: West German unions increase membership density in the face of organizational reform efforts (telephone services) or adverse market circumstances (apparel) and hold on to important levers of influence; U.S. unions face declining membership density and struggle to replace lost influence in new ways. Parallel contrasts between the United States and West Germany can thus be seen across a range of industries, regardless of market circumstances, firm or union structure, or role played in histories of product cycle development.

The argument presented here is largely confirmed by a cross-national comparison of industrial relations in the auto industries in the United States, West Germany, Britain, Italy, Sweden, and Japan. It seems to be a particular characteristic of current markets and technologies that managers need more cooperation and problem-solving input from employees at all levels of the firm; and managers can get this cooperation either by completely excluding unions or by integrating unions or works councils into their decision making in new ways. The relative lack of constraints on managerial strategies for reorganizing work in societies where organized labor is fragmented and has no established access to firms' decision-making processes often tempts managers into direct challenges to union influence, setting in motion a conflictual process that undermines the prospects for new trust and cooperation (whether unions are successfully excluded or remain entrenched). This was precisely the dynamic at work in the U.S. auto industry in the 1980s, and one could see a parallel process at work in the British and Italian auto industries. In West Germany and Sweden, by contrast, increasingly integrated autoworker unions backed up by statutory regulation and cohesive labor movements constrained management in ways conducive both to stable labor-management bargaining over the shape of new work organization and to the stability and expanded influence of workers' interest representation.[18] In Japan, labor integration into management processes has meant stability for auto industry unions, although a fragmented labor movement and the absence of legal regulation have allowed management to dominate discussions and kept unions from presenting an independent viewpoint or from reversing a modest but steady societywide decline.

Industrial Relations Settlements and the Conditions for Contemporary Union Success

Methodologically, this analysis is situated between broad, general analyses that tend to be determinist (whether Marxist or liberal; see Goldthorpe 1984b) and arguments that locate explanations only in the unique and detailed circumstances of particular countries. This latter perspective is found in a current body of insightful studies in which industry structures, social patterns, and industrial relations are woven into a social fabric that produces unique outcomes in each country (Maurice, Sellier, and Silvestre 1986; Sorge and Warner 1987). My view is that though these studies usefully depict processes at work in particular countries, it is nonetheless possible to locate critical variables (not everything is equally important) that contribute to cross-national causal explanation.

In other words, countries respond in contrasting ways to the same challenges and tasks because different institutions are in place; yet it is possible to group countries according to a limited number of outcomes (in this case concerning the stability of industrial relations and relative union success) and to explain these outcomes with reference to selected variables. This analysis thus falls in with those that see distinct national models linked to distinct patterns of outcomes. Zysman (1983), for example, offers one approach that is broadly consistent with the findings presented here: a "bargained solution" in West Germany and Sweden is contrasted to a "company-led" model of industrial adjustment in the United States and Britain and a "state-led" model in France and Japan. In the first model, labor is included in negotiations; in the last two, labor is excluded. The neo- or democratic corporatist theorists afford another important example, in which countries are grouped into two or three

---

[18] This argument parallels and is complementary to Streeck's argument that union or works council–imposed labor market rigidities drive employers upmarket toward "diversified, high quality production," with positive results both for competitiveness and for the continued influence of workers' interest representation (Streeck 1985a, 1987a).

categories along corporatist/pluralist dimensions (Schmitter 1974; Wilensky 1976; Schmitter and Lehmbruch 1979). But to the extent that these theorists are anti-corporatist (Schmitter 1982, p. 261) or emphasize unstable institutional rigidities (Sabel 1981; Streeck 1984b), the present analysis diverges. "Bargained" or "democratic corporatist"[19] political economies on the whole showed remarkable institutional stability in the turbulent years from the mid–1970s to the late 1980s, and this was particularly true for the structures representing workers' interests.

Perhaps most important, the findings presented here shed light on domestic debates regarding unions and on country-specific analyses of union decline. In West Germany, for example, numerous scholars shared the perspective in the 1980s that unions were in serious trouble, facing the threat of either "Japanization" or "Americanization" (Streeck 1984b; Hoffmann 1988). The problem was that some of these theorists had unrealistic expectations: they expected the West German labor movement to adhere to an old program for the transformation of society and "unitary unionism" that may be increasingly out-of-date (Hohn 1988). West German unions have adapted to new tasks and challenges and are stable in numbers and influence, both in comparative perspective and along a number of measurable dimensions; German analysts looking for the decline of unions would do better to look beyond their own borders.

There is, however, a conservative or neoliberal view in West Germany that unions are too strong and are standing in the way of industrial adjustment. This view was reflected in the Kohl regime's legislative challenge to union strike power (see below, Chapter 2) and in the Lafontaine current within the Social Democratic party (SPD) that called into question some of labor's most sacred cows (such as the free weekend). From a comparative perspective, West German unions are indeed influential; yet this influence appears to be flexible and considerably more in tune with the adjustment needs of industry than is true of unions in many other countries (Streeck 1987a; Thelen 1987b).

In the United States, there is widespread debate about the causes and consequences of union decline. The findings here confirm in part the pathbreaking studies by Richard Freeman and James L. Medoff (1984), Ko-

---

[19] The term is not precise and has been subject to a variety of definitions; especially controversial is its applicability to the West German case. But in both structure (centralized, inclusive interest representation) and behavior (labor-management peace bargain, extensive bilateral and trilateral negotiation throughout the political economy), Germany is closest to the smaller, more clearly corporatist societies such as Sweden, Norway, and Austria (Katzenstein 1985, 1987). Thus Wilensky (1983) places West Germany "on the margins of democratic corporatism."

chan, Katz, and McKersie (1986), and Michael Goldfield (1987) that locate the primary source of this decline in managerial values and growing employer opposition to unions (or the capitalist offensive, as Goldfield puts it). But from a comparative perspective, I argue that managerial tactics and strategies of opposition to unions are successful precisely because of the absence of particular institutional forms of constraint. Opel and Ford managers in West Germany, for example, have in the past also acted on "American" values and strategies (not least because these are American-owned firms); yet the effect has not been to interfere with the expansion of union influence. Thus the way in which union influence is institutionalized, not employer strategies or values, is the causal variable at work.

And finally, there is a debate in the United States concerning what unions should do about their current plight. One view has it that unions need to rebuild lost militance to fight more effectively against managerial opposition (Goldfield 1987; Moody 1988; Parker and Slaughter 1988); another view argues that unions need to be more open to engagement in managerial decision making (Kochan, Katz and McKersie 1986; Heckscher 1988). My argument is situated between these two positions: labor needs both integration into managerial decision making and a more cohesive movement of its own, both engagement with management on new work organization and more assertive unions.[20] The polarization of the debate into cooperation versus militance inhibits the development of appropriate strategies to rebuild the U.S. labor movement.

Unions are not in decline everywhere. There are demonstrable preconditions for contemporary union success, and these preconditions are located primarily in the structures of interest representation. We now turn to the evidence, beginning in the next two chapters with an examination of the politics of work reorganization in the U.S. and West German auto industries.

[20] See also Banks and Metzgar 1989; Herzenberg 1989. Unions, for example, could actively promote proactive strategies for new work organization (as many are attempting to do) and at the same time could unite in campaigns for new national legislation to regulate workers' and unions' participation in management.

PART ONE

PARTNERSHIP AND CONFLICT
IN THE U.S. AND
WEST GERMAN AUTO INDUSTRIES

*L*ocated at the heart of manufacturing in all the major industrial societies, the auto industry, far from fulfilling the image of a declining mature sector, remains a center of dynamic activity in technological advance, reorganization of production and work, and intensified competition among large and powerful firms (Quinn 1989). For countries with substantial auto industries, industrial relations settlements in this sector have often set patterns for national industry as a whole; and autoworkers' unions have typically played leading roles within national labor movements. In the United States and West Germany, in spite of shifts in employment from manufacturing to services and challenges to national pattern setting since the crisis years of the 1970s, auto industry negotiations continue to play a prominent role in national industrial relations. Although one cannot understand industrial relations in the United States and West Germany with reference only to the auto industry, neither can one grasp the changing contemporary dynamics of labor-management relations without looking at this industry. If unions cannot hold their own and adapt to changing circumstances here in the core industrial work force, the traditional bastion of labor strength, it is difficult to imagine that national prospects for unions elsewhere could be promising.

We begin, therefore, with an examination of the politics of work reorganization where unions are at their strongest. Because the stability and extent of workers' interest representation contrast significantly in the United States and West German auto industries, this is a good place to begin testing the argument: world market changes are driving change in industrial relations; contrasting cross-national outcomes for unions are best explained by differences in the way interest representation is institutionalized. Most important are the extent to which unions are integrated into managerial decision making and the backing for such integration by law and corporatist bargaining. The three chapters that make up Part One test this argument against extensive plant-level empirical evidence.

Conflict and Accommodation in the U.S. Auto Industry

*I*n 1915, Henry Ford started up the first mass production assembly line, offered workers five dollars a day, and transformed manufacturing; in the 1920s, Alfred Sloan took over at General Motors and wrested prominence from Ford by diversifying production, introducing yearly model changes, and vastly expanding the scope of consumer credit offerings. In the ensuing fifty years, nothing has symbolized the world-class superiority of United States manufacturing as impressively as the Big Three auto firms. The names General Motors, Ford, and Chrysler were synonomous with American industrial vitality, and the product offerings were the stuff of dreams. For Americans who came of age in the first two decades of the postwar period, young adulthood was intimately linked to the first ownership of a Chevy, Ford, or Dodge, those shiny steel manifestations of speed, independence, and vigor.

When a steady parade of comical-looking VW Beetles invaded the U.S. market in the 1950s, followed by tinny little Toyotas and Datsuns in the 1960s, auto industry executives were concerned but not overly alarmed. These were starter cars for students, young families, and the poor, perhaps a suitable transition product at the low end of the market before these customers were ready to buy a "real car." Although auto industry production, sales, and profits were always cyclical, the large U.S. auto companies, and especially the dominant firm, General Motors, appeared powerful and secure well into the 1970s in their control of the vast domestic auto market, between relatively minor niches at the low end and the luxury import segment at the top.

The dominant union in the U.S. auto industry, the United Auto Workers, appeared equally secure. Born in the labor upsurges of the 1930s, the UAW grew rapidly under the umbrella of the Congress of Industrial Organizations (CIO) to become one of the largest and strongest of American unions. The "postwar settlement" negotiated between GM and the UAW set a pattern for much of labor in the United States: steadily rising wages and improving benefits along with institutional security for the union were traded for labor peace and "managerial prerogative" in the organization of production (Brody 1980, pp. 173–211; Katz 1985, pp. 13–47). Although organized labor in the United States began to decline in overall membership density as early as 1954, the UAW was unaffected. The union remained entrenched in the core industry of U.S. manufacturing, maintained a virtual 100 percent blue-collar organization rate for large auto assembly and supplier plants, ultimately defeated GM's strategy to open nonunion plants in the South in the 1960s and 1970s, and reached the peak of its membership in 1978.

In spite of obvious industrial success for the auto firms, high membership levels and a stable position for the union, and a regular procession of contractual settlements between the two sides that allowed production lines to roll smoothly (punctuated by occasional strikes at bargaining time), there were many problems in the system of labor-management relations. Firms responded to the cyclical nature of production with periodic mass layoffs, which the union regulated through seniority provisions but which pleased no one. For production workers, work remained fragmented into tiny sets of repetitive tasks, and life in the plants was often hard and without hope of much future opportunity (Chinoy 1955; Aronowitz 1973). Labor-management relations in the plants were adversarial and often antagonistic, as drill-sergeant supervisors barked orders and union committeemen fired off grievances. By the late 1960s, black workers at plants around Detroit and young workers at plants such as Lordstown had begun to rebel; the Taylorist/Fordist production system showed signs of serious strain, as low worker morale and product quality became growing problems for the Big Three.

Nonetheless, until the late 1970s, the U.S. auto industry and its supporting industrial relations were widely viewed as successful along the most important dimensions. Firms were profitable, maintained high levels of production, and dominated the home market (the largest auto market in the world); the union maintained high levels of membership, organized the industry inclusively, and produced contracts that the membership could accept; and workers earned relatively high wages and good benefits, were compensated for layoffs by both national and contractual unemployment benefits, and could look forward to more employment security and a better, or at least a softer, job as they moved up the seniority ladder.

In 1978–79, however, disaster struck this once complacent industry. The story of a fairly sudden and far-reaching crisis in the U.S. auto industry has been told repeatedly (Altshuler et al. 1984; Halberstam 1986; Dyer, Salter, and Webber 1987). In the wake of two oil crises that substantially raised gasoline prices, consumer preferences shifted toward smaller cars, away from Detroit's "gas guzzlers." Japanese firms expanded market shares rapidly in the United States with low-cost, high-quality product offerings well suited to new consumer demand. As international competition in the auto industry intensified, the large but lumbering U.S. firms found themselves on the losing end. At the same time, a deep recession hit the economy from 1980 to 1982, consumer buying power plunged, and U.S. auto firms were forced to shut plants and lay off tens of thousands of workers. Chrysler was saved only by a massive bailout organized by the federal government; Ford reached the edge of bankruptcy and saved itself only with severe cutbacks, streamlining, and organizational reorientation; and GM stumbled into the 1980s to a future of plant closures, innovation failure and long-term declining market share.

For workers in the U.S. auto industry and for the UAW, these were devastating years. The total number of production workers employed in the auto industry dropped from 802,800 in December 1978 to 487,700 in January 1983 (Altshuler et al. 1984, p. 274). For the UAW, with over 70 percent of its membership in the auto industry,[1] membership dropped from 1.53 million in 1979 to under 1 million in 1983 (Quinn 1988). Skilled and production workers alike left the auto industry in droves, rode as long as they could on unemployment benefits, accepted early retirement and other buyout schemes, relocated to jobs at auto plants in other parts of the country, and took lower-paying jobs while waiting for plants to reopen or second shifts to be called back. In such circumstances, the UAW had little leverage for influencing company decision making or for preventing mass layoffs and dislocation. In 1979 and 1980 at Chrysler, and in 1980 and 1982 at Ford and GM, the union once again set a pattern for U.S. industry, but this time through "concession bargaining," the negotiation of substantial pay and other concessions. The UAW protected its members as best it could through Supplemental Unemployment Benefit

---

[1] The UAW's full name is International Union, United Automobile, Aerospace and Agricultural Workers of America. The UAW organizes workers in the aerospace and agricultural machinery industries and has moved in recent years to organize service and white-collar employees outside the auto industry, such as university staff.

(SUB) funds (dating from contract negotiations in the 1950s), the negotiation of a new Guaranteed Income Stream (GIS) in 1982 for high-
seniority workers, and a plethora of plant-specific programs for counseling,
job placement, and retraining.

After 1983, a vastly streamlined Chrysler and Ford, along with a still
dominant GM, returned to profitability. But unlike previous cyclical up-
swings in the postwar period, the market was no longer waiting for them
with open arms; although employment and production levels stabilized
for the Big Three, they never again reached the peaks of the 1970s. For
in the intervening years, Japanese auto firms had taken a large and permanent chunk of U.S. domestic market shares, a portion whose size was
limited to around 20 percent only by government-level Voluntary Restraint
Agreements (VRAs, which limited Japanese auto imports to 2.3 million
units beginning in 1981). As Daniel Luria succinctly summarizes:

> Between the two most recent auto sales peaks, 1978 and 1986, the overall
> U.S. vehicle market grew by 1.1 million units. But imports grew by 1.8
> million units and "transplants"—vehicles assembled in the U.S. by foreign-
> based manufacturers, alone or in joint ventures with U.S.-based firms—grew
> by 0.7 million. Traditional domestic vehicles' sales fell 1.4 million, idling
> the capacity of six Big Three assembly and five engine, transmission, and
> stamping plants, and 225,000 U.S. manufacturing workers. (1987, pp.
> 2–3)

The lion's share of the imports (and most of the transplants as well)
came from Japan.[2] U.S. auto firms groped for new production and marketing strategies as Japanese firms proved their superiority. At first, some
analysts argued that the real problem, the real source of the competitive
disadvantage for U.S. firms, was the overvalued dollar. Successive and
steady devaluation beginning in 1985, however, appeared to make little
difference, except to speed up the coming of Japanese transplants (in both
auto assembly and supply) and push Japanese product offerings further
upmarket. For 1985, market share for Japanese auto imports was 20.1
percent; after a subsequent 50 percent rise in the value of the yen relative
to the dollar, Japanese imports actually increased market share to 21.3
percent in 1987 (Keller 1988).

Why do Japanese firms appear to have such a persistent competitive
advantage over the Big Three? An important part of the answer lies in
the organization of production. According to numerous studies, Japanese

[2] By July 1987, for example, imports were up to 33.1% of the U.S. domestic market,
with 21.7% coming from Japan (*Ward's Automotive Reports*, August 19, 1987, p. 250).

auto firms have a decisive and consistent advantage in production costs, even when labor costs and fluctations in the exchange rate are controlled for (Altshuler et al. 1984; Dyer, Salter, and Webber 1987; Luria 1987; Quinn 1988). At the same time, Japanese autos are consistently rated higher in quality by consumers and independent analysts alike (see *Consumer Reports*, various issues, 1980–89).

According to all accounts, the Japanese production advantage has a number of components, including sourcing decisions, relations with suppliers, ''just-in-time'' parts delivery, and management systems. But a vital ingredient, and one that appears to make the others viable as a whole system, is the organization of work on the shop floor and the accompanying content of industrial relations (National Academy of Engineering 1982; Altshuler et al. 1984; Dohse, Jürgens, and Malsch 1985). Unions at Japanese auto firms are integrated into processes of managerial decision making as enterprise rather than national unions; they facilitate the smooth flow of production as part of a system of industrial relations that is cooperative in the extreme. On the shop floor, workers are organized into production teams that work hard and fast and eliminate many of the inefficiencies found in traditional, fragmented assembly-line work relations. This set of industrial and work relations forms a critical part of the Japanese production advantage, a conclusion that is no longer debated within the large U.S. auto firms.

In the past very troubled decade, therefore, a major strategy at each of the Big Three has been to transform both industrial relations and shop-floor work organization, to move toward labor-management cooperation and more integrated shop-floor work and committed worker responsibility. The trouble is that managers, unionists, and workers do not change their ways overnight, especially when these ways are rooted in entrenched shop-floor practices and industrial relations institutions. The process of change has been uneven, and the direction of change has varied greatly from plant to plant. Managers continue to recraft their strategies and debate internally the merits of genuine cooperative relations, while national and local unions attempt to define new roles and debate internally the merits of management's proposed changes. The politics of work reorganization has become a dominant theme in U.S. auto industry industrial relations.

Industrial Relations in the U.S. Auto Industry

From the founding of the American Federation of Labor (AFL) in 1886 until the upsurge of industrial unionism in the 1930s, the dominant unions that endured in the United States were craft-based and narrow, organized into a decentralized, nonsocialist, "business unionist" federation. Because the AFL refused to open doors to the growing ranks of unskilled and semiskilled production workers in the auto industry and elsewhere, the CIO broke away in 1935 to organize these workers. The UAW was born in these years as part of the CIO and grew rapidly, as workers occupied plants and organized whole communities to gain union recognition from the historically anti-union auto firms (Rayback 1966; Brody 1980; Green 1980). The UAW expanded throughout the auto industry, consolidated itself during World War II (with government backing), and emerged from the war as the powerful, virtually uncontested representative of the auto industry work force. In the early and seemingly wide-open postwar years, industrial relations scholars were troubled by the prospect of excessive union power; indeed, the UAW, under the leadership of Walter Reuther, made a bid for direct influence in managerial decision-making processes, demanding wage raises without increases in car prices and challenging GM to open its books to show whether this would be economically feasible. GM rode out a 113-day strike in 1945–46 to turn back union demands and to establish managerial prerogative for decisions regarding products and the organization of production (Brody 1980, pp. 183–84).

In subsequent bargaining rounds in 1948 and 1950, in a more conservative political climate following passage of the Taft-Hartley Act in 1947 (which restricted labor's strike and boycott tactics and allowed states to pass right-to-work legislation), UAW-GM contracts established a postwar settlement for the auto industry as a whole and for much of U.S. industry. In this settlement, union recognition (and institutional security) along with rising wages and improving benefits were traded off against labor peace (during the years of the contract) and full managerial prerogative in decision making regarding the product and process of production. Rights and obligations of workers, union and management were spelled out in detailed contractual language; by policing the contract, the union not only defended the workers against management abuses but helped to organize the work force for production as well. Labor and management settled into a tense, arm's-length relationship as union representatives responded to daily shop-floor complaints and made extensive use of instruments of grievance and arbitration in this system of adversarial "industrial democracy."

But in spite of industrial unionism and technological progress, life remained harsh on the shop floor in the auto as in other mass production industries. William J. Abernathy, Kim B. Clark, and Alan M. Kantrow describe the state of shop-floor relations at GM in the wake of the postwar settlement:

> There was no genuinely cooperative relationship, only an armed truce. Blue-collar employees enjoyed better pay and working conditions than they had a generation before, but the nature of their work had changed little. Jobs remained narrow in scope, with few opportunities for involvement or responsibility or initiative. Control of production remained a function of machine speeds, watchful supervision, work standards, and measurement techniques. By the mid–1950s, collective bargaining had changed a number of operational procedures, but it had not changed the long-established paradigm of production. The press to meet production targets, delivery schedules, and efficient volume levels drove the system much as it had a decade or two or three previously. (1983, p. 89)

Viewed from a comparative perspective, the critical elements of postwar industrial relations in the U.S. auto industry are the following: (1) adversarial, arm's-length relationships between labor and management at both national and plant levels, with little integration of the union into managerial decision-making processes so that management acts and the union reacts (firing off grievances against the negative effects on the work force of managerial decisions); (2) a fairly centralized national union, the UAW, engaged in collective bargaining with each of the Big Three (formerly the Big Four, including American Motors) concerning primary issues of wages and benefits, in pattern-setting processes of "connective bargaining" (Ulman 1974; Katz 1985) that regularize outcomes across and within firms; (3) active, democratic local unions (within the UAW), organized within each plant in the shop bargaining committee, that negotiate local contracts spelling out work rules including detailed job classifications and seniority-based job assignment, in a system of legalistic regulation that has been called "job-control unionism";[3] and (4) a broader context in which the UAW plays a pattern-setting role for labor in the United States, but in which the national labor federation (AFL-CIO) is highly fragmented organizationally (more than ninety unions in the decentralized federation and many others outside), has little access to government policy making, and has endured at least two decades of declining influence.

In practice, industrial relations in the U.S. auto industry (as in most of

---

[3] See Perlman 1928. For contemporary uses of the concept, see Piore 1982; Piore and Sabel 1984; and Katz 1985.

U.S. industry) gives management wide discretion regarding the organization of production, including the organization of work. The National Labor Relations Act regulates labor-management relations in unionized settings but provides no legal framework to encourage or regulate participation by unions and workers in managerial decision making. Until recently, management has had only very limited obligations regarding information sharing with the union and advance notification of changes (up to and including plant closure—it has not been uncommon for the union and work force to hear of a plant closing only two or three weeks ahead of time). Entrenched and contractual managerial prerogative blends well with American management's "no one tells me how to run my business" ideology. Because the auto industry is highly unionized, however, management must plan its technological changes and work reorganizations carefully, anticipating possible shop-floor resistance and union grievances (Slichter, Healy, and Livernash 1960, pp. 841–78). Industrial relations scholars, in fact, have argued that this advance planning actually serves management's interests, resulting in positive productivity gains (Slichter, Healy, and Livernash 1960; Freeman and Medoff 1984, pp. 162–80). Be that as it may, management's free hand must be exercised strategically because the union can and does file grievances and force modifications after the fact.

Management's free hand is most constrained in setting work rules. In pattern-bargained national and local contracts and agreements, the UAW and management have negotiated detailed job classification descriptions and job assignment procedures. Management is not free to assign workers to job classifications; this occurs through seniority bidding by workers, although management has considerably more flexibility within classifications. Although management has the unilateral right to bring in new technology and reengineer a job in the interests of production (including deskilling or upgrading skills), the union has the right to file grievances and to argue over the legal and contractual details: was the proper procedure for implementation followed? was the skill actually removed so that a lower pay level is appropriate? were proper procedures for job reassignment followed? In spite of the UAW's general acceptance of new technology in the postwar period, the adversarial relationship between labor and management and the legalistic wrangling over shop-floor details have arguably inhibited the smooth implementation of technological change and work reorganization.

Management has the unilateral contractual right to organize and reorganize production, but it must do so without violating a detailed set of shop-floor work rules. This is the paradox of "managerial prerogative":

management pays for the right to make unilateral decisions by constantly having to defend implementation in processes of grievance and arbitration and shop-floor bickering.

This form of industrial relations has been referred to as job-control unionism.[4] From the point of view of the union, however, job-control rights are very much limited by management's right to close plants temporarily or permanently and to bring in new technology and reorganize work, especially at annual model changeover time. Union committeemen are often vigilant in policing the contract and in defending workers against the effects of management decisions; and union representatives expend an inordinate amount of energy giving a lawyerlike defense to workers accused of violating company or contractual rules. The union, at least at the plant level, has little opportunity to look at the big picture, to think ahead about coming management decisions or the needs of production; "management acts, union reacts" is a slogan that aptly captures industrial relations in the auto industry in the postwar period.

Although the structure of industrial relations is adversarial by definition, there is considerable diversity from plant to plant in the nature of actual labor-management relationships, ranging from fairly cooperative to bitterly antagonistic.[5] Industrial relations are centralized at the level of national collective bargaining, for wages, benefits, working conditions, and union rights, between the UAW and each of the Big Three. Although this centralization has been an important stabilizing factor for industrial relations in the auto industry in the postwar period, it has been increasingly challenged from two directions. First, as reorganization of work has become a major tool in managerial efforts to halt the slide of the U.S. auto industry, diversity across plants has increased. And second, the organizationally fragmented nature of American labor as a whole within a decentralized political economy has offered firms opportunities to move around unions and to avoid unionization altogether.

Avoidance of unions has occurred throughout the American economy since the 1950s (Kochan, Katz, and McKersie 1986, pp. 47–80), and it has occurred in the heavily unionized auto industry as well. In the 1960s and 1970s, GM pursued a "southern strategy" to open new nonunion plants in states with weak traditions of unionism (Katz 1985, pp. 88–90).

---

[4] See Katz 1985, pp. 38–47, for a useful discussion. For a perceptive German interpretation of industrial relations and work organization in the U.S. auto industry, see Köhler 1981.

[5] These variations appear to depend on particular plant histories, managerial strategies at the plant level, characteristics of the work force, union politics, and the personalities and personal relationships between managers and union representatives that have evolved.

Although for the large assembly and major component plants this strategy ultimately failed (the UAW organized all the plants by 1982), the Big Three have continued to spin off suppliers, and unionization in the parts industry has dropped steadily since the 1970s.[6] Perhaps the biggest threat both to the UAW and to centralized industrial relations in the auto industry is now coming from the Japanese transplants, both assembly and suppliers, most of which (except for notable joint ventures with GM, Ford, and Chrysler) have remained determinedly nonunion.

The UAW is one of the strongest and most influential of American unions and has played an active, successful role both in supporting candidates for public office and in lobbying Congress and state legislatures (Greenstone 1977; Rehmus, Mc Laughlin, and Nesbitt 1978). But in a distinctly pluralistic political economy, the UAW possesses few societywide instruments to stabilize its influence in a period of rapidly changing markets and technologies.

There are few institutional constraints to prevent management from following the apparent dictates of changing market circumstances in formulating strategies for the organization of production (see Quinn 1989 for a particularly useful discussion of the overriding importance of markets on firms' decision making). Firms thus move toward ''vertical disintegration,'' outsourcing components to an increasingly nonunion sector. Within the plants where the UAW is entrenched (all of the major Big Three plants), management is sorely tempted, in a time of relative societywide union weakness, to challenge union influence either directly or indirectly in its reorganization plans. In so doing, management is simply extending the postwar logic of industrial relations in the auto industry: management makes decisions and implements them; the union defends the work force or particular groups or individuals from the negative consequences of the decisions (through grievance and arbitration or through negotiations backed up by the threat of grievances or strikes); and management fights a rear-guard action against the reactions of the union to defend or save through modification its original decisions. The dominant tenor of the system is pluralistic, adversarial, and low trust.

Increasingly, industry analysts and scholars along with managers and unionists have come to the point of view that though this system of industrial relations may have functioned well enough when American industry was dominant in the world, it has contributed to the relative decline of the U.S. auto industry in the turbulent world markets of the

---

[6] In the concluding section of this chapter, I will look at data on the declining union membership density in the parts supplier branch and in the U.S. auto industry as a whole.

past decade (Piore and Sabel 1984; Altshuler et al. 1984; Dyer, Salter, and Webber 1987; Marshall 1987). Because management and union work together in a tightly integrated team in Japan, while at the same time the two sides slug it out in the United States, it is not hard to predict which country's firms will win in head-on competition. With this perception in mind, the UAW and the Big Three have moved gradually in the past decade, and in particular since 1982, to make changes in the procedures and outcomes of industrial relations.

The direction of these changes in the 1980, 1982, and 1984 bargaining rounds at GM and Ford is well described in Katz's study of industrial relations in the U.S. auto industry (1985).[7] In these contracts, the UAW traded wage and benefit concessions against modest steps in the direction of income and employment security and expanded training opportunities (especially in the 1984 job banks). The UAW also gave its consent to wider discretion at the plant level for innovative labor-management agreements to keep plants open, keep work in-house, and save jobs. Katz's analysis showed that these contracts resulted in significant change to the three key substantive outcomes of postwar automobile industrial relations: wage rules, connective bargaining, and work rules.

In 1987 negotiations, the trend toward new cooperative relations, employment security, and innovative plant agreements accelerated; labor-management "productivity committees" were mandated for every plant to discuss improvements in production (including breaking down old rigidities in shop-floor organization) and to deepen a process now known at GM as "jointness" (labor and management working together in specified committees to share information and make suggestions for organizational improvement). These new emphases, especially employment and income security, remained important in 1990 contract settlements.

Top managers and union representatives, along with key plant managers and local unionists, have in the past few years come to the conclusion that industrial relations as well as work organization must be changed. Against entrenched interests in management, union, and work force, they have attempted to build "productivity coalitions" (Luria 1986) in a radical departure from established auto industry ways. Perhaps nowhere is this effort more visible or dramatic than in management's plant-level drive, especially at GM but also at Chrysler and more slowly at Ford, toward new team forms of shop-floor organization. This radical campaign aims at nothing less than overturning adversarial industrial relations, traditional authoritarian management, and job-control unionism.

---

[7] See also Dyer, Salter, and Webber 1987, pp. 190–98.

Management Campaigns for Team Organization

As part of an early effort aimed at higher productivity and greater managerial discretion (free of the old work rules), GM began ex-
perimenting with operating teams at its nonunion southern plants in the
1960s and 1970s.[8] Teamwork at some of these plants failed when
the plants became unionized because the work force linked teams with
avoidance of unions. The breakthrough came in 1984, with the opening of a highly successful GM-Toyota joint venture, NUMMI, that
adapted Toyota's team concept to an American context and demonstrated
the extraordinary potential gains in productivity and product quality
(see below for a full presentation of the NUMMI case). Ever since,
GM has been on a campaign to spread teamwork (and jointness and
cooperative industrial relations) to the rest of its plants in a high-powered
if not always successful "forced march" to work reorganization (Luria
1987, p. 6).

The problem for the Big Three was that Japanese firms came up with
ways of organizing production and work that produced superior results in
productivity and product quality (Altshuler et al. 1984, pp. 29–32; Krafcik
1988a).[9] A critical dimension of this superiority lay in labor-management
relations, both on and off the shop floor; management policies toward
personnel and toward the union, it turned out, mattered a great deal for
production outcomes. As the National Academy of Engineering's 1982
study, *The Competitive Status of the U.S. Auto Industry*, put it: "Despite
the popular image of Japanese superiority in advanced technology, explanation of the Japanese productivity advantage seems to be more a matter
of differences in management—process systems, workforce management—than superior automation or faster work pace" (p. 5). And as
Altshuler et al. put it two years later, in the MIT International Motor
Vehicle Program's influential study of the world auto industry: "Labor-
relations systems have only recently been recognized as powerful con-
tributors to the efficiency and competitiveness of national auto industries"
(1984, p. 205).

As it began to sink in that adversarial labor-management relations,
authoritarian management, and narrow job classifications combined to
shape a low-trust work environment in which the worker had little commitment to the product or the work, top managers began to look around

[8] Katz 1985 gives a useful introduction to the history and current meaning of operating
teams at GM (pp. 88–104).

[9] Womack, Jones, and Roos (1990) call the new system "lean production." They argue
that it is spreading and will change the way production is organized worldwide.

for new strategies. At GM, they could build on quality-of-working-life (QWL) experiments, in which small groups of workers at many plants met regularly to discuss production and shop-floor relations. Ford had a similar Employee Involvement (EI) tradition. These programs had started in the 1970s in response to worker dissatisfaction (and a few open rebellions in the late 1960s and early 1970s), high absenteeism, high grievance rates, and growing problems with product quality (sometimes attributed to a lack of concern among workers, who were required to complete a narrow set of tasks under occasional background pressure from a heavy-handed boss). Although these programs showed spotty results and were widely criticized by both work force and management, they provided a tradition and a set of learning experiences on which to build.

One central idea in the new move toward cooperative industrial relations and shop-floor work reorganization was therefore the notion that U.S. auto firms had failed to win commitment on the shop floor or tap the work force's ideas (National Academy of Engineering 1982, p. 6). A new sort of quasi-religion began to spread among the ranks of U.S. auto industry managers, especially at Ford but also at GM and Chrysler in certain departments and plants. In the interviews I conducted in the U.S. auto industry from 1986 to 1989, I repeatedly heard managers make confessions such as: We have been real authoritarian jerks; I used to be god; but now we recognize that we have to work *with* our work force; people on the shop floor have a real contribution to make if we will just let them. As a vice-president at Chrysler put it: " 'When you see a militant workforce, usually it's because you've had knucklehead types on the management side' " (Turner and Gold 1988, p. 23).

Building on the QWL/EI traditions and the new learning and driven by disastrous performance in world markets beginning in 1979, key top managers and high-ranking union officials (the latter led by Don Ephlin, who was first the UAW vice-president for Ford, then the UAW vice-president for GM) began to push from the top for cooperative labor relations and new work organization in the plants. By the mid-1980s, these strategies crystallized at GM in the drive for new team forms of work organization.

The problem was, and remains, that workers, local union officials, and middle managers are not always as enthusiastic about these new ideas as higher-level managers might like them to be (Mann 1987b; Parker and Slaughter 1988; Quinn 1989). Managerial initiatives are met with evasion, misunderstanding, negotiation, resistance, and outright opposition—and often for good reason. Beneath the statistics on trade, market share, cost, productivity, quality, and "best-practice" production, and downstream from "born-again" high-level managerial strategies, dramatic events are unfolding on the shop floor of American auto plants, including battles and negotiations over the organization of work that will have a major impact on the quality of working life, the role and influence of organized labor, and the future success of the U.S. auto industry.

Whereas advanced automation was seen by top managers as the key to renewed competitive success for the auto industry in the early 1980s, the team concept soon became the hottest strategy. This shift of emphasis came both from the expensive shortcomings of the automation solution at showplace GM assembly plants such as Orion and Hamtramck[10] and from the extraordinary success of an alternative model at NUMMI. GM managers must have been deeply embarrassed by the NUMMI outcome: with the same workers, union, and union leaders, Toyota management organized a production system that far exceeded in productivity and product quality not only the former GM plant on the same site but every other GM assembly plant in the United States as well (Krafcik 1987; Turner 1988a). Beginning even before the first car rolled off the line in late 1984 and continuing right up to the present, a steady stream of GM managers and UAW representatives have flown out on pilgrimages to view the new model in action. One result has been a major push toward new team forms of organization throughout the GM system. And Ford and Chrysler have also taken note: through their own studies of NUMMI and other Japanese-organized firms and their own nascent joint ventures, top managers at these firms have also begun major pushes toward team forms of organization.

Why are team and group forms of organization on and off the assembly line apparently superior, for productivity, quality, and flexibility, to traditional single-job organization in auto plants?[11] This is an important question because team organization seems often to be blindly accepted as virtuous these days in managerial, academic, and journalistic circles, at the same time as it is sometimes challenged from both activist and conservative bases in the rank and file. The answer has to do with the flexible allocation of manpower, the raising of work standards, and a new peer pressure to work harder, smarter, and with greater quality consciousness. When workers are organized in teams or groups, managers usually gain a greater ability to move people around (as job-control unionism begins to break down), thus keeping everyone busy all the time. When several workers and a team leader all know the tasks composing each job, man-

---

[10] See below for a discussion of the Hamtramck case.

[11] For several years, in the search for flexibility, auto firms throughout the advanced industrial world have been moving toward team forms of organization (Katz and Sabel 1985, p. 99).

agement gets more information and can more easily regularize work standards across jobs and push for the steady and uniform raising of these
standards. And when workers can be pulled together in a group responsible
for one part of production and the quality of its output, peer pressure can
be shifted away from traditional shop-floor "slow down, you'll work us
out of a job" consciousness to a new emphasis on collective productivity
and quality of output. There is no doubt that the current effort by auto
industry managers to introduce teams is a form of speedup: Stephen Wood
(1986) has referred to the new work organization as "team Taylorism";
Mike Parker and Jane Slaughter (1988) have pegged it as part of a system
of "management by stress." But however one judges the new managerial
initiatives, they have spread rapidly from plant to plant and have gained
considerable support from union and work force, along with vocal and
sometimes well-organized opposition.

Management efforts to set up teams on the Japanese model or otherwise,
it must be said, are notorious for their failures.[12] Harry Katz, Thomas
Kochan, and Jeffrey Keefe, for example, found no positive correlation
between teams and productivity in the U.S. auto industry; in fact, they
found a negative relationship (1988).[13] They did find, however, a correlation between increased worker participation in shop-floor decision making and productivity, leading them to the conclusion that teams can be
beneficial only when linked to real input from workers (thus fulfilling the
promise to workers that there is something in this for them, too). Luria
finds a correlation between work reorganization and performance only
when reorganization is linked to product redesign (specifically, the design
of the product to match production efficiency requirements; Luria 1987).

John F. Krafcik (1988a) and John Paul MacDuffie and Kochan (1988)
present evidence to demonstrate the necessary linkage, for good economic
performance, of clusters of innovative industrial relations, human resources, technology, and production practices (teams, for example, linked
to decentralized production practices such as just-in-time inventory and
closer labor-management cooperation). Team organization, to be suc-

[12] See, for example, Robert Cole's study (1989) of the contrasting problems and strategies
for "small group activity" in Japan, Sweden, and the United States. Cole discusses the
problems that American traditions of labor-management conflict cause for attempts here to
move organizations toward a small group orientation.

[13] This is a plausible finding, given that teams are new at many U.S. plants and are thus
at the early "bug-filled" stage of transition to new work organization; Big Three managers
often lack a commitment to the thoroughgoing reform within their own ranks necessary for
successful team organization (as we will see in the case studies below, especially at Van
Nuys and Hamtramck); and team organization exists more on paper than in reality at many
U.S. auto plants.

cessful, must be part of a larger whole, a new production system in the auto industry that includes a new social organization of the factory. Part of the problem, however, is that managers in the United States have not yet decided on the precise nature of the new production system or new team organization. Managers appear fairly unanimous in the belief that labor-management relations should be more cooperative; but how much substantive input the union should be offered and how much real participation and responsibility the worker on the shop floor should be given are subjects of intramanagement debate and ongoing trial-and-error experimentation in the plants.

Plant managers even in the same firm are pursuing contrasting strategies in their approach to work reorganization and new industrial relations. Given the broad societywide decline of the labor movement, managers have been tempted to pursue an aggressive strategy toward labor as product and labor markets in the auto industry loosened. The Big Three have all pursued variants on a "cooperative labor strategy" that has included a major effort to work with key national-level UAW officials on the need for new work organization and industrial relations; heavy pressure on local unions, including the threat of plant closure and "whipsawing," for work rules concessions and a more cooperative approach; and the offer of a new form of incorporation—informal voice in new areas of managerial decision making and employment security for at least part of a unionized work force—in return for major shop floor concessions.

Firms have also made major investments in new technology, closed plants and laid off many workers, closed or spun off unionized supplier plants, and moved production offshore, all of which have challenged union influence and reduced (among the remaining core work force) the labor-management trust necessary for the success of a cooperative strategy (Quinn 1989). Management has cut its unionized work force back toward a core level and pushed for the plant-by-plant adoption of flexible internal labor practices, new industrial relations, and teamwork, thus pursuing contradictory but simultaneous adversarial and cooperative strategies toward work force and union.[14]

[14] Important interfirm differences have existed, of course, both in the challenge faced and the strategies pursued. GM, for example, was the most cash rich and thus was best placed to pursue a high-technology strategy, pouring $10 billion into advanced automation between 1982 and 1987; but this strategy backfired at least in the short run as bugs in the new equipment and lack of adequate training and corresponding human relations reform crippled production at some of the showplace plants. After the disaster of 1979, Chrysler was lucky. Although top managers would have liked to have made the same kind of investments as GM and watched enviously from the sidelines, Chrysler was forced by financial constraints to take a more gradual, incremental approach to technological change

At GM, Ford, and Chrysler, the drive toward teamwork on the shop floor in selected plants has often meant a substantial reduction in the number of job classifications, the easing of "rigidities" in the assignment of personnel (such as seniority provisions), and the establishment of joint labor-management committees to set up new programs and discuss problems, to move away from the grievance-oriented relations of the past. In this emerging vision (now a reality at a few plants), workers work more flexibly on the shop floor (rotating jobs, integrating new tasks such as quality inspection into production work, working in teams) with a greater commitment to the plant and to product quality, and union representatives participate in consensus-building discussions and help smooth implementation of new technology and work organization. All of these innovations, however, challenge traditional union roles and bases of influence; indeed, UAW efforts to respond and adapt to the new managerial strategies have pushed the union repeatedly into trial-and-error situations and internal discussion and debate, at national and local levels, aimed at virtually forging a new organizational identity.

The UAW Grapples with Work Reorganization

For the UAW, the Big Three management's drive toward work reorganization, and especially toward work teams, represents a major challenge. In whatever form it takes, the new organization moves away from several of the tenets of the established postwar industrial relations system (compare Slichter, Healy, and Livernash 1960 with Katz and Sabel 1985; Kochan 1985; Kochan, Katz, and McKersie 1986). Two examples will show the significance of these changes and the depth of the challenge to organized labor.

First, a major basis for union presence and strength in the auto industry (as throughout much of the unionized work force) has been on the shop

---

and work reorganization and thus avoided GM's expensive plant-level failures (Turner and Gold 1988). Ford, for its part, had great success in the 1980s relative to GM (as reflected in market share changes, profitability, and cost-per-car differential). Analysts attribute the relative Ford success, with varying emphasis, to cohesive international organization and coordination of production, relative vertical disintegration (Ford produces 50% of its parts in-house compared to 70% for GM), more cooperative labor-management relations, promoted in part through the EI program, and popular product design (e.g., the Taurus and Sable). But the limits of the Ford model may have been reached in the absence of major work reorganization; Ford itself is certainly pushing team systems and flexible labor allocation reforms similar to those of GM and Chrysler, and for the same reasons (e.g., superior Japanese performance in production).

floor as defender of seniority-based allocation for multiple, well-defined job classifications. This has been one of the main things that local union representatives do and one of the main services they provide for their members. Managerial work reorganization initiatives are demanding a substantial weakening of this power: big reductions in the number of job classifications, a more flexible allocation of shop-floor labor, and a co-operative labor-management relationship that includes less use of griev-ance and arbitration, the legal means through which local unions make their clout felt. Second, another basis for union strength both at the national and local levels has been national and pattern bargaining and the resulting relative uniformity of pay, working conditions, rights, and work organi-zation. Current managerial strategies aim at getting local unions to compete with one another as plant-by-plant negotiations are conducted and a wide variety of outcomes are reached. In return for the weakening of traditional shop-floor power and national-level solidarity, the union and its members have won limited employment security (limited before 1990 by market circumstances, always the main reason that autoworkers get laid off any-way),[15] increased training opportunities, and some increased input (usually informal) into managerial decision making.

Market circumstances (overcapacity, intense competition in world mar-kets and in the U.S. domestic market) have undercut the capacity of the union to bargain from a position of strength. In this context it is perhaps remarkable that the UAW, as one of the strongest unions in the United States, has been able to remain entrenched in the auto industry and continue to provide its members with important new protections. But the union position remains a difficult one for two reasons in addition to the general market circumstances. For one thing, unions in the United States have little history of integration into managerial decision making, as unions do, for example (in different ways), in Germany, Sweden, and Japan. This means that managerial initiatives such as the current drive toward work reorganization are taken at the outset without much reference to union concerns; and the union has to scramble from scratch to figure out how to influence management and come up with negotiable positions. In addition, the UAW suffers as do all American unions from the fragmented and declining state of U.S. unionism. In the absence of a cohesive labor movement and of external legal or political constraints on management, the nonunion option is viable (as Nissan at Smyrna, Tennessee, and Honda at Marysville, Ohio, have shown). Big Three managers are emboldened

---

[15] Income security was substantially improved in the 1990 contracts.

to use direct pressure and the threat of disinvestment or plant closure as a basis for negotiation.

How has the union responded? Because the traditional basis of national-level UAW strength has been at the industry and firm level (broad collective bargaining with an emphasis on wages and benefits), key national union leaders have taken a broad view of economic and political realities: the market challenge, the need for new social organization, the unavoidable impact of general weakness in the labor movement. But because the traditional basis of local union strength has been on the shop floor—in work rules and job-allocation enforcement through grievance procedures at the plant level—some local union leaders have vigorously opposed new management schemes for work reorganization, such as teamwork. And local union officials as well as workers in the plants have been well placed to observe that changes imposed on the work force have all too often been accompanied by little substantial reform or "humanization" of managerial authority.

These contradictory influences have resulted in considerable internal union conflict, between the national and selected local unions, and within locals. The national union, through its regional directors, has attempted where possible to make coalition with local union leaderships to negotiate with management for the introduction of new social organization (reduction in the number of job classifications, more flexible job allocation, shop-floor teams, cooperative industrial relations, informal union voice, enhanced employment security and training opportunities). Local unions and work forces, however, have in many cases come over to new organization only under heavy pressure from management (threat of plant closure or disinvestment).

As a strong, fairly cohesive union firmly entrenched in its industry, the UAW has been able to negotiate important protections for both the work force (such as the job banks in 1984 and more comprehensive, though still limited, employment security in 1987) and the union (union security, extensive full-time union representation even in a nonadversarial system, as at NUMMI). But the UAW has seen its membership significantly reduced and has lacked a consistent strategy of its own for responding to managerial initiatives (e.g., alternatives for work organization). Whether accommodative or oppositional, union strategies regarding work reorganization have as yet rarely been proactive (taking initiative, proposing alternatives, and negotiating for them).[16]

---

[16] The UAW has embarked on the laborious process of developing its own concepts of new work organization (see United Auto Workers 1989, pp. 61–68; see also the "New

The severity of the market challenge and the general fragmentation of organized labor have strengthened management's hand against local plant (both union and management) opposition; job classifications, for example, have given way gradually on a plant-by-plant basis under heavy managerial pressure. This process accelerated under provisions of the 1987 GM-UAW and Ford-UAW contracts, which provided for enhanced employment security and the establishment of plant-level joint committees to improve efficiency.

Local unions remain entrenched in the plants, and the national UAW leadership must consider local union politics for its own internal majority coalition; at the same time, management at the plant level often resists the new ways that appear to threaten traditional bases of managerial power by bringing the work force and union into new levels of decision making for the firm.[17] Together, these dynamics have resulted in considerable resistance to management's reorganization initiatives, making for a rocky transition and patchwork plant-by-plant pattern of success and failure. As Davis Dyer, Malcolm S. Salter, and Alan M. Webber put it:

> Moreover, at the level of the individual plant, the progress toward practicing the new philosophy embodied in the 1982 and 1984 contracts has been notoriously spotty, depending almost entirely on the character of the plant manager and the president of the UAW local.
>
> Simply continuing this pattern will not secure a competitive future: the rate of change is too slow and the scope of change too narrow. (1987, p. 269)

Extrapolating from current trends, the most likely general outcome appears to be a gradual, rocky, plant-by-plant transition to experimental new systems of work organization, with an auto industry work force substantially reduced in size from its 1978 peak, with the UAW integrated in a limited way into managerial decision making (through joint processes and committees at the firm and plant levels) but perhaps less legally and

Technology" Resolution adopted at the same convention). But these concepts have not as yet been translated into consistent plant-level bargaining strategies.

[17] Managerial resistance is arguably more important in this regard than union resistance. Where management has changed its ways substantially, as at NUMMI, the union and work force have gone along with new work organization much more readily. Where management has said, in effect, "you get teams but we'll keep running the show in our traditional, authoritarian way"—one persuasive interpretation, for example, for persistent team-system problems at the GM Van Nuys plant—union and work-force resistance stiffens. Managerial resistance, of course, is facilitated by the larger political and economic context, which makes possible the continuing aggressive posture toward union and work force.

formally entrenched. Competitive success is problematic (in part because of the problematic nature of the transition to new work organization), and the union faces a smaller membership, a less densely organized industry, and a more uncertain role.

As one would expect, management pressure for union concessions of traditional bases of influence combined with plant-by-plant changes in industrial relations have provoked considerable political conflict within the UAW. There are winners and losers in the new organizational changes, especially with the spread of shop-floor teams, and the losers usually refuse to go quietly. UAW locals for the most part have long traditions of active union democracy, with incumbent leadership regularly voted out of office as contending caucuses campaign for support. Proposed changes in work organization and industrial relations have in some cases galvanized the work-force electorate into two blocs: those favoring the changes and those opposed (with many others in the middle and undecided). The opposition groups are often led by an uncomfortable alliance of conservative, older workers with high seniority (who fear losing their favored status in new, integrated team systems) and activist workers favoring a more militant and less cooperative trade unionism. Favoring the changes are many union leaders, who see both personal and organizational advantages from enhanced "jointness," allied with younger, lower-seniority production workers, who have at once the most to fear from disinvestment and mass layoffs and the most to gain from new team organization (since their current jobs tend to be the harshest).

At some plants, these opposing groups turn out to be roughly equal in size; intense political campaigns for and against new contracts as well as for local union elections have resulted in close votes on many occasions. Typically, management works out an agreement with local union leadership for new work organization, including the establishment of new joint committees (to give the union new voice to replace old job-control rights, and which incidentally create new full-time union positions and increase the appointment power of the union leadership); a reduction in the number of job classifications; and the implementation of experimental or plantwide team organization. The agreement is then submitted to the membership for ratification, usually under the spoken or implied threat of disinvestment (no new model or outright plant closing). If the opposition wins the vote, it is not unusual for management to step up the pressure for plant closing and call for a second vote to give the rank and file the opportunity to "get it right."

Internal local union conflict also plays itself out within the national union. Although national union leadership has been stable and fairly united in its accommodative stance toward new work organization, national union representatives (from the GM, Ford, and Chrysler departments within the UAW and from the regional offices) have had to push management at the plant level to live up to promises and at the same time give support to local union coalitions that favor change. Along the way, the national union has had to fight against considerable internal opposition.

In 1982, a group called Locals Opposed to Concessions almost defeated the UAW-GM national contract (Milkman 1982; Dyer, Salter, and Webber 1987, pp. 205–8). In the 1984 contracts, the UAW, with establishment of the job banks,[18] moved forward in its strategy of trading wage restraint and a willingness to encourage plant-level changes in work rules in return for enhanced employment security and union input. Again an active opposition campaigned against the contract at GM, which passed by a vote of 57 to 43. Beginning in 1988, a new political grouping within the UAW called New Directions pulled together opposition groups from the local unions (including local union leaders opposed to teams and to the national union's accommodative strategies). Although New Directions was defeated in its bid for national executive board positions at the 1989 convention, the group announced its intent to form a permanent movement within the UAW, in part to oppose new management schemes for work reorganization and teamwork.

How do we gauge the stability and extent of workers' representation in the U.S. auto industry in the contemporary period? Clearly, the picture that emerges from this overall story is one of instability. Because the institutions of industrial relations in place were not compatible, in many ways, with the new competitive needs of industry, industrial relations had to change, and the bases of influence and the roles played by the UAW have had to change correspondingly. The outcomes, for a new stable settlement between labor and management and a stable union role, remain undetermined. In the final section of this chapter, we will look more closely at the three indicators of workers' interest representation (as described in the Introduction), showing the following patterns: (1) union membership density that is declining, as the organization rate for parts supplier firms drops and as Japanese transplants remain nonunion;[19] (2) modest improve-

---

[18] The formal name is JOBS, for Job Opportunity Banks. These are training and income maintenance funds for displaced autoworkers; the training and allocation programs are jointly run by labor and management and funded according to the 1984 contracts by $1 billion from GM and $280 million from Ford. Funding was increased modestly in the 1987 contracts.

[19] In contrast to union organization rules in West Germany, when the UAW organizes a plant in most states where the auto industry is concentrated (the "non-right-to-work"

ments for the remaining work force in protections against the effects of new technology and work organization, including enhanced employment security and training opportunities through the job banks; and (3) the absence, from the UAW side, of a consistent set of proposals for the shape of new work organization, so that the accommodative strategy remains one that accepts and attempts to modify managerial initiatives such as the team concept.

To look concretely at the politics of work reorganization and changing labor-management relations, we now turn to case studies of five plants where management has attempted to bring in new team organization. We begin with the widely acclaimed international model, the GM-Toyota joint venture known as NUMMI, in Fremont, California.[20]

NUMMI: The New Shrine in the West

In fact, NUMMI has achieved its gains through far greater regimentation of the work force than exists in traditional American auto plants. Tight specifications and monitoring of how jobs are to be done, a barebones work force with no replacements for absentees and a systematic and continuing speedup are the methods used.

We use the term ''management by stress'' to describe this system, which often goes by the names ''team concept'' or ''synchronous manufacturing.''

Mike Parker and Jane Slaughter, *New York Times*, December 4, 1988

The workers' revolution has finally come to the shop floor. The people who work on the assembly line have taken charge and have the power to make management do their jobs right. . . . The revolution is not happening everywhere—yet. But it is happening at Nummi. . . .

Its spectacular success, which has attracted attention in the United States and Europe, is not due to advanced robotics or sub-union wages.

states), through a successful certification election, the plant has 100% membership for the blue-collar work force; everyone is required to join. But new parts suppliers and the large Japanese assembly plants, Nissan in Tennessee, Honda in Ohio, and Toyota in Kentucky, have so far resisted unionization. This was demonstrated most dramatically in the summer of 1989, when the Nissan work force at Smyrna voted against union representation by a 70-to-30 margin.

[20] The facts and interpretations presented in the next five sections are based on a reading of labor-management agreements, other union and management documents and publications, newspaper and trade press articles, a visit to each plant, and, most important, a series of in-depth interviews and discussions, conducted between May 1987 and November 1989, with workers, union representatives, and managers at each of the five plants.

It is due to a revolutionary team production system run by the workers themselves. That system was worked out jointly with the plant's Japanese and American managers by the third partner in the joint venture—the U.A.W. And it is the U.A.W.'s rank-and-file workers who are making the team system work.

That's not the revolution some people were looking for. But it's a revolution a lot of real trade unionists have worked hard to bring about.

Bruce Lee, regional director, UAW, *New York Times*,
December 25, 1988

The old GM plant in Fremont, Calfornia, opened in 1962 and closed in 1982.[21] During its twenty years of operation, the plant fairly characterized work organization and industrial relations in the U.S. auto industry. Standardized goods (with many options) were produced for usually dependable mass markets in a production system notable for the many job classifications (well over one hundred), a seniority-based system of job control, high absenteeism and very high grievance rates, and highly adversarial industrial relations that at the most peaceful could be termed armed truce (following Harbison and Coleman 1951). The work force at Fremont earned a reputation as one of GM's most militant, but this militance was not at all atypical of relations within the U.S. auto industry.

In March 1982, the plant closed. In the midst of the worst Big Three auto sales slump in postwar history, Fremont became the fourth West Coast auto plant to shut down, leaving only GM's Van Nuys plant west of the Rocky Mountains. Workers were notified three weeks before closure; for many, the loss of this job inaugurated a roller coaster of dislocation and trauma that would culminate in what might be termed a "transformation of world views"[22] by the time NUMMI opened in 1984.

There were virtually no comparable union-wage manufacturing jobs in the area around Fremont (Caterpillar, Mack Trucks, Peterbilt, and Ford Milipitas had all closed in recent years in response to rising competition and economic downturn). Many workers maintained income for a time through standard unemployment benefits and union-negotiated supplements, known as Supplemental Unemployment Benefits and Guaranteed Income Stream (ten years seniority required). SUB payments were limited, however, and workers lost GIS if they refused a GM job in another part

[21] An earlier version of this section on NUMMI appeared in Turner 1988a, pp. 14–24. A German version appeared in Muster and Richter, eds., 1990, pp. 78–87. For generally favorable accounts of NUMMI, see Stansbury 1985; Krafcik 1987; and Brown and Reich 1989. For a critical account, see Parker and Slaughter 1988, pp. 100–122.

[22] For a useful and suggestive discussion of the ways in which workers' worldviews are transformed at particular historical moments, see Sabel 1982.

of the country. In this forced relocation, twenty-five hundred of the six thousand laid-off workers took new jobs in Oklahoma City, St. Louis, Kansas City, and other places. But because of the continual rumors that the plant might reopen under GM-Toyota management, many left their families behind in Fremont.

The UAW was powerless to prevent plant closure; labor in the United States has so far been unsuccessful in promoting broad plant closure legislation of the kind common in many other advanced industrial societies (although legislation requiring sixty-day advance notification for plants with one hundred or more workers was finally adopted by Congress in 1988; see Ehrenberg and Jakubson 1990). Nor was the union in a position to present management with alternative production or work organization strategies as a basis from which to bargain to keep the plant open. Finally, 1982 was the year in which active labor-market policies were slashed under the new Reagan government, at a time of perhaps unprecedented need, thereby reducing the already limited options for retraining and placement in new jobs.[23] The absence of government policies and union strategies that could have minimized worker dislocation reflects the very substantial limitation on union influence (political, industrial, firm-level, and plant-level) in the past decade and a half of intermittent economic crisis and industrial adjustment.

As a strong union with national contracts, however, the UAW was able to ensure its displaced members of much better protections than most laid-off American workers can receive. These protections included SUB and GIS; union-wage job opportunities elsewhere in the country; some counseling services, including tie-ins with local retraining and placement centers; and the hope of a future union job at the new plant if only workers could hang on for a couple of years.

The local union had a rocky history of relations not only with GM plant management but with the national union (the local, in fact, had been in trusteeship before the plant closure). Although there was much difference of opinion regarding union strategy within the local UAW, within the national UAW, and between the two, the threat of permanent closure of this and many other unionized plants effectively cut the ground from under proposed militant approaches and reduced the leverage of more uncompromising local union activists. The national UAW adopted a policy of working with the new GM-Toyota management to ensure that the plant would reopen. The national union moved in by way of the regional office,

---

[23] In 1982, CETA (the Comprehensive Employment and Training Act) was abolished and replaced by a much smaller JTPA (Joint Training and Partnership Act).

made key alliances with local union leaders, and dominated the subsequent three-year bargaining process, leading to a letter of intent in 1984, a full-fledged contract with NUMMI in 1985, and a fairly consensual union-management relationship that continues to the present day.

Cooperation, however, did not mean rolling over. Although the union gave up a good deal in the way of traditional job control (job classifications and seniority rights), it bargained successfully on other key issues: for the rehiring of former GM workers,[24] for top union-wage scale, for employment security (guarantees of no layoffs), for union recognition, and for full-time union representation in the plant (NUMMI management argued that part-time representation would be sufficient in a new non-grievance-oriented, cooperative relationship—the UAW won this one and now has fifteen full-time local representatives).

The transformation of local union leaders' worldviews demonstrates perhaps most dramatically the changed attitudes among the work force that have made the NUMMI plant highly productive and successful. Current local union leadership both inside and outside the plant is dominated by the cooperation-oriented Administration Caucus. These union leaders file very few grievances; encourage and actively practice the consensual talking out of problems from the shop-floor level on up; are big supporters of NUMMI, its product, product quality, and model of work organization and industrial relations; receive a steady flow of business, production, market, and personnel data from NUMMI management; engage in informal participation at various levels of managerial decision making from which the UAW has historically been excluded; and perhaps most indicative of all, locate union shop headquarters in the same office with management's labor relations (so they can "interface").

Yet these union leaders are for the most part not former members of the more moderate union factions but former rank-and-file militants from

---

[24] No seniority rights were won in this regard, but all former workers were given applications, the union became involved in the hiring process, and relatively few former workers who wanted these jobs were in the end excluded. Former union activists were rehired, including the old militant union leadership; 75 to 80% of the current work force in 1988 was former GM-Fremont workers. Thirty-three hundred former Fremont workers applied for jobs at NUMMI; some dropped out along the way, a few were screened out for drug, alcohol, and excessive discipline problems, and the rest were rehired. No one has yet done a comprehensive study of former Fremont workers not hired at NUMMI (the Fremont work force totaled seven thousand at its peak in the 1970s, compared to two thousand five hundred at NUMMI), but it appears that some retired (including early retirement), some settled in their new GM jobs in other parts of the country and chose not to apply to NUMMI, some found other jobs during the period of dislocation and kept them, and some chose not to apply or withdrew their applications during the screening process when they saw what the new system looked like.

the old plant.[25] In a fairly short time span (around two years), these union leaders underwent major attitude changes in response to pressure from the national union; pressure from NUMMI; the desire to save and provide jobs for "their people," after a disastrous period of dislocation and in the absence of other viable alternatives; and exposure to a new system of management and work organization, which offered a great deal on its own merits to win them over and convince them that this system was in fact better for their members.

Just as the dominant part of local union leadership was won over, so was a substantial portion of the former (and current) work force. During two years or more of dislocation, people found low-paying jobs, kicked about on benefits without much to do and with great anxiety about the future, or moved to places like Oklahoma, where they found themselves in new GM jobs but at the very bottom of plant seniority lists (in spite of ten, fifteen, even twenty years of service at the Fremont plant) and thus in the hardest assembly-line positions. When these workers finally returned to the new NUMMI plant for a week of unpaid screening and testing (the application process), they did so in a less militant and often even grateful frame of mind. Although skepticism about the new management system was widespread among the returning work force, that skepticism gradually gave way for many to a newfound plant loyalty as people discovered the relief of steady union wages; employment security (a no-layoff contract); a management system in which their old drill-sergeant bosses had been replaced by team and group leaders, who combined the roles of problem solver, facilitator, and boss, and at least in theory (if not always in practice) sought the input and consensus of the work force; a system of labor-management relations in which they themselves were expected to partic-ipate, at least in team meetings, and in which their input regarding prob-lems of production and work organization was encouraged; a system of work organization based on a more equitable distribution of the work load (a dramatic difference from the old system); and a system of production that emphasized cleanliness, efficiency, and high quality, in which one could much more easily (than under the old system) take pride in the product produced.

The first two hundred workers hired were the team leaders, who have played a key role both in the reintegration of the old work force and in the current operation of the production system. Team leaders were care-fully selected by management from among applicants on the basis of

[25] Before the plant closed in 1982, there were four caucuses within the local union, which one participant described to me as conservative, moderate, militant, and sectarian left.

attributes such as experience, problem-solving ability, leadership, communication, and general "people" skills. The original team leaders were sent to Japan for three weeks to work in production and receive training at a Toyota plant; they were paired off individually with Japanese trainers, who were responsible for educating them in the workings and benefits of the Toyota production and labor-management systems. In Fremont, these team leaders were given extensive additional training, both before and after their trips to Japan, in company policies, consensus building, the just-in-time inventory system, team organization, work standards, "kaizen" (constant improvement), market circumstances, and human relations.

Team organization exists throughout the plant. There is only one job classification for production workers and two skilled trades classifications; teams are typically composed of either all production workers or all skilled workers.[26] Most teams consist of four members and a team leader (five in all); the four members in a production team typically rotate among jobs while the team leader coordinates, checks equipment, monitors parts stocks, solves problems, repairs defects when possible, makes sure the right parts are put on the right cars, and fills in for members who are absent or at the restroom. Inspection is incorporated into the work of the teams. Teams meet regularly (twice a month) for half an hour at the end of a shift on paid overtime to discuss production problems; the team has considerable discretion in the organization and apportioning out of the work load assigned to it by management. Suggestions for improvements and the resolution of problems by team members, team leaders, union representatives, and managers are discussed at team meetings, where consensus is sought. Management, of course, has the final say, especially regarding work standards; but NUMMI "corporate culture" encourages managerial decisions that have been discussed and agreed to by those affected.

The role that teams play in promoting high work standards and continual, worker-initiated improvements in these standards is perhaps the key aspect of NUMMI social organization. High work standards (the number

---

[26] NUMMI production begins with huge steel coils and ends with Chevy Novas, Toyota Corollas, and as of 1988 the Geo Prizm (which replaced the Nova). NUMMI has a highly automated stamping plant, a body shop and a paint shop, both populated by a mix of people and robots, and an assembly line that is not highly automated (that is, it is relatively "low tech," as are most auto final assembly lines), where 900 of the 2,100 blue-collar employees in the plant work. Along the way, a substantial number of components are added from outside production sources, including engines and transmissions from Japan, by two separate receiving departments, "Overseas" and "North American."

of tasks completed within one cycle, usually around sixty seconds) is central to high productivity at NUMMI, and management's "kaizen" concept emphasizes the responsibility of all employees to strive for continual improvement in work standards. Management claims that a large majority of the work force has participated in the suggestion program, demonstrating widespread acceptance of the emphasis on high work standards and the willingness of many to "work smarter," if not harder and faster. The team system, led by the specially trained team leaders, encourages peer pressure for the raising of work standards (called speedup by critics inside and outside the plant), as opposed to traditional "slowdown" union consciousness.

Union structure in the plant consists of a network of union coordinators (sixty-seven in all, often team leaders), who attempt to resolve problems through discussion at the lowest level and who receive two hours overtime pay a week for this extra work, and fifteen full-time representatives. Very few grievances are filed; the emphasis is on discussion and consensus up and down the line. Management policy is explicit and written regarding exactly how many infractions (such as absences) will result in discipline, up to and including termination. In most cases of discipline, union agreement has been secured; often, discipline is discussed in advance with union representatives, and informal negotiation results in consensus before action is taken.

In spite of the team system and consensual organizational philosophy, management retains its ultimate prerogative in matters of work standards ("there are sixty working seconds in every minute, regardless of a worker's seniority"), equipment use, sourcing decisions, product and other strategic planning. What is new is that the union gets a steady flow of information and is often brought in on early discussions regarding issues such as equipment use, hiring policy, scheduling, and work standards. Union rights in these arenas of discussion and decision making are informal, yet the opportunity for input and in some cases influence appears to be substantial. Union representatives claim to have an active influence in areas of traditional managerial prerogative.

What the union does not have is a strategy of its own for work organization and industrial relations (beyond cooperation). This is definitely management's game; the team system and problem-solving climate, the cooperative labor relations and processes of consensus, the emphasis on high work standards—NUMMI management has implemented very much the system that it preconceived. The UAW has managed to negotiate substantial modifications (such as the fifteen full-time representatives and, in a 1988 agreement, the right to participate in the selection of team leaders and in the establishment of a clear set of criteria for their selection), but for the most part the union has, given some input, reacted to management's initiatives in an accommodating way. One gets the sense that union leadership at both the local and regional levels is feeling its way along in an imported system that so far has worked out surprisingly well.

What do the workers think of this new model? Survey research remains to be done, but the political success from 1986 to 1990 of the union's Administration Caucus suggests the popularity or at least acceptance of the system. In the 1988 local union elections, Administration Caucus candidates were successful in balloting for most of the top union offices. But the opposition People's Caucus won many of the union coordinator positions and remained very much in evidence in the plant, especially in final assembly with the greatest concentration of workers. The opposition has concentrated its criticisms on four main issues: the speed of the line (and the constant pressure to work harder and faster, not just smarter—this is a critique of the crucial kaizen approach to work standards); the close (and too friendly in this view) relationship between union and management; the unequal distribution of privileges in the plant (the same people, it is claimed, get pulled off the line for training and for the "soft" project jobs); and the top-down way in which the local union is run (with constant consensus meetings with management held behind closed doors). The People's Caucus calls for a tougher and more democratically accountable union as independent representative of the work force. The NUMMI workforce apparently shares this concern; in June 1991, opposition candidates improved on their previous showings (stable vote totals around 40 percent between 1986 and 1989) to win a majority of key posts in local union elections.

The point to emphasize about internal union conflict at NUMMI, however, is that the team system does not seem to be in jeopardy as a result of union politics. My guess is that a victory for the opposition will result in more grievances filed, a more adversarial relationship between labor and management, perhaps a few more concessions extracted for the work force, without basically changing the NUMMI system or model. At best, the People's Caucus will attempt to present an alternative vision of what NUMMI could be—a more democratic and equitable version—as a new basis for negotiation, based on a more assertive and proactively engaged unionism. It seems likely that management could find common ground with a new union leadership that accepts the team system in its main points.

There is, therefore, a new model of industrial relations in the United

States, and this model is linked inseparably to a new model of work organization. That this model includes the union in a central position is evidence of the strength of the UAW as a national union. That this model is essentially a product of management conception and execution, implemented only after a humbling and traumatic period of dislocation for the work force, testifies to the limitations of union influence in the United States in a period when market circumstances have undermined labor's bargaining strength.

In its efforts to spread the NUMMI model to other U.S. auto plants, GM has come up against widespread explicit as well as implicit resistance in the ranks of both management and labor. Those who oppose the NUMMI model are both conservative—managers holding on to traditional forms of power; older workers defending seniority rights—and rank-and-file activists and union leaders defending traditional, arm's-length, adversarial unionism or the class struggle. The trouble with these oppositional viewpoints is that they generally fail to consider thoroughly enough the real, unavoidable changes in the world market that have made work reorganization imperative, and they fail to produce realistic alternatives in work organization to management's team concept. But those on the labor side who favor NUMMI and other parallel drives toward cooperation and new organization all too often do so uncritically, without considering the real risks for both union and work force.

In fact, world markets demand that the U.S. auto industry develop new industrial relations and new work organization. The old ways simply cannot compete on open markets with the high-quality, low-cost products of a Japanese system based on shop-floor teamwork, high work intensity, and subordinate, cooperative enterprise unionism. NUMMI offers an alternative, which includes the union (unlike most other Japanese plants in the United States) and results in world-class productivity and product quality. Workers in many cases like the teams and appreciate the opportunity to rotate jobs and give input; they like the clean, efficient environment and the fact that they are treated with new respect. Team leaders (about one in every five workers) are especially pleased at their new responsibilities and leadership roles. No one appears to miss the old drill-sergeant bosses and the tension of constant labor-management antagonism that characterized the old plant.

Nevertheless, there are problems with the NUMMI model, and some of these take political shape in the People's Caucus critique. High productivity combined with outsourcing (both domestic, as for seat production and cafeteria work, and foreign, as for engines and transmissions from

Japan) means fewer jobs at the plant than before,[27] and this also means fewer unionized auto industry jobs in the United States than might otherwise be the case. Substantive training opportunities for production workers remain limited as the wide cleft between skilled and production groups stays unchanged. Cycle time is short (around one minute), and there is great pressure to maintain high work standards, to work fast and intensely; the earlier waiting and buffer time is largely gone at NUMMI, as virtually everyone works "sixty seconds in every minute." There is great pressure to avoid absenteeism, which means that people sometimes come to work sick and those who are sick too often are forced out.

In perhaps the opposition's most telling critique, the merging of labor and management viewpoints does raise the danger of an American version of enterprise unionism, stripped of its strong independent base. I have argued that the local union, backed by the national UAW, has so far played a role that is independent enough of management to have pushed NUMMI in new directions (to include, for example, full-time union representation and joint selection of team leaders). But the danger of the union losing its identity should not be ignored.

Spreading the Model with Great Difficulty: GM-Van Nuys

In order to be an ongoing and successful organization, Van Nuys must change its fundamental ways of operating. In order to accomplish this change, a new agreement is necessary to provide the framework to produce a world class quality vehicle which is competitive in the marketplace, while at the same time serving the needs of our employees. . . .

The framework for change is a team organization. In a team organization, the work performed in the various departments will be assigned to business teams . . . Each team will be responsible for such things as safety, product quality including specifications, cost reduction, meeting budgets and schedules, overtime equalization, training and job rotation, absentee coverage, job layout and methods, inspection, repair and housekeeping . . . It is recognized that the team concept will dramatically

---

[27] This is true even when one controls for the fact that the current plant has one assembly line for car production compared to the old plant's two lines (one for cars, one for trucks). Outsourcing is a problem for the union at NUMMI; but this is not the key to understanding the plant, as some critics have suggested. The old plant also outsourced engines and transmissions (although now they come from Japan); what is new, for example, is the outsourcing of seats—but in this, NUMMI is following a process widespread throughout the auto industry, in both the United States and West Germany.

change the existing system and structure, expanding the responsibilities of all employees. Accordingly, higher rates of pay will be justified. . . .

The parties further recognize that due to the rapidly changing nature of our business brought about by global competition, it is necessary that this agreement not be static, but be a Living Agreement.

—CPC Van Nuys, Local 645 UAW, "Local Team Concept Agreement," 1986

Eliminating workers—that's what the team concept is all about.
—Pete Beltran, president, Local 645 UAW, May 23, 1987

GM management invested a major effort to adopt the lessons of NUMMI in the Van Nuys assembly plant in Los Angeles, California.[28] But the experiment produced no great success story and faced major problems from two directions, the work force and union and middle management. A team system modeled after NUMMI was implemented throughout the plant on both shifts in 1987, but no glowing productivity, quality, or cost improvements had yet been advertised as of 1989, and from every account the plant faced a continuing rocky future for labor-management relations and the team system.

Built in 1947, the Van Nuys plant in the 1980s mass-produced Chevy Camaros and Pontiac Firebirds, about two hundred thousand a year.[29] These cars sold for about $20,000 each and thus occupied a "specialty niche," a market fact that might seem to make the plant a more conducive target for multiskilled and multitask team organization. In 1985, GM reassigned an energetic, "rising star" plant manager named Ernie Shaefer from the innovative Fiero plant in Pontiac, Michigan, to take over at Van Nuys. In 1986, with the plant facing the threat of closure from GM headquarters, Shaefer negotiated a new "team concept" local agreement, including drastic reductions in job classifications and plantwide team organization, with the shop bargaining committee. The new contract was presented to the work force as a way to raise productivity and product quality, increase the participation and responsibility of workers, improve

[28] For a detailed account of labor-management relations at Van Nuys from an engaged, partisan point of view, including a highly critical interpretation of the coming of the team system, see Mann 1987b. For a useful comparison of Van Nuys and NUMMI, see Brown and Reich 1989. See also various articles in the *Los Angeles Times* (e.g., March 12, 1987, Part I, p. 28, by Richard Paddock; August 18, 1987, Part IV, pp. 1, 22, by Harry Bernstein). An earlier version of this Van Nuys study appeared in Turner 1988b, pp. 12–16.

Beltran quote reported in *Daily Labor Reports*, Bureau of National Affairs, No. 101, May 28, 1987, p. A–5.

[29] As of 1988, the Van Nuys plant employed 3,800 hourly workers (union members).

the quality of working life, and convince GM headquarters that the Van Nuys plant was worth keeping open. On a first vote, the rank and file, apparently convinced by arguments that the team system would undercut union protections, reduce job mobility, eliminate many of the "good jobs" that high-seniority workers usually occupy, and result in speedup, rejected the agreement. But on a second vote, under stepped-up pressure from plant management and the shop committee, and with the heavy threat of plant closure hanging in the air and the second shift on layoff, the agreement passed by a small margin (53 to 47).

The union itself, and not just the work force, was badly split on the issue of team organization. The shop chairman (the highest-ranking local UAW official inside the plant) and his allies negotiated and supported the agreement as an appropriate response to intensified market competition, one that could both keep the plant open (by convincing top GM management that here was a cooperative work force willing to improve performance dramatically) and serve workers' interests in expanding the area of responsibility and making work more interesting. Between 1986 and 1989, roughly half the work force supported this point of view in various elections (for union offices and for contract and agreement approval), with the largest base among younger production workers, those with the hardest jobs and thus the least to lose (and perhaps the most to gain) from reorganization.

On the other side, a solid coalition of older, high-seniority workers (with the most to lose from reorganization) and more militant trade unionists (opposed to labor-managment cooperation and perceived union-weakening teams) stood against the innovative arrangements. Until 1988, this group was led by Pete Beltran, for nine years the popular local union president (the top local union officer, based outside the plant in the union office), who in 1987 gave up his presidency and ran for shop chairman to gain more influence inside the plant. Beltran and his allies had organized and led an impressive Labor-Community Coalition for several years to pressure GM to keep the plant open, using the threat of a widely organized southern California boycott of GM products (in the largest new car market in the country; Mann 1987b). Some of the leaders of this group became leaders of the opposition to team organization, seeing in the new arrangements a renewed management campaign to whipsaw the work force into concessions using the threat of plant closing. Management's negotiation of teams with the shop chairman in explicit opposition to the union president effectively polarized the union and work force into opposing camps.

In the fall of 1986, GM announced that the Norwood, Ohio, assembly plant, the only other plant producing Camaros and Firebirds, would be closed (it had been clear for quite some time that either Norwood or Van Nuys would close); and management moved to implement the team system at Van Nuys. With the help of $20 million from California's Employment Training Panel, a training program was set up. First, 125 instructors were selected from among the work force and taught to be trainers; then 1,100 team leaders were selected and trained for ten weeks each (in the team concept, work standards, consensual leadership, and human relations); and finally, in May 1987, the entire remaining work force along with supervisors on both shifts received seven days of training, and the new system went into effect. Job classifications were reduced in number from over seventy to two production (team member and team leader) and seven skilled classifications; people for the most part kept their old jobs but the entire work force, like it or not, was reorganized into NUMMI-style teams.

In early June, however, hotly contested local union elections resulted in the ouster of the pro-team shop chairman (Richard Ruppert) and his replacement by the local president (Pete Beltran), who had opposed the new agreement (Mann 1987b, pp. 267–328). As was the case for the team concept elections, the vote was very close and resulted this time in a mixed outcome: although Beltran ousted Ruppert to gain the decisive shop chairman position, Jerry Shrieves, a Ruppert ally and team concept supporter, won election to Beltran's old job as local president. So the union leadership split continued, with the top positions switched. The new shop chair proceeded to pull the union out of all the joint labor-management committees that had been set up to administer and facilitate the team system. It was too late to turn back the clock on teams—the earlier agreement had been signed and ratified and the team system was in place, if only for a very short time. But the team system that remained was now very much management's project, without consensual industrial relations and with only the reluctant participation of much of the work force.

Management attempted to move around the new shop chairman and his allies by drawing whoever would participate into the joint processes: bargaining committee members, team leaders, the new union president (Shrieves), and union officers appointed by the national union.[30] In this effort, management and pro-team unionists had some success; the team

---

[30] At each plant, there are a small number of full-time "nonpolitical" union positions that are not subject to election. Health and Safety is one example, Quality of Working Life is another. Appointed by the national union, these representatives usually back the national union position, which for the most part has been supportive of team organization. At Van Nuys, the QWL officer played an active role in support of teams and the new joint labor-management processes. The national union itself officially supported the team concept at Van Nuys without playing the activist role it played at NUMMI.

system stayed in place and joint discussions for implementation and facilitation of the system found new life. Jerry Shrieves filled the vacuum
left by Beltran's withdrawal from the joint processes and became the leader
from the union side of efforts to make the reforms work and push management to live up to its promises regarding new dignity and respect for
the workers. In this effort, Shrieves found considerable resistance on the
part of middle management: group leaders (management's front line, in
charge of several teams), for example, invaded team meetings and often
ran the show in the old authoritarian fashion. Pro-team unionists found
their energies all too often dissipated on two fronts: trying to win over
doubters of the new system in the work force and fighting rear-guard
actions against determined opponents; and leaning on management to fulfill
the "humanization" and substantive participation intent of the agreement.

The difficulties, limitations, and instability inherent in moving around
the democratically elected shop chairman were apparent. Although repeated attempts were made by managers and pro-team unionists to win
Beltran over to the new system, he remained opposed in principle. And
his views continued to find considerable resonance among the work force,
for at least two reasons. For one thing, management's unwillingness to
undergo its own thoroughgoing internal reform (absolutely essential in the
switch to a new "democratic" firm culture) made many team members
skeptical of the team system and management's intent; what workers found
back on the shop floor was in many cases not what they had been promised
in training. And for another, GM continued to offer no guarantees about
the future status of the plant. Workers and union sought the commitment
of a new future model assignment in return for the very substantial organizational changes to which they had agreed; but no commitments were
forthcoming from the firm.

In early 1988, a sales slump required the temporary layoff (for four
weeks, as it turned out) of half the work force at Van Nuys. Past practice
and contractual provisions mandated that the low-seniority half of the
work force be laid off and the remaining workers consolidated into one
shift. Management did not want to use the traditional approach, however,
because this would have broken up teams and disrupted the implementation
process. So management, with the support of the pro-team unionists,
presented a plan to alternate shifts on layoff (two weeks at at time), to
keep the teams together and share the burden of low sales among the
entire work force. With unemployment benefits and SUB funds, the laid-
off workers would get most of their pay, and Shrieves and his allies sold
the plan as offering paid time off for all. But in the context of mistrust

at Van Nuys, the plan was perceived as an attack on vital seniority rights; it was defeated on a first vote and then narrowly passed, under renewed pressure, on a second vote. Once again, the work force was bitterly divided.

Seniority rights, in fact, were substantially protected in the new team system at Van Nuys (unlike at NUMMI, where they virtually went out the window because all workers hired when the plant opened in 1984 were new hires). Workers kept their old jobs when the teams were set up, and seniority remained the deciding factor in reassignment to open positions. But seniority rights were weakened in two ways: in new restrictions placed on bidding rights and in selection of team leaders (for which seniority was only one of several criteria). In a climate of considerable mistrust, workers' perceptions of the management layoff plan emphasized not the objective benefits for all (which is what workers at Lansing saw, as we will see, when presented with the same plan) but a managerial ulterior motive aimed at further weakening seniority rights.

As Beltran and his allies on the shop committee and in the work force continued to boycott the joint processes, tension reached a high point in the spring of 1988 in a rapid-fire series of events: management fired Beltran for allegedly lying about past absences (claiming to be on union business on his lost time vouchers, when management claimed he was not); management unilaterally outsourced the cushion room at a cost of 130 union jobs, a heavy-handed slap in the face to notions of mutual respect and joint decision making (even the pro-team union contingent was excluded from this decision process); and Plant Manager Shaefer, the manager most closely identified with substantive support for the team system, was promoted to a new job in Detroit. The first two of these events engendered a backlash on the shop floor and could hardly be expected to contribute to the atmosphere of trust that team systems require, while the third left supporters of the team concept twisting in the wind, uncertain about management's commitment to work reorganization at Van Nuys.

As it turned out, the new plant manager was a "hands-on" leader who worked actively with union supporters to make the team system succeed. But he lasted only a year or so before being reassigned, once again leaving workers doubtful about GM's commitment to the plant and setting off new rumors of a possible future plant closing. And the new plant manager's positive accomplishments were, in the eyes of the work force, at least partially offset by widespread resentment about the cushion room action and the decision to fire Beltran. Although a NUMMI-style team system existed on paper throughout the entire plant and appeared to work successfully in a few areas (such as the body shop), skepticism about the system remained widespread at Van Nuys and successful operation was spotty two and a half years after plantwide training and implementation.

Beltran and the local union vice-president (who was fired on a similar charge) finally agreed to a deal to accept retirement, with full benefits, rather than be fired. In 1989, a new election was held for shop chairman, and this time Richard Ruppert, the former shop chairman whom Beltran had defeated in 1987, was elected. Ruppert and Shrieves, as allies, reestablished the full "jointness" process with management and moved forward in support of the team system. Perhaps now they would be able to turn things around and make teams work at Van Nuys, with demonstrable results in productivity, product quality, and work-force satisfaction. But considerable damage had been done, and their efforts continued to collide with resistance from both management and work force. And as unionists do throughout the U.S. auto industry, they continued to work and bargain around the edges of management's team plans, without a well-developed and long-term perspective of their own on new work organization.

What accounts for the difference between NUMMI and Van Nuys?[31] One common view, especially in management circles, is that because the plant was never closed, the work force did not suffer enough to be willing to embrace the new system. But this argument is flawed: workers at Van Nuys in fact suffered through considerable uncertainty and dislocation. The entire second shift (half the work force) was on long-term layoff, some of the workers were recent transfers from other plants that had closed, and everyone had experienced the years-long threat of plant closure (GM Van Nuys was prominent on the list of plants considered for permanent shutdown for several years in the early to mid-1980s). Management was able to get majority acceptance for the new plan and had a golden opportunity to solidify a pro-team system in the work force through extensive training programs and initial team implementation.

Another interpretation offered is the strong organized presence of union militance at the Van Nuys plant. Union representatives and workers organized an impressive Labor-Community Coalition, several years in the making to keep the plant open in the face of GM's closure threats (rounding up politicians and church and community leaders to support a boycott of GM products if the plant closed). But again this argument fails to hold water: it is based on the assumption that union militants will necessarily oppose "class collaborationist" systems of cooperation. In fact, a number

---

[31] The analysis here parallels an argument made by Brown and Reich (1989). N.B.: In July 1991, GM announced the 1992 closing of the Van Nuys plant.

of coalition activists and supporters became team leaders and supporters of the new system, and at NUMMI, it is former union militants from the old GM plant who today head the cooperation-oriented Administration Caucus.

Both of these arguments focus on resistance in the rank and file, and indeed there has been much opposition, based ironically on a de facto coalition between left-leaning activists opposed to cooperation with management (especially on management's terms) and more conservative and traditional older workers concerned about preserving seniority rights. Both of these forces have in common an understandable wariness about what they perceive to be management's drive to weaken traditional union protections and bases of strength with only doubtful promises, informal input, and "joint processes" offered in return—that is, management's apparent drive in the direction of enterprise unionism. Even the pro-team union leaders spent much of their time pushing and arguing with management to live up to the promises of the new system, which hardly helped to win over the opponents.

A better interpretation emphasizes management's failure to reorganize itself more adequately for the tasks at hand. The critical difference between NUMMI and Van Nuys is the presence at NUMMI of a new management approach, strategic orientation, and focus on human relations. Management at Van Nuys saw to it that the instructors and team leaders were trained, as was the work force (although perhaps too minimally) but overlooked substantial screening and retraining for front-line supervisors (group leaders) and other middle managers. Because foremen in the auto industry have traditionally been drill-sergeant types, either a whole new breed is needed or else middle managers need extensive retraining and a vastly reformed approach to the work force, to elicit trust, input, cooperation, and active participation in the new system. The view I heard from both NUMMI visitors to the Van Nuys plant (sent down by GM and the UAW to assist reform initiatives) and Van Nuys workers was that management was asking for a major transformation of workers' attitudes and job descriptions while shop-floor management often kept to the same old authoritarian styles.

Why is traditional management so intransigent? This is an important question because the pattern is widespread throughout U.S. auto plants and U.S. industry in general. Is it particular American managerial values, the entrenched "no one tells me how to run my business" culture? Perhaps, but I would prefer to focus on the political opportunities for the continued expression of such values, which are not peculiar to the United States but have shown up strongly in other societies as well. Here I would point to the importance of two key variables: because labor was unable or disinclined in the past to break through into company decision making, managers have no history of sharing such processes with workers and unions. And because unions lack the backing of appropriate laws or corporatist bargaining structures (including a cohesive labor movement), an aggressive managerial posture is both viable and predominant throughout U.S. manufacturing in the current period of ongoing work reorganization.

Teamwork Troubles at Hamtramck

Another plant where GM has made a major effort to introduce teams is at the new flagship plant, Hamtramck (pronounced ham-*tram*-mik), located in an ethnic, low-income neighborhood of Detroit known as Poletown (the neighborhood was partly razed to make way for plant construction).[32] In this case, team organization was combined with the latest advanced automation, including such innovations as a Robogate system for flexible electric robot welding in the body shop, extensive automatic guided vehicle (AGV) applications (including just-in-time parts delivery), an advanced paint module in which the body is painted entirely by robots, and windshield installation by robots (Berry 1986). The plant cost $600 million to build and was billed as a showpiece, along with similar new plants at Orion and Wentzville, for GM's advanced technology and enlightened human-relations organization strategy. But problems with the technology, the teams, and labor-management relations caused great difficulties at this plant from the very start.

Construction of the plant began at Poletown in 1981, and the first car came off the assembly line in 1985. The Hamtramck plant was built to produce Cadillac El Dorados and Sevilles, Oldsmobile Toronados, Buick Rivieras, and the specialty Cadillac Allantes. The work force was hired principally from three other GM plants that closed in Detroit, and the workers were allowed to carry over their seniority. Because sales were slower than anticipated (or the other side of the coin, because of overcapacity and the production of similar models at the new Orion plant), Hamtramck has operated on only one shift (with fluctuating overtime) for most of its life span, employing about 3,200 hourly workers (out of 4,700 total employees). As of 1988, the junior seniority date at the plant was from 1976, meaning the hourly work force was composed of workers with twelve years or more experience in auto industry production.

[32] For a useful introduction to the Hamtramck plant, see the *Detroit Free Press* Special Issue on "Poletown," September 8, 1985.

From 1985 to early 1986, press reviews of the new plant expressed excitement about this bold high-technology effort and GM's big investment in rejuvenating auto production in the United States. Trade press journalists toured the plant and were impressed by the AGV forklifts delivering parts along the assembly line and robots installing windshields; they wrote of the team concept as an idea whose time had come. But by mid–1986, press reports began to turn negative; the technology was not working out, there were too many bugs, perhaps GM's great high-tech gamble had turned into an expensive boondoggle. And this was true not just for Hamtramck but for Orion and Wentzville as well.[33] As a rather dramatic statement of technological failure, parts delivery AGVs and windshield robots were removed from the plant for failure to perform up to expectations.

Similar shortcomings plagued the introduction of innovative work organization. In some ways, GM had ideal circumstances at Hamtramck for the implementation of a new team system of work organization. The plant produces specialty, upmarket products, which removes some of the pressure of labor costs; the plant was brand new, a greenfield operation, with a chance to make a fresh start in labor-management relations and shop-floor organization; and GM's major investment in the plant and obvious long-term commitment could have helped lay the groundwork for the development of high-trust relations. The work force, it is true, was made up of seasoned older workers perhaps set in their ways; but as we have seen at NUMMI, where the average age in 1987 was forty-two, older workers are capable of working well within a new system provided management organizes it appropriately.

The union was involved from the start in negotiations and joint committees at Hamtramck, including negotiations for the initial team concept training for the work force. All workers, in joint hourly and salaried groups, were given ten days of training in human relations, team skills and consensus decision making, ergonomics, economic awareness, problem solving, and team development. As veterans of the ups and downs of work in the auto industry, these workers probably approached their new jobs in very much the same mind-set as workers at NUMMI first did: grateful to have a job after a previous plant closure and layoff, skeptical about the team system management was placing them in, and hopeful that the promises of expanded dignity and participation expressed in the training were true.

[33] Developments at Orion and Wentzville parallel those at Hamtramck in the essential points of the story.

Teams started out very large at Hamtramck, ranging from twenty to sixty members. Teams elect their own team coordinators (TCs), who serve for 120 days and are eligible for reelection. The TC leads the weekly half-hour team meetings and fulfills many of the functions of a traditional foreman, monitoring work and product quality, administering overtime, checking equipment and parts stock, relieving on the line in emergencies, and facilitating team meetings. Although there is only one production classification at Hamtramck (called "technician"; and there are seven skilled classifications), there are many different jobs within a team. When the plant first opened, workers were encouraged to rotate jobs; and to the extent that they learned other jobs they were supposed to be rewarded through a pay-for-knowledge program (by learning seven different jobs they could reach top pay scale for a production worker).

A small part of the plant was set aside for production of the very expensive new Cadillac Allante. Here teams of high-seniority skilled workers put the car together, using bodies shipped over from Italy and engines from another plant. Instead of cycle times of about one minute as in most of the plant, workers perform a wide variety of tasks in twenty-seven-minute cycles; instead of an assembly line, the car moves around on AGVs, stopping for the necessary time at each work station. In this part of the plant, with much less time pressure (given the top-quality, high-cost product), the team system has appeared to work well.

In the rest of the plant, however, the team system did not work out with anything remotely approaching NUMMI's success, and this continued to be the case four years after initial implementation. There was frequent turnover among TCs (who either "burn out" or are voted out of office), causing considerable leadership instability on the shop floor; there was not much substantive pay-for-knowledge in practice; job rotation occurred only here and there; and workers' dissatisfaction with the system remained widespread on the shop floor (as indicated by 1989 union election results, discussed below).

One problem has been the merging of three workplace cultures. Workers were hired from three different former GM plants, and each group came in with distinct patterns of social relationships and labor-management histories. Another problem has been low use of capacity; with the second shift on continuous layoff from 1987 to 1989, rumors that one of the three very similar new plants would close (Hamtramck, Orion, or Wentzville) were hardly advantageous for building morale and commitment among workers. A third problem has been failures in the new technology and persistent bugs that divert energy from smooth production. It may well be that GM simply tried to do too much, eschewing incremental change for the sudden introduction of state-of-the-art technology, major work reorganization, and innovation in industrial relations.

None of these problems, however, seem necessarily fatal for the successful introduction of a team system, had it been properly organized and implemented. Union leadership supported the team system and participated in a variety of joint committees and activities. After the ten-day initial training, there was at least widespread interest and perhaps hope among the work force for the new system. Management appeared to have a good opportunity to make a fresh start.

Once again, however, the problem that stands out is management's failure to reform itself thoroughly and to keep to the innovative program and expanded worker participation that it had promised.[34] As the line reached full speed and production pressure mounted, managers in many cases simply fell back on their old ways of doing things, making unilateral decisions even when these decisions conflicted with the intent and the promise of the new system. Claiming that job rotation, as workers learned the new jobs, was hurting production, management stopped an already widespread and popular practice. Management let effective pay-for-knowledge slip away when it agreed to pay everyone top scale at the outset but then failed adequately to encourage or facilitate the learning of additional jobs. Training for the pivotal TCs was inadequate and largely on the job, contributing to problems in coordinating the teams and rapid turnover of TCs. And management offered no follow-up training for the work force in the first three years to reinforce and build on the initial ten days of learning. Managers themselves were inadequately trained for the fundamentally reformed labor-management and team relations that existed on paper and had been promised to the work force. From the front-line foreman level up to the plant manager, the old unilateral ways of operation remained entrenched (according to both union and management sources). And it did not help in the building of a sustained climate of cooperative relations and trust that Hamtramck had three different plant managers in the first four years of operation.

Under the circumstances, it is not surprising that disillusionment was widespread among the work force, and these feelings were reflected in local union politics. In 1986, the first local contract negotiated between management and the union was rejected by the work force. A year later, in October 1987, a new contract containing a few improvements for the workers was finally approved. In 1988, a strong opposition to the incum-

---

[34] Managers for the Hamtramck plant, like the work force, had been hired from among the ranks of the three other closed GM plants.

bent union leadership consolidated itself within the plant, building on widespread resentment about working conditions, shop-floor relations, the team concept, and union-management cooperation that was not benefiting the work force. In 1989, the opposition swept into office and took over the shop bargaining committee.

At first, tension increased between management and the new union leaders, who refused to go along with management's game plan. The new shop committee demanded more concrete commitment from management to carry through on its promises, in return for union cooperation. The new leadership pushed management, and according to sources in the plant, a decent working relationship began to develop after a few months. The union, for example, has pushed management for more real worker participation on the shop floor through the teams; and union representatives have been there, playing a more visible role than before, to enforce agreements. Even a Hamtramck middle manager told me that prospects for the team concept and a more engaged and mutually committed labor-management relationship had improved since the new, more "militant" shop committee took over.[35]

One major change that occurred between 1987 and 1989 was a switch to teams of smaller sizes. When the old twenty- to sixty- member structure turned out to be unworkable, smaller pilot teams were set up with positive results. By 1989, most of the plant had been converted to teams of four to eight workers (in some cases as large as fifteen). Communication, rotation (which is now up to the teams to decide on), problem solving, and rank-and-file leadership (the smaller teams each continue to elect a TC) all appear to work better in smaller teams; and this change may bode well for future prospects for the team system at Hamtramck.[36] In addition, there are, and have been from the start, a core of people in both management and union who are genuinely committed to organizational transformation and who are working very hard to make the team system and joint labor-management relationship work. Ironically, organizational innovation at Hamtramck may now have a better chance with a "tougher" shop committee in place, as a reluctantly innovative, foot-dragging management finds itself up against a stronger countervailing force.

Hamtramck may yet evolve into a successful case of work reorganization

---

[35] This was a manager who herself was critical of management's inadequate commitment to cooperative relations and genuine work-force participation.

[36] I have seen no data on the relation between team size and effectiveness; as Van Nuys demonstrates, small teams can also fail. But experiences at NUMMI and Lansing suggest that smaller teams have a better chance of success; and this is certainly the conclusion that managers at Hamtramck have drawn.

and "new industrial relations." As of late 1989, however, four years after the opening of the plant, it still had a long way to go. It remained to be seen whether management's internal reforms and work organization policies would prove substantial enough to evoke widespread commitment among the work force and an enduring cooperative labor-management relationship.

Homegrown Solutions (1): Lansing

Work reorganization in the auto industry in Lansing, Michigan, received considerable attention in trade journals and even in the national press in the mid-1980s, mainly for two reasons. First, the Reatta Craft Center has been hailed as a new model of non-assembly-line group production using skilled workers. Numerous organizational innovations have proven possible here in the small production runs of an expensive specialty car (the Buick Reatta); but the problem that remains is how to adapt such innovations for use in mass production, still by far the dominant form of auto industry production.[37] Second, around 1985, a series of articles appeared praising high-technology innovations in the largest GM Lansing plant (BOC North and South), which had just been changed over to produce new model Oldsmobiles, Buicks, and the Pontiac Grand Am. In particular, writers noted the decline of the assembly line and its replacement with AGVs, which brought work to each station and allowed the worker adequate time to do the job, inspect the work, and pass it along.

By 1987, most of the AGVs were gone, booted out of the factory by management for excessive downtime; and the assembly line was still very much alive. But this sprawling facility (known in Lansing as Plant No. 1, the largest of the six Lansing auto plants—known also as Lansing A and B, or Lansing North, South, and Center) is deserving of notice now for the successful development of a homegrown model of work reorganization and cooperative industrial relations that has significantly boosted productivity and quality of output.[38]

---

[37] The same dynamic was present at the Hamtramck plant: highly skilled, well-functioning teams for Cadillac Allante production compared to spotty team success in the larger part of the plant geared to mass production. The same question arises in the next chapter, when we consider successful group work in the skilled tool-making shop at the Ford-Cologne plant.

[38] These developments at Lansing, in contrast to the Reatta and AGV stories, have not received the press and analytic attention they deserve. For one exception, see Marjorie

Lansing Plant No. 1 employs 7,800 hourly workers (out of 8,500 altogether); workers are high seniority, with the most recent hires dating from 1980. Workers at Lansing are organized into teams of ten to twenty-five, each led by a full-time bargaining-unit team coordinator selected by seniority. The TC is responsible for knowing all the jobs in the team, facilitates, checks on parts, equipment, and quality of output, and fulfills many traditional supervisory functions. Weekly team meetings are led by the team chairperson, who is elected by the team; participation in the meetings is voluntary but popular, with interest high in the ongoing discussions of problem solving, production and quality improvements, labor-management relations, and general business developments. For many years, Lansing has had a relatively low number of job classifications, but several people at the plant emphasized to me that it was not the number of classifications that was critical but rather getting people to work together as a team.[39] There does seem to be a pervasive process at work, from team meetings to various levels of joint labor-management committees and activities, in which workers actively participate in discussions and decisions regarding productivity and quality improvements, set within a climate of trust.[40] And overlaying the innovations and continual improvements in work organization is a consensual labor-management relationship in which union representatives are drawn into discussions and decision making right up to the plant manager level. A productivity coalition is clearly at work in Lansing.

What is remarkable is that these successful innovations have been made without following the NUMMI model, that is, without several elements usually considered necessary for the success of team systems: the weakening of seniority rights in job allocation, promises of employment security

---

Sorge, "GM and UAW a Team at Lansing," *Automotive News*, April 29, 1985, pp. 6, 18. For an earlier version of this section, see Turner 1988b, pp. 17–21.

Actual hard productivity data for most auto plants, including Lansing, are either confidential or political and thus of questionable reliability. According to sources at the plant as well as at UAW headquarters, Lansing's Plant No. 1 is among the top-performing GM plants.

[39] The results at both Van Nuys and Hamtramck, where the number of job classifications was drastically reduced without correspondingly substantial performance improvement, reinforces this point of view. And Katz, Kochan, and Keefe (1988) found no independent relationship between economic performance and the number of job classifications.

At Lansing's Plant No. 1, there is one basic production classification, and this structure, according to plant sources, dates from the earliest local agreements in the 1940s.

[40] There are forty employees assigned full time to various participation programs, twenty from management and twenty from the union (whose wages are paid by the company). This represents a significant investment, which, according to plant management, pays off.

(contractual or informal), job rotation,[41] pay-for-knowledge (which NUMMI does not have but which is in place at several other team-organized plants), mandatory team participation, or the "significant emotional event" (plant closure or the prolonged threat of closure). Rather, the changes at Lansing developed over several years in a climate of trust in which a stable union leadership encountered a management that appeared genuinely committed to participation of the work force and union in decision making.

Lansing is quite conscious of itself as an alternative to NUMMI. I heard a comparison here of a Japanese management approach to consensus, in which top management makes a decision and then groups of lower managers and workers discuss it until they all agree with that decision, with a more genuinely participative approach. The claim at Lansing is that workers, lower-level managers, and union representatives are consulted before decisions are made and are encouraged to participate in the decision-making process, from minor shop-floor decisions to strategic planning at the level of the plant. And workers and union representatives at Lansing appear proud that they have made successful changes without giving up traditional seniority rights or independent union strength. Though not yet as productive as NUMMI, Lansing made major improvements in the space of a few years in a nongreenfield plant, without ever shutting down.

Lansing thus is an alternative model of successful work reorganization, one that may be more generally appropriate than NUMMI given established features of industrial relations and work organization in the U.S. auto industry. The comparison with Van Nuys is instructive. There management intervened in union politics in a controversial way, using threats of plant closure to convince slightly more than half the work force to accept a NUMMI-type system; the price of this heavy-handed approach was considerable backlash and resistance on the shop floor. At Lansing, by contrast, the union and work force were brought into discussions in a more comprehensive, open, and less heavy-handed way, with a much more favorable outcome for smooth work reorganization and labor-management relations. The repercussions are clear: when at Van Nuys management offered an innovative layoff agreement (during volume reductions in early 1988) designed to share the burden and benefits between those with low and high seniority, workers responded with distrust and required two votes and a bitter political debate before they narrowly accepted the package. At Lansing, by contrast, the obvious benefits for the entire work force of a virtually identical package (including time off with 95 percent pay for

[41] In the first couple of years of team operation, job rotation was not a regular feature of the system. Now this is up to the teams; rotation exists in some areas but is not yet widespread.

high-seniority as well as low-seniority workers when unemployment and SUB benefits were combined) were quickly recognized and the plan passed by 90 percent. At Van Nuys, management's initiative was perceived by many as another attack on seniority rights; at Lansing, where seniority rights, for example, are reinforced in the selection of TCs, the package was perceived as a boon to the workers as well as to plant production. By alternating shifts on layoff, the plant could keep its teams together (which was the same reason management at Van Nuys wanted the package), and all workers at the plant could take two weeks off with close to full pay.

A unilateral management decision was made to outsource seat production at Van Nuys, at a cost of 130 jobs. Lansing also came under pressure from top GM management to cut costs by outsourcing seats. But at Lansing, management took the problem directly to the union and to the workers in the cushion room, initiating a months-long series of discussions and brainstorming sessions; as a result, the workers themselves came up with a plan in 1987–88 to reorganize, cutting a few jobs to save the rest. Management accepted the proposals, found new assignments for the few displaced, and made a commitment to keep production in the cushion room in-house in spite of corporationwide pressure to outsource.

Acceptance of the changes at Lansing during this period was indicated by the absence of substantial opposition to the dominant Unity Caucus in the local union. The Solidarity Caucus unsuccessfully challenged for power in the early 1980s and subsequently dropped out of sight. Both union and management appear to have taken a patient, persuading, non-authoritarian approach to the work force, with positive results. In 1986, for example, workers wary over the pressure inherent in the sudden implementation of a team system voted to accept the teams but make participation voluntary. As a result, participation dropped to 30 percent. But neither union leadership nor management responded with stepped-up pressure and a second vote (as was common at other GM plants). Rather, they set out to persuade workers of the benefits of genuine participation, with the result that the voluntary participation rate rose to the 80 to 90 percent range by 1988.

An opposition group called You and I emerged in 1988, critical of the team system and "jointness," especially the appointment of new full-time union representatives (such as quality and safety coordinators) to serve in joint labor-management capacities. But in union elections in 1990, the group was decisively defeated by the incumbent union leadership.

Critical to Lansing's success was the innovative approach of management. Led from 1985 to 1989 by Frank Shotters, a self-proclaimed "participatory manager,'' plant management was cut back from seven levels to four to enhance direct communication and clear responsibility, management staff meetings were opened up to the union, and managers at all levels went through screening and retraining to replace authoritarianism with a new participative approach. Two levels between the supervisors on the shop floor and the plant superintendent were eliminated: the general foreman and the assistant superintendent. Communication runs directly from supervisor to superintendent, and the supervisor, who previously tended to be a ''gopher'' for the general foreman, now has expanded responsibilities. Between the supervisor and superintendent, but outside the chain of command, a new position called manufacturing coordinator was created to serve as a resource and facilitator for the supervisors. Perhaps most important, managers themselves, from top to bottom, were involved from the start in the discussions that resulted in this process of organizational reform; although substantial changes in personal style were asked of many managers, they did not face firings or layoffs: managerial ranks were thinned out through attrition.

Managers were thus trained and themselves engaged in the process of building a more humane, participatory work environment. And the results were positive: offered genuine worklife-enhancing reforms without a major assault on traditional protections and union bases of strength, workers and union representatives responded by supporting the new system.[42]

Homegrown Solutions (2): The ''Wars'' End at Lordstown

The GM J-car plant at Lordstown, Ohio, producing Chevy Cavaliers and Pontiac Sunbirds (along with a separate minivan line until 1992) offers another homegrown variant of work reorganization, not as successful at first as Lansing but showing strong potential nonetheless.[43] Even more explicitly than at Lansing, Lordstown offers an alternative to NUMMI.

[42] In 1989, a new plant manager's attempt to abolish the teams was greeted with protest from union and rank and file. Teams were reinstalled, with an emphasis on smaller groups of eight or so, to allow a focus on working out specific problems. It should be emphasized that teams at Lansing do not represent as radical an experiment in new work organization as NUMMI; Lansing is nonetheless a cooperative, participatory case with strong union involvement.

[43] For a partisan account of the earlier battles at Lordstown, see Aronowitz 1973. On the more recent, contrasting developments, see John D. Oravecz, ''Lordstown,'' *Ward's Automotive World*, August 1985, pp. 49–51; and James Risen, ''Age Eases 'Blue-Collar Blues' at GM,'' *Los Angeles Times*, June 10, 1987, pp. 1, 18–19. An earlier version of this section appeared in Turner 1988b, pp. 22–24.

Lordstown is a fascinating plant to look at: in the 1970s, "wars" (as managers and workers today refer to them) took place here when a young 1960s generation of workers confronted the speed, brutality, and authoritarian management of assembly-line work in a showplace, fast-paced, high-technology plant (Aronowitz 1973).

In the 1980s, these same workers, a decade or so older, and many of the same managers, were aiming toward a new model of labor-management cooperation. Beginning in the early years of the decade, discussions between plant management and veteran shop chairman (and former militant) Al Alli laid the groundwork for a new approach. As Alli puts it, management took the initiative (led by Bernie Brown, the personnel director), the union responded, and a gradual process of building trust began, based largely on the understanding that market circumstances were likely to destroy both sides. Various joint programs were set up and discussions intensified in 1985 and 1986, culminating in a local agreement aimed at reorganizing work in October 1986. As one manifestation of the changed labor-management relationship, the two sides agreed to open local contract negotiations early so as to speed the implementation of new shop-floor and union-management relations. Brown, backed by a supportive plant manager, had to take on old-guard middle managers within his own ranks; Alli had to fight off the potentially lethal "in bed with management" charge. After a heated ratification campaign, the new contract was approved by the membership.

Job classifications for production workers were reduced from 116 to 35 (still a large number compared to 1 at NUMMI), and a new understanding was reached on flexibility for skilled workers in crossing traditional craft lines. A group structure (words like "team" and "team concept" are taboo at Lordstown, to emphasize that this is not Japan, not NUMMI, and not enterprise unionism) was set up for the plant; groups of about fifteen, composed of two units of seven workers each, were led by group coordinators, selected by seniority.[44] All group members had 120 hours of training in the first two years of implementation, in communication, human relations, world economics, and the like; in addition, though each worker had a base job, he or she could learn all seven jobs in the unit to qualify for a higher rate of pay. The extent of job rotation at Lordstown is left up to the groups; each worker is required to validate knowledge of the seven jobs every six months.

[44] "Team concept" became a loaded term by the mid-1980s, signifying for many plant-level union activists a management-led, Japanese-style productivity drive, with little in the way of positive shop-floor benefits for workers (see below, Chapter 3, for a fuller discussion of the difference between "teams" and "groups").

Along with the group structure, a dense network of joint labor-management committees and discussions developed, in which workers appointed by the union serve in full-time positions such as training, competitive assessment, and strategic planning for the plant. The competitive assessment coordinator, for example, works with management and independently as well to study competing products, analyze markets, and bring the findings to the shop floor. The union representative for strategic planning serves on the management planning committee and brings all information concerning future product decisions for the plant directly to the union shop chairman.

As indicators of the new relationship at the plant, both grievance and discipline rates dropped substantially between the early and late 1980s. And as at Lansing, management responded to pressure from headquarters to outsource the cushion room by taking the problem to the workers. Joint teams of workers, union representatives, and managers flew around the country visiting cushion rooms and outside seat manufacturing plants to study best available production. Management at Lordstown made a commitment to keep 160 cushion room jobs in-house through the end of the current model (1991). And through joint discussions including shop-floor workers, union and management came up with a plan to keep encapsulated glass production in-house for windshield module installation.

What accounts for the changed relationship between labor and management that made new work organization possible? Press accounts focused on the fact that these formerly militant workers were older now and had families and mortgages. Though this may be part of the story, the same is true at auto plants all over the country, yet there are wide variations in plant-level outcomes. And the same critique applies to explanations that emphasize increasingly competitive market circumstances, which at Lordstown had the effect of bringing labor and management together. A fuller explanation requires looking at the ways in which management reformed itself, attempting to root out one-sided command leadership and replace it with a more collaborative approach. When management did this at Lordstown, union leaders and many workers responded, becoming active participants in plant operations and decision making.

But just as management could take substantial credit for a reformed relationship with labor, entrenched drill-sergeant supervisors (supposedly now "advisers" for two or three groups) undermined the experiment. In union elections in May 1988, the incumbent leadership cited persistent boss problems on the shop floor as a major factor strengthening the opposition. In fact, union politics have always been lively at Lordstown. When the 1986 agreement was ratified by the work force, it received a

57 percent yes vote but faced strong attacks from an opposition that denounced collaboration and the "team concept in disguise." In the 1988 elections, an opposition slate (based both on the older militant tradition and on a newer conservative view) again campaigned against the groups and the collaborative process, charging the incumbents with being too close to management and assigning the new "cushy" joint-type jobs on the basis of favoritism rather than seniority. After a lengthy, hard-fought campaign viewed by both sides as a referendum on the new organization and labor-management relationship, Alli and his slate were returned to office and the process continued. Alli won the largest majority of his political career in 1988.

The Lordstown plant was still very much in transition and the changes still relatively new. GM had excess capacity throughout its manufacturing operations, and with the van line scheduled to close in 1992 (for consolidation at Flint), Lordstown workers continued to fear for the life of their plant. Productivity and quality failed to show dramatic improvement in the wake of the 1986 agreement; but by 1990 the plant was performing well in company audits. If market circumstances and top GM brass permit the plant to keep or boost capacity, Lordstown may well be on the road to successful performance and a new model of work organization that incorporates the union and work force while retaining seniority rights, multiple job classifications, and a strong union role.

Conclusion

What stands out from a study of the politics of new work organization in U.S. auto plants is the very wide range of outcomes, both for work reorganization itself and for industrial relations and the union role. The wide range is apparent from a look at four GM assembly plants and one GM-Toyota joint venture; but these plants were selected as cases of active work reorganization. If all the GM auto assembly plants are included in the sample, the range is even wider, including, for example, plants where workers have rejected teams (Oklahoma City) and plants where management and union have expanded processes of "jointness" and loosened up work rules without introducing teams (as at the refurbished Linden, New Jersey, plant, home of a new generation of Chevys, the Beretta and Corsica; Milkman and Pullman 1988).

And the range expands even more when Ford, Chrysler, and the new Japanese transplants are included. Most ominous for the union, the Japanese auto assembly plants in the United States (Honda, Nissan, and

Toyota), with the exception of the unionized joint ventures, have successfully introduced Japanese-style work organization (radical work reorganization from an American perspective) without including the UAW or any other union.[45] From all indications, these plants are equally successful in productivity, product quality, and avoiding unionization. The decision to exclude unions is a deliberate one for most Japanese firms that open plants in the United States; the potential to avoid unionization is one of the decisive criteria in plant location and hiring policies for the transplants. The success of such strategies was demonstrated dramatically in the summer of 1989 when the UAW lost a union certification election at the Nissan plant in Smyrna, Tennessee; in spite of a major UAW organizing effort (effectively countered by a company anti-union campaign), the work force voted by a 70-to-30 margin against the union.[46] Television news broadcasts showed enthusiastic groups of cheering workers, waving American flags and signs saying "Union Free and Proud." In the case of the transplants, management has consciously used more cooperative relations with the work force and more enlightened working conditions to keep the union out. If this trend continues, and if the transplants continue to expand production volume and U.S. market shares, the UAW faces an increasingly threatening dual (union/nonunion) industrial relations situation at the core of the U.S. auto industry.[47]

Ford was a more profitable and generally successful auto firm than GM in the 1980s (although Ford's market share in the late 1980s still trailed GM's by approximately 35 percent to 20 percent), and work reorganization and industrial relations outcomes have been more stable from plant to plant. Industry analysts are divided over the extent to which Ford's relative success has to do with good (and perhaps lucky) product designs and effective organization of production and how much it has to do with improved labor-management relations (manifested, for example, in the Employee Involvement program since 1979). High-capacity utilization at

[45] This is also happening extensively in the parts supplier branch of the industry, characterized by large numbers of smaller plants, where Japanese transplants are making rapid inroads in part to service the needs of the Japanese assembly plants in the United States.

[46] See Doron P. Levin, "U.A.W. Bid to Organize Nissan Plant Is Rejected," *New York Times*, July 28, 1989, pp. A1, A8; "Nissan Workers in U.S. Test Union and Industry," *New York Times*, August 12, 1989, p. 8; Jane Slaughter, "Behind the UAW's Defeat at Nissan," *Labor Notes*, September 1989, pp. 1, 12.

[47] Luria projects from available data and current trends a rise in transplant production, from 600,000 cars sold at retail in 1986 to 1.7 million in 1992, accompanied by a corresponding drop in traditional domestic car production (Big Three) from 7.6 million in 1986 to 5.9 in 1992 (1987, p. 4). While these figures include NUMMI and two other unionized joint ventures, they also include the three large nonunion transplants.

Ford has no doubt boosted workers' morale, especially at a time of plant closings for GM; and Ford definitely seems to have learned better than GM how to manage a modern production system, including its personnel. Ulrich Jürgens, Thomas Malsch, and Knuth Dohse (1989, pp. 215–21) argue, for example, that rationalization in the early 1980s, including the integration of quality inspection into production, worked well at Ford because the union was included and given full information in advance about the changes. In the current moves toward shop-floor teams at Ford, management continues to work with union leadership in an effort to make the changes gradually and smoothly, avoiding the turbulence at GM. According to union representatives within the Ford Department at the UAW, Ford appears so far to be taking a "back-door" approach, bringing teams into new facilities within a plant with union cooperation and using workers who volunteer for the new work organization. But the extent to which this has been done, and the tenor of labor-management relations, varies considerably from plant to plant.

Chrysler developed a standard "modern operating agreement" (MOA) for its plants, which includes a large reduction in the number of job classifications and a switch to shop-floor teams and cooperative industrial relations. Chrysler's work force, however, has shown a propensity toward militance ever since the firm rebounded from near bankruptcy (saved in part by substantial concessions by workers). The extent to which the plants have accepted and begun to implement MOAs varies considerably. The Detroit Jefferson Avenue plant, for example, accepted a full MOA; but in the face of a growing and projected sales slump, the firm announced in late 1989 that Jefferson Avenue would close. At Sterling Heights, by contrast, a new plant producing the popular Dodge Shadow and Plymouth Sundance, the work force, led by an anti-team union president, turned down a team organization agreement (causing Chrysler to claim that it was going with a modified MOA at Sterling Heights).

The range of work organization and industrial relations outcomes within the U.S. auto industry is thus wide, ranging from new nonunion plants (transplants), to plants with conflictual and still traditional industrial relations, to plants with traditional but more cooperative industrial relations, and finally to plants in which team organization is accompanied by an integration of the union into new levels of managerial decision making. Although outcomes may be gravitating toward variations on the latter model for Big Three plants, the changeover is rocky and is often accompanied by heavy managerial pressure (the threat of plant closing or disinvestment), which undermines the trust necessary for a successful team system or cooperative labor-management relationship. In the transition, the union is giving up some of its traditional shop-floor power (in job classification and regulation of assignments and high grievance rates) in return for enhanced union input, "jointness," and worker participation. The new role of the union is being carved out on a plant-by-plant basis, with the future position of the union in relationship to the firm still very much an open question.

What accounts for the wide range of outcomes in different plants within the U.S. auto industry? Although a systematic interplant comparative analysis within the United States is beyond the scope of this book, I would suggest that the wide range of outcomes is a product primarily of the wide discretion that contemporary U.S. institutions of industrial relations make available to management. It takes two sides to develop a labor-management relationship, but management, I would argue, is the critical variable (i.e., managerial behavior and strategy) in U.S. auto industry work organization and industrial relations. Differences in the composition and history of the work force and union politics at NUMMI and at Hamtramck, for example, do not appear substantial; nor do such differences between Van Nuys and Lordstown (Van Nuys had a considerably less adversarial tradition before the 1980s than did Lordstown). Product segments, market circumstances, work-force demographics, union history—none of these appear useful in explaining the cross-plant variations. Management's approach to the work force, however, its ability to reform its own practices fundamentally and to offer the union and work force genuine participation, appears to make all the difference. When management succeeded in doing this at NUMMI, Lansing, and Lordstown, labor-management cooperation developed rapidly and shop-floor teamwork became a reality; when management failed to accomplish these key tasks at Hamtramck and Van Nuys, reform processes ran into serious trouble. Milkman (1990) argues persuasively that in most cases in the American auto industry (as in other industries), bureaucratic inertia has prevented management from making the reforms necessary to use its available discretion in constructive and innovative ways.

If wide managerial discretion accounts for the range of outcomes, the argument here, to be tested in the cross-national analyses to come (in Chapters 3 and 5), is that wide managerial discretion itself is accounted for by institutional industrial relations variables. In particular, management in the United States has wide discretion in the current era of work reorganization because the union has no tradition of integration into processes of managerial decision making (to constrain management from within), and the United States lacks laws on participation or corporatist bargaining structures, including a cohesive labor movement (to constrain management from without). Management has wide discretion, in other words, because management is relatively unconstrained by labor.

Given the wide range of plant-level outcomes, how do we characterize the stability and extent of workers' interest representation in the U.S. auto industry in the period under discussion, from 1982 to 1989? The wide range itself is indicative of a generally unstable union role, and this is the first point that should be emphasized. Beyond general instability and uncertainty, however, there is nonetheless a consistent set of findings for the three variables that operationalize (in this study) the stability and extent of workers' interest representation.

First, union membership density has experienced a steady decline. This decline has not occurred at the case-study plants presented in this chapter, where contractual union-shop agreements keep the hourly work forces 100 percent organized. But in the auto industry as a whole, there are two important (and ominous) sources of decline in union density. One is in the parts supplier branch of the industry; Stephen Herzenberg (1989) has produced data showing that in the independent (non–Big Three) parts supplier branch, unionization dropped from over two-thirds in the mid-1970s to around one-third in 1986. This drop in union density at the independent suppliers (which include a growing number of determinedly nonunion Japanese-owned parts plants) helped drive the overall auto parts sector unionization rate down from 92 percent in 1975 to 67 percent in 1985.[48] The second source of decline is in the recent establishment of three new nonunion Japanese assembly plants: Honda at Marysville, Ohio; Nissan at Smyrna, Tennessee; and Toyota at Georgetown, Kentucky. Whereas by 1982 the UAW could boast virtually full blue-collar unionization at U.S. auto assembly plants (after the defeat of GM's "southern strategy"; Katz 1985, pp. 88–90), by 1989 three of the approximately thirty-five auto assembly plants in the United States had remained nonunion under Japanese management. And though production cutbacks, employment streamlining, and additional plant closures were widely foreseen for the Big Three plants in the early 1990s, the highly successful Japanese transplants were expected to expand output, market share, and percentage of the overall auto assembly work force. After the UAW's defeat in its 1989 attempt to organize Smyrna, unionization prospects at the Japanese transplants appeared problematic. Overall unionization in the U.S. motor vehicle industry dropped from 95 percent in 1975 to 77 percent in 1985, and the trend appeared to be continuing downward.[49]

[48] Herzenberg 1989, pp. 14–15 and Table 3 at the end of his paper.
[49] Ibid.

The second variable is protection of the work force against the effects of productivity-improving technological change and work reorganization. In this area the UAW made substantial improvements in 1984 and 1987 contract rounds with GM and Ford (and these gains were carried over in 1985 and 1988 negotiations with Chrysler). After a six-day strike at GM in 1984, the union and company agreed to set up an innovative, jointly run jobs bank to provide for workers displaced because of the introduction of new technology, work organization, new outsourcing, or corporate reorganization (Katz 1985, p. 176). Displaced workers were put into a jobs bank, where they retained full pay while they either got new training, filled in for another worker who was in training, or did "nontraditional" work (which in practice varied across a wide range from plant to plant, from community service, to helping with training programs, to outright busywork, to virtual inactivity). Ford set up a similar program in 1984; and the jobs banks along with employment protection guarantees were expanded in the 1987 contracts. Ford set up a Secure Employment Levels (SEL) plan, and GM set up a virtually identical Guaranteed Employment Numbers (GEN) program. Under SEL and GEN, 1987 employment levels at Ford and GM were guaranteed throughout the three-year contract period, except for attrition (on a two-for-one basis) and cutbacks resulting from decline in sales volume. In 1987, both Ford and GM made renewed commitment and funding to the jobs banks. These contract gains for the UAW, traded off against a commitment to work with the companies at the firm and plant levels to improve productivity and product quality, including developing work reorganization plans, far exceeded previous employment security measures in the U.S. auto industry (or in most other industries).

There were, however, at least four important limitations to these contractual forms for protecting the work force. First, the sales volume exception gives the companies a large loophole through which to continue to close plants and lay off workers in response to adverse market circumstances; as we have seen, the threat of plant closure and widespread displacement remains prominent in the consciousness of autoworkers at many U.S. plants. Second, contractual protections do not guarantee the worker a place at the same pay and status level; makework in the jobs banks (with negative effects on self-esteem) and bumping to a lower pay classification (in the interest of preserving a job) are both commonplace under the new protection plans. Third, workers in the jobs banks or the protected "pools" often receive no new training, which was a primary intent of the agreement. And finally, pay security is guaranteed only as long as funding for the jobs banks lasts; and funding levels were not established to handle major dislocation. Katz estimated, for example, that GM's 1984 agreement to contribute $1 billion would take care of only four thousand workers per year (Katz 1985, p. 177). And Jim Harbour (1987) makes a similar claim for the 1987 contract: GM's $1.3 billion would cover only twenty six thousand workers for one year.[50]

The UAW's methods for protecting the work force against the effects of new technologies and work organization, therefore, are path-breaking in the context of U.S. industrial relations. But they still contained major limitations and loopholes (which the UAW hoped to cut into steadily in future negotiations and did to some extent in 1990), and they were modest in comparison to similar measures negotiated by works councils in the West German auto industry, as we will see in Chapter 2.

The third variable indicating the stability and extent of workers' interest representation in the current period is the promotion of an independent union vision of work organization. In this regard, the UAW had plans on the drawing board (and this may be a good sign for the future) but had yet to produce a great deal in the way of consistent policy. At none of the innovative plants considered here had the UAW come forward with its own well-developed concepts. Although union representatives in every case made important suggestions and negotiated significant improvements and protections for the work force, and the implementation of teams or groups often became a joint project, neither the national nor the local unions had yet put forward their own broad proposals for new work organization. Teamwork has so far come to the U.S. auto industry as a management project; the UAW has now made this a joint project, but jointness regarding work organization has meant union modifications of management concepts rather than vice versa or a negotiated settlement between two strong, contending views.[51]

The 1980s was a decade of turbulence for industrial relations in the United States, and the auto industry was no exception. The case studies have revealed fundamental change and reform, new models that stand

---

[50] This figure is out of approximately 370,000 hourly GM workers, and the contract is for three years. Ford contributions and funding limitations are similar and proportional to Ford's size relative to GM.

[51] A partial exception is GM's Saturn plant in Springhill, Tennessee, where operations from the strategic level down to the shop floor have been jointly designed by teams that include UAW members. As Saturn headed toward full operation in 1990–91, union leaders, including the now retired Don Ephlin (until 1989 the UAW vice-president in charge of the GM Department and a key player at Saturn from the start), were hopeful regarding Saturn's model-setting potential for the U.S. auto industry.

as signs of hope, and new adaptive union roles. The UAW, through joint processes at the firm and plant levels, is increasingly integrated into some levels of managerial decision making. But developments are uneven, with wide plant-level variation and a generally rocky transition to still uncertain outcomes. The absence of an appropriate statutory and political framework in the United States places the UAW (and other U.S. unions) in some jeopardy at the hands of adversarial or anti-union management, even as new cooperative-participatory models develop and the union gains new input. Nonunionism is on the rise, even in the highly organized auto industry. Whipsawing has become a standard management practice, as managers pressure UAW locals and work forces to grant concessions on work organization. And the danger of an American version of enterprise unionism cannot be discounted as locals at different firms and plants go their own joint, productivity-enhancing ways.

In the contemporary period, perhaps only legal regulation or corporatist bargaining by a cohesive labor movement could provide the necessary bulwark against the spread of nonunionism and union decline. Already existing excess capacity in the auto industry as a recession approached at the onset of the 1990s made the situation that much more difficult for the UAW. As Luria (1987, pp. 23–24) put it:

> Massive excess capacity in both assembly and parts confers on U.S. automotive management a "loaded gun" with which to seek changes in traditional work practices. Thus management is likely to get much of what it seeks. The press will note growing instances of rank and file disgruntlement, and a continuing split between "cooperationists" and "resisters" in the labor leadership. When push comes to shove, however, all stripes of labor leader, at all levels, will do what they think they have to do in order to save plants from closure.
>
> What we don't know is whether the automotive economy that will emerge from the fray in the 1990s will be one that can hold its own in the market place while providing high living standards for its American workers. Will the labor-management engagements we foresee result in bargains that anchor and nurture wealth-creating automotive activity in unionized frostbelt factories? Will any of the changes in work organization actually have any positive effect on the quality of work life? In short, will heretofore purely management prerogatives really be shared, or will "joint" remain an adjective modifying only plant-level programs that don't involve major strategic investments? . . .
>
> Capital mobility is a formidable weapon: the very fact that the *option* of moving production exists reduces the pressure on management to trade sig-

nificant unilateral prerogatives for more labor cooperation. . . . UAW victories have been limited to protection for current members' incomes, and have not yet extended to guarantees concerning what will be produced or where. The weakness of unions in the U.S. today no doubt heightens the temptation on the part of management to go for an outright win.

CHAPTER 2

Partnership and Engagement in
the West German Auto Industry

Following the devastation of World War II, the phenomenal rise of West German manufacturing in the 1950s assured the prominent place of West German industry in the postwar world economy. For American observers, nothing was more symbolic and indicative of the German "economic miracle" (*Wirtschaftswunder*) than the flood of Volkswagen Beetles that descended on U.S. shores, beginning as early as 1949 with the first Bug import; and indeed the auto industry, with both strong domestic sales and exports, has been a main engine of West German economic success throughout the postwar period.

By the early 1970s, however, the Bug was dying out, driven from its dominance of the small-car market in the United States by a new flood of Toyotas and Datsuns. West German high-volume producers (VW, Opel, and Ford) scrambled for new product and marketing strategies when economic crisis beginning with the first oil shock in 1973–74 combined with the rapid growth of Japanese auto exports to threaten sales and market share both at home and abroad. Auto industry analysts predicted crisis for the West German auto industry, especially in the period 1979–82 as recession deepened and the full extent of the Japanese production advantage (in both cost and product quality) became known.[1] Among managers and worker representatives in the West German auto industry these years became known as the "Japan shock"; and at Ford-Werke (the German

[1] Japanese production cost advantages over West German auto firms parallel those found in the U.S.-Japanese comparison, and for similar reasons. See above, Chapter 1, and Altshuler et al. 1984; Flynn 1984–85; and Schumann et al. 1988.

Ford subsidiary), a sweeping process of managerial reform and production reorganization since 1979 is commonly known as "after Japan." Japanese auto firms continued to drive the Germans out of the high-volume market segment in the United States,[2] and the Japanese market share within Western Europe and West Germany itself moved steadily upward.[3] West German firms faced a crisis situation by the early 1980s that resulted in the widespread perceived need to reorganize production.

At the same time, some analysts drew a direct connection between the strength and influence of organized labor, reflected in welfare state spending, high wages, and the need for firms to engage in lengthy negotiations with worker representatives before reorganization, and problems of industrial adjustment in West Germany and other Western European societies (Scott 1985; Olson 1982; Crozier, Huntington, and Watanuke 1975). "Eurosclerosis" became a common term in academic and policy circles, indicative of the problems in newly competitive world markets faced by societies in which old, entrenched interest groups (especially labor) held sway. In West Germany, scholars analyzed the connection between structural unemployment and rigidities in the labor market (Windolf and Hohn 1984) and variously predicted the decline of the unions, social instability (with negative consequences for democracy), and failed industrial adjustment. Prospects for organized labor were predicted to be especially gloomy as a newly elected conservative-liberal regime in Bonn proclaimed its intention to engineer a major change in direction (*die Wende*) that would undercut excessive union power and trim the welfare state down to size.

But the analysts who made such predictions of doom were wrong. Talk of Eurosclerosis was replaced by concerns among policy makers in Washington, D.C., about the coming 1992 "European juggernaut," well before the dramatic opening up of Eastern Europe in late 1989. Perhaps most notably among the major Western European nations, West German in-

---

[2] From 1970 to 1983, the share of auto exports sent to North America by German firms dropped from 40% to 12% (Dyer, Salter, and Webber 1987, p. 79).

[3] Japanese market share, for example, reached 11.1% of the combined Western European market by 1988, including 14.8% of the West German market and even higher percentages in traditional German markets such as the Netherlands (27.5%), Belgium and Luxembourg (20.5%), Denmark (32.9%), and Switzerland (31.1%). Protected markets in France and Italy kept the Japanese out (3.0% and 0.9% shares respectively) and thus offered German firms at least temporarily easier sales competition (data supplied by VDA and IG Metall). What is noteworthy is the steady rise of Japanese market shares in most European countries: in West Germany, for example, from 3.7% in 1978 to 15.0% in 1986 (data supplied by the European Metalworkers' Federation), in spite of informally agreed-upon Japanese export restraint.

dustry, along with its institutions of industrial relations, showed remarkable resilience in the years after 1982. West German auto firms, in particular, weathered the crisis without mass layoffs (in marked contrast to U.S. auto firms), diversifed, moved upmarket to some extent, rationalized production and began to reorganize work, and by 1988–89 had reached new sales and export records. The German Metalworkers Union (*Industriegewerkschaft Metall*, or IG Metall) held on to its high membership levels and density, expanded protections for its members, retained a stable position of influence within the plants through union-dominated works councils, and began to promote its own vision of work reorganization as part of a general pattern of plant-level productivity coalitions throughout the auto industry.[4]

Wolfgang Streeck argues that the West German auto industry's remarkable and perhaps unexpected competitive success of the past fifteen years is in part an unintended consequence of the industrial relations system, and in particular the role of works councils and the IG Metall (Streeck 1985a, 1987a). As Streeck put it in a recent formulation of the argument:

> In a context of unmitigated world market pressure and institutionalized responsibility through codetermination and legally regulated collective bargaining (*Tarif-autonomie*), strong trade unions and the rigidities they impose upon management not only do not hurt but may indeed help in that they press firms to embark on more demanding and, in the long run, more successful adjustment strategies. (1989, p. 150)

This argument sounds very much like an updated, internationalized version of a classical industrial relations analysis in the United States, expressed in its most comprehensive form by Sumner H. Slichter, James J. Healy, and E. Robert Livernash in 1960:

> If one single statement were sought to describe the effect of unions on policymaking, it would be: "they have encouraged investigation and reflection." Some unions are in fact only a slight check on management; other unions run the shop. But whether the union influence is weak or strong, it always

---

[4] See Thelen 1987a for a perceptive account of IG Metall's strategic and organizational adaptation. Thelen's argument takes issue with analyses from both the left and right within Germany that see primarily union decline and fragmentation, or the "Americanization" of German industrial relations (see Hoffman 1988; Hohn 1988). The research and analysis presented here, with the benefit of a comparative perspective, confirm the more optimistic assessments of Thelen, Streeck (1989), and Jürgens, Malsch, and Dohse (1989).

tends to force management to consider the probable consequences of its
proposed decisions and to adjust those decisions accordingly. (p. 952)

Slichter et al. wrote this not about West Germany but about the United
States, but as we have seen in Chapter 1, this favorable assessment of the
consequences of labor-management relations is currently very much in
question throughout U.S. industry. In this chapter and the next, I will
systematically compare contemporary union success in the U.S. and West
German auto industries and explore the reasons why this traditional American industrial relations analysis is today perhaps more relevant abroad
than at home.

In Streeck's analysis, West German unions and works councils, in
particular the IG Metall and IG Metall–led works councils in the auto
industry, have imposed external labor market rigidities (no layoffs) and
high wages on firms while accepting a system of internal labor market
flexibility (see also Katz and Sabel 1985). Firms have been forced to train
and retrain the existing work force and develop a strategy of upmarket
"diversified high-quality production," in which market success offsets
high manpower costs; at the same time, internal flexibility has permitted
managers to reorganize and make better use of the available manpower.
Industrial relations, in this view, is thus a major contributor to the success
of the West German auto industry in contemporary world markets.

It is clear, however, that internal flexibility as often depicted by American observers (note the Katz and Sabel 1985 discussion of the "German-
Japanese model") is overrated, at least for the West German auto industry.
Although technically management has much broader rights regarding allocation of manpower in West German industry than in the United States
(in the absence of the myriad of job classifications and corresponding
seniority-based job allocation found in U.S. auto plants), in fact all reassignments are subject both to complex wage security provisions (Dohse,
Jürgens, and Malsch 1985, p. 120) and to works council approval. Each
working day begins with negotiations and discussion between managers
and works councillors regarding who is to be moved around, and quite
often shop-floor workers effectively (if informally) resist such "flexibility." For all longer-term reassignments, including those resulting from
work reorganization, the works council can effectively block management
moves so that consensus is sought before the use of West German industry's famous shop-floor flexibility. Representation of workers' interests in
West Germany can and does interfere effectively with management's unconstrained allocation of labor.[5]

[5] In the course of my interviews in the West German auto industry, I often heard

It is not so much the flexibility as it is the daily processes of negotiation between management and a powerful union-dominated works council that ensure smooth adjustment. When management and works council, after lengthy discussion, finally agree on both the framework and the specific details of work reorganization, implementation is smooth because most of the interests in the plant have been considered and the agreed-upon changes can be explained to the rank and file by their elected representatives—and further negotiations can be made around the margins in this system of permanent bargaining. Representation of entrenched interests has arguably contributed to the West German auto industry's ability to adjust, rather than to its sometimes predicted ossification.

If dire predictions both for the West German auto industry and for union decline have so far proven wrong, major challenges stand squarely in view. There is continuing overcapacity in the world auto industry and specifically within Western Europe; the long-term creeping expansion of Japanese market share in Europe shows no signs of abating, and the Japanese have followed the Germans upmarket, now challenging not only VW, Opel, and Ford but BMW, Audi, and Mercedes as well; Korean firms are moving into the low end of the German and other European markets as powerful new competitors, just as they are in the United States; West German firms are receiving unexpectedly strong challenges from other revamped European firms such as Fiat and Peugeot; and the uncertainties surrounding the coming of more free-flowing internal markets in Europe after 1992 presage a further intensification of competition. In response to these ongoing challenges, the pace of work reorganization has escalated in the West German auto industry over the past few years, and negotiations between representatives of management and labor have intensified. From its base in the works councils, the IG Metall has begun to negotiate not only the terms of work reorganization but the substance (including the use of new technology and the design of new jobs).

Industrial Relations in the Federal Republic

In some ways, the development of postwar industrial relations in West Germany parallels developments in Japan. In both countries, resurgent

---

complaints from managers that they were too limited in their shop-floor flexibility in labor allocation, even at VW, where the LODI agreement supposedly grants unprecedented new flexibility (see below, the VW-Wolfsburg section). Rather than viewing the United States as rigid in this regard and Japan and Germany as flexible (the common perception; see Katz and Sabel 1985), it makes more sense to place West Germany in the middle, between the United States and Japan on this important dimension.

socialist labor movements were tamed by conservative, pro-business forces in the early 1950s as a new industrial relations order took hold. The West German labor movement lost a major political battle when the Adenauer government passed the Works Constitution Act (*Betriebsverfassungsgesetz*) in 1952, setting up a dual system in which plant-level works councils were legally separated from union control. As the years went by, the labor movement's stated historic mission to transform society, articulated in the DGB's Munich Program of 1949, gave way to negotiations with employers, employer associations, and political groupings within the capitalist system for immediate gains for workers and modest social reforms (Bergmann and Müller-Jentsch 1983; Markovits 1986).

But the "taming" of the West German labor movement was a far cry from the defeat of nationally organized independent unionism in Japan and the incorporation of organized labor into enterprise unions (see below, Chapter 5). West German labor retained its independence through a structure of sixteen national industrial unions (later seventeen, and now sixteen again), organized into one labor federation (the Deutscher Gewerkschaftsbund, or DGB).[6] Although the Allied occupation forces would not let West German unions have a centralized labor movement (the DGB is formally decentralized, with power residing in the member unions), unionists settled for a cohesive labor movement.[7] In spite of the perceived danger of company unionism (called "yellow unionism" in Germany) inherent in the dual system, the works councils, especially in the auto industry, came to be dominated by members of DGB unions and increasingly became vehicles for the expression of union interests.

The structure and postwar evolution of industrial relations in West Germany have been well described at length elsewhere (for useful English-language presentations, see Adams and Rummel 1977; Bergmann and Müller-Jentsch 1983; Markovits 1986; Katzenstein 1987; and Thelen 1987b; for the best English-language study of industrial relations in the West German auto industry, see Streeck 1984a). The structure and required

---

[6] There are three other labor federations in West Germany: the Deutscher Beamten Bund (DBB) for civil servants; the Deutsche Angestellten Gewerkschaft (DAG) for white-collar workers; and the Christlicher Gerwerkschaftsbund Deutschlands (CGB), a Catholic workers organization. But these three other federations have had relatively small membership totals and have played only a minor role in West German industrial relations, for the most part excluded from influence in collective bargaining and on the works councils. There are more white-collar workers in the DGB, for example, than in the DAG; in 1981, the three smaller federations had a combined membership of 1.6 million, compared to 7.9 million for the DGB (Markovits 1986, pp. 9–12).

[7] See below for a depiction of West Germany's postwar labor movement; the Introduction gives the definition of a cohesive labor movement.

and permissible activities of works councils, unions, and managers within this system are well regulated by law (the Works Constitution Act). In addition, the actual behavior of the parties as well as the negotiated outcomes are the product of political and organizational decisions and the relative success of contending strategies within the legal framework—and both the laws and the outcomes of particular strategies, conflicts, and negotiations have shaped the current institutional arrangements.

The key characteristics of contemporary industrial relations in West Germany, in its actual workings, are as follows: (1) works councils legally independent of both union and management, democratically elected by the entire work force, empowered by law, precedent, and plant- and firm-level agreements to consult with management before the implementation of decisions affecting personnel (including work organization and the use of new technology) and in many cases to participate actively in managerial decision-making processes (with veto rights), especially in matters of personnel policy (such as hiring, firing, training and retraining, and reassignment in the event of work reorganization and technological change); (2) close union–works council relations, with the works councils usually dominated by union members, who are chosen to run either individually or as part of a list, usually from the ranks of the union-organized shop stewards (*Vertrauensleute*); works councillors are thus often union activists who work closely with the local union office (*Verwaltungsstelle*) as well as the shop-floor union representatives (in representational work that is significantly overlapping); (3) regional collective bargaining that is nationally coordinated by centralized unions and employer associations and that establishes guidelines for pay levels and groupings as well as working hours and conditions, setting the framework within which managers and works councillors operate and negotiate for the contractual period; and (4) a cohesive labor movement, organized into one principal labor federation, the DGB, composed of sixteen industrial unions; although the DGB is formally rather decentralized (Wilensky 1976, p. 51) the federation and labor movement as a whole are given relative cohesiveness by the small number of unions, the industrial (and often multi-industry) and centralized nature of these unions, and perhaps most important, the centralizing role of one dominant union, the IG Metall.[8]

---

[8] IG Metall has served as a pattern setter in wage bargaining and in the more recent emphasis on the shorter workweek and on work reorganization; and this union is by far the largest in West Germany and within the DGB. In 1986, IG Metall had 2.6 million members out of 7.8 million total in the DGB; the second largest union was less than half as big (the ÖTV, with 1.2 million members) (Kittner 1988, pp. 54, 66, 67).

Not included in this list of the four principal characteristics of postwar industrial relations

This system is highly regulated by a legal and political framework. The framework includes both law (including the Works Constitution Act) and regularized bargaining among centralized interest groups (business and labor). This "corporatist" bargaining takes place in a variety of forums and at a number of levels, from (nationally coordinated) regional collective bargaining, to political processes that result in social and labor market policies, to the tripartite institutions that run West Germany's vocational education system.

How does this industrial relations system work in practice? There are many things, especially in areas of personnel policy, training, and work organization, that management cannot do without first consulting the works council. In areas such as the introduction of new technology and job design, management is required to give information to the works council and listen to comments and suggestions before implementation (Works Constitution Act, article 90); in these areas, however, management often does what it wants regardless of the wishes of the works council, once the consultation obligation is fulfilled. But in other areas, management must either get agreement from the works council or, in the event of stalemate, face the prospect of binding arbitration. Decisions are handed down by a joint labor-management "settlement board" (*Einigungsstelle*), with half its members chosen by the works council, half by the employer, and a neutral tie-breaking chairperson agreed on by both sides (article 76).

Under the Works Constitution Act, works councils have important co-determination rights that affect work reorganization. These include working hours, piecework rates and bonuses, and monitoring of work performance (article 87); working conditions, when employers violate accepted principles of "human-suitable" job design (article 91); hiring, firing, transfers, assignment to pay groupings or job classifications (articles 95 and 99); and training and retraining (article 98). In all these cases, in-

---

in West Germany is codetermination at the top level of the firm—the legally mandated inclusion of unionists and works councillors on company supervisory boards. Whereas the works councils, the other pole of codetermination, engage in daily discussions, negotiations, and representation work, the supervisory boards meet only a few times a year. For the worker representatives on these boards, this is an occasion to hear of company financial and strategic planning; this is not an insignificant forum, and the access to information and the ability to speak out directly at the top levels have sometimes served union and works council interests, as well as smooth labor-management negotiations. But except in the iron, steel, and coal-mining industries, which have parity representation on the supervisory boards, the minority position of labor on the boards has meant that codetermination at this level plays a minor role compared to the daily activities at the works council level. As Markovits puts it, "If real codetermination exists anywhere in West Germany, it does so at the plant level" (1986, pp. 59–60).

cluding works council claims that full information regarding the affairs of the firm was not disclosed (articles 106 and 109), disagreement is subject to binding arbitration by the settlement boards, whose decisions can be enforced by labor courts. Works councils can and do use these rights to make their voices heard on issues of new work organization.[9]

In spite of West German industry's often cited shop-floor flexibility, management is therefore not free to reorganize work, given the myriad of personnel issues involved, without extensive discussion and negotiation with the works council. Management decision making along with the implementation of new work organization may be slowed down in this consensus-building process (and the actual content of decisions may be changed), but once agreement is reached, management has an important ally in the works council for winning the work force's acceptance of the changes and for smoothing implementation.

From the point of view of worker representation, there are two institutional vehicles for the expression of interests in this dual system, the union and the works council. For the works council, consultation and codetermination rights guaranteed in the Works Constitution Act, first established in 1952 and subsequently amended and strengthened in 1972, ensure an integration of sorts into managerial decision-making processes (and this integration can range from marginal to a rather deep penetration, depending on the particular industry, firm, or plant). Works councillors are elected by the entire work force, serving part time in smaller plants, with a mix of both part-time and full-time councillors in larger plants; and they work under a "peace obligation" (article 74) and a "trustful cooperation" clause (article 2), which together require that they work with management in the interest of a smoothly running production of goods or services. The integration into managerial decision-making processes and their election by a plant work force combine to mean that works councillors must consider closely the interests of the firm or plant.

The dominant union in a given industry, however, is usually in a position, as the most strongly organized presence among the work force, to select candidates and win most of the positions on the works council.[10] Works council majorities are thus typically made up of active unionists, with histories of participation in the internal politics and education of

---

[9] Works councils sometimes use their codetermination rights (backed up by binding arbitration) to gain leverage in other areas, where they have only consultation rights. See below, for example, in the section on Ford-Cologne.

[10] Over 80% of all works councillors are union members, and the overwhelming majority of these are members of one of the sixteen industrial unions of the DGB. (Because of a recent merger, the seventeen unions of the DGB are now down to sixteen.)

centralized national unions. In the dual system, then, active unionists, operating from bases in national industrial unions, find themselves in a position to influence firms' decision making directly, to promote the interests of the work force as well as those of the national union and broader working class from this base within the firm, and to facilitate the smooth operation of the firm by supporting negotiated conditions of work and terms of change. In practice, works councils are often in a position to force managers to consider the interests of the work force and occasionally broader social interests; managers are in a position to force works councillors to consider the interests of the firm or plant. The result is negotiated solutions to plant- and firm-level problems.[11]

The union, for its part, must consider the interests and points of view of its most influential members at the local and often regional and national levels, the works councillors; and this is another way of saying that unions must closely consider the interests of the firm as well as the plant-level work force. Yet the union has two important avenues for articulating its interests within the industrial relations arena, regional (nationally coordinated) collective bargaining at an industrywide or even multi-industry level, and the works councils at the plant and firm levels. Unions thus have effective instruments for the expression of interests both at a centralized level, in negotiations and sometimes open conflict with the highly centralized employer associations of West German industry, and at a decentralized level, through union influence, embodied in the dominant

---

[11] Local unions in the United States and elsewhere, of course, even when well integrated into a national union structure, have always had to consider the interests of the plant or firm; if the plant closes or the firm goes under, the work force goes under, too (and this was recognized long ago in the U.S. industrial relations literature; see Barnett 1969 [1926]). But rarely have local unions had to consider the interests and decision-making processes of the firm as closely as is the case in postwar West Germany. There is an important contemporary body of literature in Germany that emphasizes the dual loyalties of the works councils and argues that works councillors are inevitably forced to choose firm over broader union interests, leading to the demise of national union strength and the rise of "productivity coalitions" and "plant syndicalism" (Hoffmann 1988; Hohn 1988; Windolf and Hohn 1984). Although this literature is useful for understanding the dilemmas that works councillors face and for bringing out general decentralizing trends within West German industrial relations, the evidence presented in this book does not corroborate the central argument, especially the works councils' role in the demise of national union strength; such an argument is in any case belied by the much more serious decline of unions in the 1980s in countries without dual systems or works councils. What intrigues me is how so many works councils seem able to reconcile apparently conflicting interests, contributing in an arguably significant way to a set of national outcomes that include success for West German industry in world markets *and* the stability of union membership rates (over twice as high as rates in the United States) as well as the relatively secure place of workers' interest representation within the West German political economy.

corps of union-oriented works councillors at the plant and firm levels.[12] In an era of work reorganization on the shop floor, the role of the works councils has expanded along with the efforts of the unions to disseminate information and exert influence at this level; and one can identify a de-centralizing trend within West German industrial relations and the building of plant- and firm-level productivity coalitions (Streeck 1987b; Windolf 1989). But as Kathleen Thelen (1987 a and b) has persuasively argued, centralization and decentralization, at least in the case of the IG Metall, are no zero-sum game; far from undermining central union strength, the expansion of the use of works councils as arenas for the expression of union positions has arguably contributed to the flexibility and contin-ued strength of West German unions in a period of worldwide union weakness.[13]

To sum up, industrial relations in West Germany are characterized by continual bargaining at the plant and firm levels, punctuated by intense periods of regional and national negotiation (at three-year intervals since 1984 for the IG Metall) between centralized unions and employer asso-ciations. Strike rates are low in this "consensual" system, although strike threats are credible and occasionally lead to dramatic periods of open conflict (as in the massive six-week-long strikes and lockouts in the metal-working and printing industries in 1984), which demonstrate the inde-pendence and conflict potential of West German unions.[14] From the perspective of industrial relations, West Germany shows key attributes of "democratic corporatism,"[15] with interests aggregated within a relatively cohesive labor movement and centralized employer associations, engaged

---

[12] See, for example, Hohn 1988, p. 170, on the practical identity of works council and plant-level union.

[13] The empirical presentations in this chapter and in Chapter 4 support Thelen's thesis, at least for the auto industry (which she looked at) and for the telecommunications and apparel industries (which she did not). See also Jacobi and Müller-Jentsch 1990 on the basic institutional stability of West German industrial relations in a period of adaptation and adjustment.

[14] The ability of unions to wage successful strikes was challenged in legislation passed under the conservative-liberal government led by Helmut Kohl, most notably in the con-troversy over paragraph 116 of the Work Promotion Act (*Arbeitsforderungsgesetz*, or AFG; see Silvia 1988). The strike threat apparently remains credible, however, as demonstrated in the series of warning strikes that preceded a favorably arbitrated (from the union point of view) contract settlement in the printing industry in early 1989 and in the negotiations and warning strikes that preceded IG Metall's successful 1990 bargaining round (which established the thirty-five-hour workweek).

[15] This is a term used by both Wilensky and Katzenstein. Wilensky (1983) puts West Germany "on the margins of democratic corporatism"; Katzenstein (1985) argues that West Germany is the large country that is most similar to the smaller democratic corporatist societies of Western Europe.

in periodic "subpeak" bargaining at the regional level (nationally coordinated). Outcomes of regional negotiations generally reflect a de facto national-level industrial peace bargain between labor and capital, as do the legal apparatus of codetermination and the tone and outcomes of continuous plant- and firm-level bargaining between works councils and management.

There are, of course, considerable industry-, union-, firm-, and plant-specific variations within West German industrial relations (just as there are in every country, no matter how the institutions place in categories of corporatism or pluralism), and it is in part to these differences that the new literature on sectoral or "meso"-corporatism speaks (Cawson 1985; Schmitter 1988). There are plants within the same industry, and even within the same firm, that are very different in levels of works council influence and strength. At the national level, there are industries in which unions have considerable clout, with corresponding influence on well-organized and effective works councils; the auto industry (organized by IG Metall) and the postal and telecommunications services of the Bundespost (organized by the Deutsche Postgewerkschaft) are prime examples. At the same time, there are industries in which unions have less clout and works councils are weaker and less independent of management; parts of the machinery industry (also organized by IG Metall) and the apparel industry (organized by Gewerkschaft Textil-Bekleidung) are examples.[16] From the point of view of unions and works councils, industrial relations in West Germany work much better in some industries than others; but even in the industries where unions and works councils are weaker, union membership rates have generally been maintained (Kittner 1988) and important levers of influence have been retained (at the very least through works council negotiation of required social plans for displaced workers). Even in these industries, workers' interest representation is arguably better off than it is in most advanced industrial societies in this period of widespread turmoil and decline for unions.[17]

There is a serious downside to this generally (and certainly comparatively) positive picture of industrial relations in West Germany. This is

[16] The difference between auto and postal and telecommunications services on one hand and machinery and apparel on the other can be accounted for in part by the difference between large-firm and small-to-medium-firm industries. But this is not a full explanation because there is also considerable variation across both large firms and small-to-medium firms.

[17] But see Altmann 1987 and Altmann and Düll 1990 for insightful discussions of the new and serious problems faced by works councils and unions as technological advance increasingly integrates rationalization, both within and across firms. Compare Kern and Sabel 1990, who propose major decentralizing revisions in union strategy.

the reality of social exclusion (*soziale Schliessung*), which locks millions of workers and would-be workers out of stable employment opportunities in the core work force, where jobs and working conditions are protected by works council bargaining. Hans-Willy Hohn (1988) argues, in fact, that the very logic of the behavior of workers' interest representation—unions supporting the expansion of the rights and influence of works councils combined with the close identification of works councils with the plant and with the interests of the already employed work force at the plant—has contributed significantly to a deepening segmentation in the labor market in which those on the inside are protected and secure while those on the outside are denied entry. The term "two-thirds society" (*zwei-drittel Gesellschaft*) has come into common usage in contemporary West German discourse; the left-out third are the unemployed and the underemployed, including high percentages of women, foreign workers, and the unskilled.

There is considerable debate in the West German literature concerning how to interpret this phenomenon; one point of view, from both the left and the right, sees deepening segmentation as a reflection and a result of union decline. As unions have lost clout in the political arena and at the same time handed over the locus of bargaining to firm-oriented works councils in the industrial relations arena, they have lost the capacity to fight effectively for societywide reforms that could break down segmentation and have been reduced to a support organization for the works councils. Although the evidence and analysis presented in this book, especially from a comparative point of view, will not support a "decline of the unions" thesis in West Germany, it is nonetheless clear that polarization of the labor market into haves and have-nots poses major problems for West German unions, threatening long-term social stability and raising the danger that unions become entrenched only as the representative of a core work force that is declining in number.[18]

Works Councils, IG Metall, and Rationalization in the Auto Industry

The auto industry is a useful starting point for an understanding of how West German industrial relations have adapted to the market turmoil of

---

[18] Unionists argue that they recognize these problems and are attempting to combat them through job creation resulting from bargained reductions in the length of the workweek; consistent demands for the hiring of new apprentices; a "qualifications offensive" to upgrade the skills of the unskilled; and the political defense of social legislation.

the past fifteen years and the perceived need for ongoing reorganization of work (including both technological change and the redesign of work). As in the United States, the auto industry has often played the role of trailblazer in the use of new technology and the development of new production concepts and work organization. And West German auto-workers, perhaps even more so than in the United States, play a pivotal role within the West German labor movement (Streeck 1984a).

Autoworkers make up about 40 percent of the membership of the IG Metall (which also organizes the steel, machinery, and electronics indus-tries) and serve as pattern setters in plant-level negotiations and leaders in regional bargaining rounds. The IG Metall, in turn, plays the role of pattern setter for West German labor as a whole in regard to wages, working conditions, and hours. In the wake of IG Metall's prolonged strike in 1984 for the shorter workweek,[19] for example, negotiations for shorter working hours have spread throughout West German industry. Although the auto industry is atypical in the sense that this is where union and works councils are perhaps at their strongest, industrial relations arrangements here at the core of West German industry set patterns as well as a general model toward which unions and works councils in many other industries aspire. Industrial relations in the auto industry show both the possibilities for influence and the limits faced by unions and works councils in postwar West Germany.

The influence of workers' interest representation has been tested sharply in the past twenty years in the West German auto industry. First, wildcat strikes and widespread unrest among the rank and file in the period from 1969 to 1973 expressed not only complaints about wages but a grow-ing dissatisfaction, especially among younger workers, with traditional assembly-line work (Bergmann and Müller-Jentsch 1983, pp. 260–63; Markovits 1986, pp. 111, 116, 205–36.) The breakdown of shop-floor discipline was seen as a major threat by managers and union alike and accounted in part for labor's successful push under a Social Democratic–Liberal (SPD-FDP) government in 1972 for an amended Works Consti-tution Act, expanding the rights of works councils as well as union pres-ence in the plants. Rank-and-file dissatisfaction in the auto and other industries drove the Social Democratic party (SPD) to develop "human-ization of work" programs in the 1970s, in which researchers in con-junction with unionists and managers developed alternatives for work organization (such as job rotation, job enrichment, and work teams) and

---

[19] The workweek was down to thirty-seven hours by 1989 and scheduled for thirty-five hours by 1995, as a result of collective bargaining rounds in 1984, 1987, and 1990.

set up pilot projects to test the new concepts. From this time on, humanization became a major theme for the IG Metall, and the union developed its own group of researchers to study the effects of new technology and to propose alternative means for organizing work.[20]

In 1973, metalworkers in North Baden–North Württemberg, who have often led the way in national pattern setting, campaigned for a new Wage Framework Agreement (*Lohnrahmen-Tarifvertrag II*). After a five-day strike by fifty-seven thousand workers, concentrated on Daimler-Benz and Bosch in the auto industry, the IG Metall reached agreement with the employers association (Markovits 1986, pp. 229–32). Among other provisions, the new framework contract for all metalworkers in the region placed limits on the division of labor; no work unit could be less than 1.5 minutes (contrasted to usual auto plant cycle times in the United States of one minute or less). The IG Metall was subsequently unable to spread this agreement to other areas of West Germany, but issues of work humanization were now on the bargaining agenda.

In the mid-1970s, economic crisis raised the prospect of large-scale U.S.-style layoffs in the auto industry. Although these were for the most part averted, works councils even in the most historically harmonious of cases, such as Volkswagen, were forced into acrimonious negotiations with management that threatened to break into open conflict—resulting in increased awareness on both sides of the need for better planning for the use of personnel, including training and retraining, along with market and production strategies that ensured the stable employment of a core work force (Streeck 1984a; Koch 1987).

In 1978, another strike in North Baden–North Württemberg, in which autoworkers played a major role, resulted in an improved "rationalization protection" package (Markovits 1986, pp. 245–51; Thelen 1987b, pp. 221–29). Although IG Metall was again unsuccessful in spreading the provisions of this contract to other regions, the emphasis on the effects of work reorganization spread throughout the union to become one of the major concerns of works councils in the auto industry in the present period.

The interest of union and works councils (and to some extent mangement) in issues of work organization were at first driven by rank-and-file dissatisfaction, wildcat strikes, and demands for the humanization of work. Throughout the 1970s, and continuing to the start of the 1980–82 reces-

---

[20] Job design (*Gestaltung*) alternatives are developed within the IG Metall principally in the Department of Automation and Technology. They are also developed at independent research institutes such as the Institut für Sozialwissenschaftliche Forschung in Munich, where proposals and accompanying analyses are made available to both labor and management.

sion, interest in the reorganization of work (and a limited number of actual initiatives) came from the side of workers' interest representation or was prompted by managerial fears concerning workers' behavior. Increasingly, however, and especially in the past decade, work reorganization has become a major strategy for management, not to humanize work but to cut costs and increase productivity and flexibility. The need to respond to such strategies has given works councils and the IG Metall an added push to take up these issues and develop negotiating positions.

Why has management been moving to rationalize and reorganize work in the past decade, with a speed perhaps unprecedented in the history of the West German auto industry? The answer lies in market circumstances and the availability of new technologies. At the beginning of this chapter, the long-term success of the West German auto industry was acknowledged. But it was also noted that success in the 1980s came in the face of worldwide overcapacity, in particular in Europe, and the dramatic rise of Japanese (and now Korean) competition.

It is well known now that the steady worldwide rise of Japanese market share in the auto industry (and this is true for other industries as well) is not just a result of marketing strategies or well-organized state-led promotion of exports. It is also based on decisive production advantages that make possible the marketing of low-cost, high-quality cars (Altshuler et al. 1984; Quinn 1989; Schumann et al. 1988). At first, as in the United States, Japan mounted an effective competitive challenge and secured increasing market share in small cars. This in itself was perceived as a major threat to the West German high-volume producers (VW, Opel, Ford), whose major offerings had always been small cars. These firms responded beginning in the mid- to late 1970s by rationalizing (with new technology and work organization to cut costs and increase production flexibility), diversifying (offering a range of new products), and moving upmarket (improving product designs, quality, and the range of options offered) to stay ahead of the Japanese challenge. West German firms also concentrated on the European market, which is partly closed to the Japanese (especially in France and Italy).

These strategies, combined with the relatively unchallenged position of the specialty producers (especially Daimler-Benz, BMW, and Audi), allowed the West German auto industry to avoid the huge setbacks faced by U.S. auto producers, but Japanese auto firms, production advantages still intact, have begun in recent years to move decisively upmarket. Though basic Toyotas and other small cars continue to hold market share at the low end, Japanese firms have followed the Germans upmarket, diversifying their own options and product offerings. And now, dramatically, Japanese firms are beginning to offer high-quality, top-of-the-line direct competitors for the Mercedes and BMW. Honda, for example, is offering a new model that is reputed to match a typical Mercedes in quality at two-thirds the cost. It is the widely voiced opinion of German auto industry managers and analysts today that no market segment will remain secure from Japanese and other competition.[21]

Market challenges of the past decade have thus driven West German auto firms in all market segments to rationalize, bringing in new technology and reorganizing work at a rapid pace. Reorganization of the shop floor has resulted in new production concepts, including, for example, the introduction of programmable (flexible) automation that is overseen by versatile, appropriately trained production workers, called systems monitors (*Anlagenführer*). In many cases, traditionally fragmented assembly work has been reintegrated to some degree, especially to include quality inspection, and many production workers' jobs have become multitask and have acquired new responsibilities. The study of new production concepts and new work organization has become very much a growth industry in West Germany for industrial sociologists and political economists, and analyses of the actual outcomes are widely debated. Kern and Schumann, for example, present a fairly positive picture of current developments in the auto industry (and other industries as well), identifying general trends toward upskilling, expanded responsibility, and the reintegration of work, leading perhaps toward an end to the division of labor (Kern and Schumann 1984; Schumann et al. 1988). Others see a darker future, pointing to a polarization of the work force into a multiskilled elite and an unskilled corps of highly regimented production workers. In a recent important contribution, Jürgens, Malsch, and Dohse (1989) paint a more complex picture in which new production concepts vary in content across firms (as well as nations) and in which simultaneous trends exist toward greater autonomy and responsibility on the shop floor *and* enhanced managerial control. In this view, what is happening in auto plants is not

---

[21] The emphasis here is on competition from Japan. But West German firms also face major competition in European markets from other auto producers such as Fiat and Peugeot (and in 1988 and 1989, VW and Fiat ran neck and neck as European market share leaders). Intense competition among European producers reflects in part the unwillingness of governments to let large auto firms die, even in an oversupplied market which must produce its losers. But German firms have fared well in intra-European competition; the argument here is that the big challenge for the Germans, as for the Americans, comes from Japan—although the Japanese challenge is exacerbated in an already oversupplied European market. The European Commission, for example, predicted a rise in Japanese market shares in autos to 20% in West Germany by 1992 and 15% in the European Community as a whole (EMF 1988).

only a change in the division of labor and an adaptation to new technology, but a change in the form and content of management functions, as quality circles and teamwork spread (Jürgens 1987).

But no matter how one analyzes the current developments in work organization, it is clear that major changes are under way. As in the U.S. case, these changes are driven by market circumstances, in particular the intensification of competition with the arrival of new world-class Japanese competitors; and the new market threats have pushed managers toward strategic change on a number of fronts, including the reorganization of work. And as in the United States, it seems to be a particularity of new technologies and work organization that managers need more input and cooperation from workers on the shop floor—at least in part because such input and cooperation are key elements in the Japanese production advantage.[22] Managers in West German auto firms, therefore, have in the past few years introduced quality circles on the U.S. model (at VW and Ford, for the firms considered here) and have begun to consider new forms of shop-floor teamwork.[23]

Work reorganization in West Germany, however, requires considerable discussion and negotiation with works councils. Although plant management is legally free, after consultation with the works council, to bring in new technology and organize production as it sees fit, it must negotiate the terms of change (because proposed change affects the work force or individual workers) before changes are implemented. Works councils have thus increasingly been pushed into discussions and negotiation about work organization, both by managers in need of agreement and support for implementation and by workers and shop stewards concerned about the effects of change. And as works councils have moved squarely into the work organization arena, the IG Metall has been called on to provide information and suggest strategies. In part as a response to works council demands, but also as part of its own new strategic orientation, the union has moved increasingly in the past decade to develop information and negotiating strategies regarding technology and work organization and to spread these to the works councils (IG Metall 1984a; Thelen 1987a).

The IG Metall has been in a position to build on past studies and

[22] For a fuller discussion of the perceived link between employee participation and production outcomes, see Chapter 1.

[23] Kern and Schumann argue not only that teams are an appropriate organizational form given new markets, technologies, and changes in work organization, but that the identifiable trends in the auto industry toward new integrated forms of work and the breakdown of Taylorism include the spread of teams or groups. How far this goes is highly dependent on workers and their representatives (Kern and Schumann 1984, pp. 48–51, 99–136).

negotiations beginning in the 1970s concerning humanization of work. Although the SPD- and government-sponsored humanization campaign never really took off and direct participation never spread beyond the research groups and pilot projects, the concepts of humanization spread through union ranks and through the ranks of the auto industry works councils. The notion that work could and should be more interesting and less monotonous and stressful, and that worker representatives could take up these issues as legitimate subjects of bargaining, became accepted by many unionists and works councillors; and these initial discussions laid the groundwork for a much more proactive role on the part of workers' interest representation by the mid- to late 1980s.[24]

To the extent that humanization interests existed on the works councils in the 1970s, the expression of such interests was significantly weakened in the face of the 1980–82 recession and the escalating managerial drive for shop-floor rationalization. IG Metall's paper on the auto industry, written the same year that Kern and Schumann's book was published, argues that the union must get involved in work organization precisely to oppose deskilling and work intensification in management's pursuit of the "Olympic-class team" (IG Metall 1984b). And Norbert Altmann (1987) identifies, for German industry as a whole, opposing union "manpower orientation" and managerial "centralistic automation" strategies.

Subsequent union and works council strategies concerning the reorganization of work can be divided into two approaches: first, defense against the negative effects on the work force of technological change and work reorganization, which in the German discussion falls under the general term "rationalization protection"; and second, the development and promotion of an independent union vision and strategy for the shape and content of new work organization.

The main efforts of works councils in the auto industry, supported by union advisers, have focused on the first approach, the need to protect workers against unemployment, displacement, lower pay, and unfavorable job reassignment as management rationalizes production. This approach can be divided into two parts: rationalization protection agreements and a "training offensive." In both of these areas, German autoworkers have been considerably ahead of their U.S. counterparts. Protection measures,

[24] Kern and Schumann, for example, note that in their first study of work organization, published in 1972, they found no independent works council influence on new technology and work organization. But in their studies conducted in the early 1980s in the auto industry, they found that the works councils had become partners in firms' decision making and that the shape of work reorganization was now the result of negotiation and compromise (Kern and Schumann 1984, pp. 117–18).

both regional/contractual and plant-level agreements, have improved steadily in the past decade, to the point that autoworkers in the large plants are virtually assured of employment security, pay protection of unlimited duration, and retraining rights. Overlapping with rationalization protection, the training offensive has aimed at securing the maximum funding and rights and opportunities for training and retraining and has emphasized the common interests of labor and management in developing a more highly skilled work force. In part as a result of union and works council efforts, the West German auto industry work force is arguably more highly skilled than any other in the world.[25]

The training offensive overlaps with the development of an independent union vision of new work organization. But in itself, the promotion of training is more protective than proactive unless it is linked with answers to the question, training for what? As we have seen, the development of a comprehensive union vision and strategy regarding new work organization was missing in the U.S. case in the 1980s. In part this is so because at least in the postwar period it has not been the role of unions in the United States, West Germany, or almost anywhere else to help management plan the organization of work. To the extent that unions have taken up such questions, they have done so through grievance and negotiation to challenge or modify management plans in the interest of individual workers or groups of workers.

For most of the postwar period, the IG Metall has been no exception to this general rule. Like the UAW, the IG Metall has a strong tradition of "letting management manage." From the earliest work humanization initiatives right up to the present day, a strong position exists among many IG Metallers, at national headquarters in Frankfurt and elsewhere, against the proactive intrusion of the union into issues involving the organization of work. "Why should we help management plan production? Why should we help management raise productivity (which will only cost us jobs and create problems for us with our members)?" say these "traditionalist" voices, who see plenty of work for the union already in negotiations and conflict for better wages, working conditions and hours, rationalization protection, and broader social issues.[26]

---

[25] This is true in part because an oversupply of apprentices (resulting from labor demands for high levels of training) has increasingly meant that even un- or semiskilled production jobs are filled by fully trained, skilled workers. The German auto industry thus possesses a reservoir of skills that gives managers and worker representatives numerous options as they contemplate the shape of new work organization.

[26] This perception is based on a series of interviews that I conducted at IG Metall headquarters in Frankfurt in 1988–89, along with interviews at works council offices in

And yet in the past decade, clear union positions on the nature of new work organization have begun to emerge, the result of internal discussion and debate and in response to a steady stream of works council demands for more information and support on issues of new technology and job design. From several different departments of the IG Metall (Economics, Automation and Technology, Works Councils), proactive proposals and strategies for work organization have been put forward, and in some cases, with organizational backing, these plans have been taken to the works councils. The example with the most far-reaching implications, and the one that has now been taken up by the works councils of almost every major West German auto assembly plant, is the union-led campaign for group work (*Gruppenarbeit*).

IG Metall Campaigns for "Group Work"

Initiatives in the U.S. auto industry for various forms of teamwork, including the team concept, have come principally from the management side. The UAW at the national level has lent conditional support to these new forms of work organization and has entered into discussions with top management and with local union leaders regarding what changes are acceptable and how best to implement them. At the local level, union leaders and members have debated the new proposals and in many cases have negotiated the terms of change as well as some modifications in the substance of new forms of teamwork. But in all cases, the initial planning and proposals have come from management. In West Germany, by contrast, at least until 1985, initiatives aimed at developing new forms of teamwork in the auto industry have come primarily from the union side. In the course of the past ten to fifteen years, the IG Metall has developed a well-reasoned vision of new work organization accompanied by concrete proposals for implementation; the union calls the new concept *Gruppenarbeit*, which I translate as "group work."[27]

---

several auto plants and at local union offices (*Verwaltungsstellen*) in several cities (where much of the representation work concerns a major auto plant).

[27] *Gruppen* means "groups" and *Arbeit* means "work." *Gruppenarbeit* as the term is used by IG Metallers (as well as other unionists and industry researchers) is defined in different ways but generally refers to a new work organization based on responsible groups of workers, as opposed to traditional assembly-line organization in which individual workers each perform a limited set of tasks.

Terminology here is important. Just as the Lordstown workers are explicit in using the term "groups" to mark off their organizational innovations from other plants' "teams" or

There have been three phases in the development of union-promoted group work in the West German auto industry (Muster 1988c, pp. 62–63). Serious discussion regarding new work organization first began in the union in the early 1970s, in response to unrest and dissatisfaction among the rank and file and as part of the humanization of work campaign. Unionists backed by academic and industry researchers proposed setting up work groups with internal job rotation and new responsibility as a way to overcome assembly-line alienation and the fragmentation of work. These discussions emerged as part of a broader discussion within the SPD, in power at the time and grappling with issues of social reform and economic and industrial democracy. Management at VW and Ford showed a willingness to experiment, and group work pilot projects were set up at Salzgitter (VW) and Saarlouis (Ford); but these projects proved short-lived, soon to be abandoned and considered failures in retrospect. From the management side, the experiments were viewed as uneconomical; from the union side, the concerns were the fear that union and works council representation was undermined as the new groups made their own decisions and the perception on the part of many workers that this was really just another management effort at speedup.

In the second phase, new ideas and proposals were bounced around within the IG Metall from around 1979 to 1985, and some of these appeared on works council–management bargaining tables, in most cases without success.[28] The new proposals arose in response to management rationalization campaigns and were put forward as a way to protect pay and job content and to overcome polarization of the work force as new technology made some jobs obsolete and created demands for new skills. Proposals to group workers into cross-trained and equally paid units were closely linked to both rationalization protection negotiations and the training offensive. But although firms made concessions on pay protection and training, managers proved little interested in moving the added step forward into a wholesale new system of organization.

The third phase began about 1985 and is characterized both by an upsurge of union–works council plant-level bargaining for group work and by an increasing managerial interest in new forms of teamwork (Hölterhoff 1988; Jürgens, Malsch, and Dohse 1989, p. 295). Managers who

---

"team concept" (which they perceive as based on a more Japanese-style approach, including a weaker union role), so IG Metallers are insistent on the term *Gruppenarbeit*, especially given management's new interest in teams (*Teamarbeit, Team Konzept*), based on observations of Japanese and recent U.S. work organization innovations.

[28] See, for example, the Opel-Bochum case that follows.

flat out rejected works council suggestions for group work before 1985 now began to discuss the issue with interest and to put forward their own concepts and proposals (such as Opel's production groups—*Fertigungs-gruppen*—as influenced by GM's NUMMI and other team organization plants). Based on learning from abroad and a perceived intensification of competition in the auto industry, managers began looking to new team systems of work for similar reasons as did managers in the United States: lower costs, higher productivity, better product quality, and a more flexible use of labor, in part through increased cooperation, input, and responsibility from group-organized shop-floor workers.[29]

On the union side, there is considerable concern that management's intentions include the weakening of union influence and works council representation functions (in the transfer of discussion and decision making to the shop-floor group) as well as the squeezing out of the traditional production work force, to be replaced with new "Olympic-class teams" of young skilled workers. In response to the perceived dangers inherent in management's new interest in teamwork, the IG Metall has sharpened its strategic focus on work organization issues, a change that is reflected in resolutions adopted beginning at the 1986 convention (Jürgens, Malsch, and Dohse 1989, p. 349), and in the increasing educational work by union representatives from national headquarters directed at auto plant works councils. The increased focus by union representatives, informed by give-and-take between union and works councils and the preliminary discussions between works councils and management, has resulted in a well-developed union-promoted concept of group work that is now being put forward for negotiation at most West German auto assembly plants.

Although management concepts regarding teamwork were in the process of development and remained as yet somewhat vague, varying considerably from firm to firm, the union concept, with ample space for local and shop-floor adaptations, was well developed by the late 1980s. The twelve main principles of group work (*Eckpunkte zur Gruppenarbeit*) can be summarized as follows:[30] (1) a broad assignment of varying tasks for

---

[29] Streeck (1989, pp. 131–34) discusses management's newfound interest in teamwork. But the emphasis is misplaced in his claim that the coming of teams is based on managerial initiative and that the problems for acceptance lie on the union side. Streeck misses the history of group-work promotion by the IG Metall as well as the current dynamics of (sometimes union-led) negotiation.

[30] The *Eckpunkte zur Gruppenarbeit* have been widely circulated to the works councils in the form of unpublished educational material. The presentation here is a summary translation based on Muster and Wannöffel 1989, pp. 39–54.

the group (including long cycle times); (2) group competence in decision making in such areas as job rotation, division of the work, quality control, and training needs; (3) decentralization of the plant decision-making structure; (4) selection of production organization and technology suitable for group work (based on decentralized technology and production concepts); (5) equal pay for group members; (6) equal opportunity for all, including special training where necessary for the disabled and the socially disadvantaged, to participate in group work (''group work as solidaristic work organization''); (7) support for the personal and occupational development of individuals and the group; (8) regular group meetings, at least one hour per week; (9) representation of group interests within the established plant system of interest representation; (10) voluntary participation in the groups; (11) pilot projects to test the functioning of group work before broader implementation; (12) a joint steering committee at the firm level, with equal labor and management representation, to oversee and coordinate the implementation of group work and the activities of the groups.

At this point, the story would not be complete without the mention of two rather remarkable individuals. IG Metall concepts of work organization do not reach the works councils by mail (they would be ignored if they did); rather they are personally delivered by union representatives, who discuss the main points with the works council chairperson, other interested works councillors, and the assembled works council as a whole. Concepts are then revised in a back-and-forth flow between union and works councils (the above *Eckpunkte* were several years in the making); works councils, in this case, were won over to the (initially quite threatening) idea of group work in a prolonged, years-long process of education. Because works councils are legally separate from the union under the dual system, the national union has no formal authority to influence their acceptance of new ideas and bargaining positions on work organization, such as group work. Union representatives must first educate and win over the works councils and then work closely with works councillors to develop strategies for bargaining at a particular plant and for the spread of these new ideas down through the ranks of the shop stewards and the work force. The two IG Metall representatives[31] most closely identified with group work in the auto industry, and most responsible for spreading interest in group work to the works councils, are Siegfried Roth and Manfred Muster.

[31] The German word here is *Gewerkschaftssecretär*, or union secretary. This union representative is not an elected official or department head, but a hired staff member, often well educated, who is based at the IG Metall national headquarters in Frankfurt.

Siegfried Roth has coauthored several articles that emphasize the suit-ability (and superiority) of group work for high-technology applications in today's workplace and in the "factory of the future" (Roth 1988; Roth and Königs 1988) and has coedited a book compiling diverse contemporary viewpoints on group work from works councillors, unionists, scholars, and politicians (Roth and Kohl 1988). Assigned to work with Ford works councils, Roth has done important educational work, helped to formulate a works council bargaining proposal for submission to the company, and played an important role in setting up an impressive pilot project at the flagship plant in Cologne. It is fair to say that the Ford general works council, with many other claims on its time, would have been much slower to develop interest in the new group work issue without Roth's painstaking and patient intervention since 1985.

At VW, Opel, and Daimler-Benz, the name Manfred Muster is syn-onymous with group work. Working from within a socialist tradition (which in itself is mainstream IG Metall), Muster has arguably done more than anyone else in West Germany to develop and spread the new union version of group work. Muster's articles on group work appear regularly in journals and books (Muster 1988a, 1988b, 1988c), and more than anyone else he has been responsible for the development and adaptations of the above twelve principles (*Eckpunkte*). As an organizer, Muster is exceptional, combining technical knowledge that runs the full length of an auto plant's shop floor with an unrelenting persuasiveness and a will-ingness to listen and constantly revise his own thinking. Muster's organ-izing work at VW, Opel, and Daimler-Benz has had a great deal to do with the spread of interest in group work at these plants, the setting up of pilot projects, and the arrival of serious labor-management group work bargaining sessions.

The rising emphasis on work organization issues, and in particular group work, on the part of auto plant works councils cannot be explained solely by reference to the work of effective organizers like Roth and Muster, but neither can their role be ignored. The tendency of social scientists to discount leadership, in search of greater scientific objectivity, sometimes flies in the face of everyday perceptions of reality and perhaps undermines the credibility of social science. Nevertheless, some institutions facilitate the work of organizers and leaders much more than others. The particular institutions of industrial relations in West Germany, including both unions and union-influenced works councils, with the latter assigned clear rights to bargain on a variety of substantial in-plant issues, make possible the development and spread of union concepts of work organization, and fortuitously for West German labor, talented organizers have been there to step into the available roles.[32]

In contrast to the U.S. case, characterized by management strategies to reorganize work and intraunion debates about whether to cooperate or negotiate, the West German auto industry has both a well-developed union concept for group work and developing management concepts and strategies. The union view is rooted in the SPD-led humanization of work efforts of the 1970s and thus has distinctly political origins; it is hard to imagine the humanization campaign backed by government funding taking off in the absence of an SPD-led government, with close ties to the unions, concerned about rank-and-file unrest, and ideologically committed to greater economic and industrial democracy. Developing management views of teamwork, by contrast, appear to have external roots: in the QWL and EI traditions of GM and Ford in the United States and, above all, in the Japanese production model. The actual shape and structure of new teams or groups, if indeed they materialize in a widespread way in the West German auto industry (which now appears likely because both sides are pushing in this direction), will be determined as a result of bargaining between two strong and overlapping positions. For the union and works councils, the *Eckpunkte* represent a bargaining position; no one expects wholesale adoption, and the practical question is what can be negotiated. For management, the questions are what aspects of the union plan are compatible with company efforts to raise productivity and flexibility and at the same time lower costs and where the line should be drawn in pursuit of its own contending plans for work reorganization. Negotiated agreement seems likely given the current spread of pilot projects, the generally co-operative plant-level tradition, the recognition of both sides that work reorganization is on the agenda, and the parallel claims by both sides of the need to raise productivity in the interest of competitiveness (and even the union and works councils are meticulous in justifying their group work proposals with cost and productivity data). Nonetheless, bargaining will be difficult, posing management's desire for more controlled and "lean" systems (Krafcik 1988b) against labor's interest in buffered, autonomous group organization. The most important rounds of negotiation and implementation lie ahead.

---

[32] The U.S. case is a useful counterpoint in this regard. Talented organizers and conceptual thinkers of the ilk of Roth and Muster also exist within the UAW. But past history and still embedded traditions that exclude the union from management decision-making processes (and that in the past afforded the union few incentives to put resources into work organization issues) mean that such talents are directed into other areas. The result, as we have seen in Chapter 1, is that the UAW has yet to promote actively, in the plants, a consistent union vision of the shape of new work organization.

For a closer look at actual processes of negotiation, the following sections will consider the politics of work reorganization in the 1980s at five important assembly plants of West Germany's high-volume auto producers: VW-Wolfsburg, Opel-Bochum, Opel-Rüsselsheim, Ford-Cologne, and Ford-Saarlouis.[33]

Social Partnership at Wolfsburg: The VW Model

Like all West German auto firms, Volkswagen is a product of special historical and market circumstances.[34] As a creation of the Nazis in 1938, the Volkswagen plant at Wolfsburg (then and now the largest auto plant in West Germany) entered the postwar period with no union tradition, located in a company town in a rural area (in Lower Saxony near the border with East Germany), with a work force demoralized by the war and military defeat and fearful that the plant would be shut by military occupation authorities (the British).[35] The result was a company-dominated works council at Wolfsburg after the war (analogous to company unionism in the United States), with IG Metall membership of around 20 percent in the early 1950s and a cooperative labor-management relationship dominated by common survival fears and company paternalism.

But just as company unionism at AT&T in the United States was trans-

[33] I focus on the mass-market producers to afford a more controlled comparison to developments in the U.S. auto industry, where all firms are high-volume. Specialty producers such as Daimler-Benz and BMW face special market circumstances, including competition that is less cost-based, which may permit a greater range of production innovation (Quinn 1989). Surprisingly, however, this does not seem to be the case in Germany, where past rationalization efforts and current group-work negotiations are moving along very similar tracks at Daimler-Benz, VW, Ford, and Opel (according to interviews at IG Metall headquarters and at the one Daimler-Benz plant that I visited).

[34] There are six large VW auto plants in West Germany, three of which are assembly plants (Wolfsburg, Hannover, and Emden). Wolfsburg is the original and by far the largest plant; Volkswagen has its headquarters here as does the general works council (an increasingly important body made up of representatives from each of the six individual plant works councils). As of March 1989, the Wolfsburg plant had 62,200 employees and produced about 4,000 cars per day: 2,600 to 2,700 Golfs, 700 to 800 Jettas, and 500 to 700 Polos (data provided by Volkswagen AG in Wolfsburg).

For Ford and Opel, the special circumstances are their respective positions as German subsidiaries of U.S. firms (Ford and GM, respectively); for Daimler-Benz, BMW, and Porsche, the special circumstances are the upmarket, high-cost, and quality market niches they occupy as specialty producers.

An earlier version of this section on the VW Wolfsburg plant can be found in Mishel and Voos 1991.

[35] For a useful history of industrial relations at Volkswagen, see Koch 1987. For much more condensed versions in English see Brumlop and Jürgens 1986; and Streeck 1984a.

formed into nationally organized independent unionism in the CWA in the postwar period (see below, Chapter 4), so the IG Metall turned things around at Wolfsburg in the 1950s and 1960s. Working within the framework of labor-management cooperation, IG Metall made use of the dual system to run candidates in the works council elections, securing its first works council majority in 1955 (Koch 1987, pp. 89–91). From that date forward, the union has steadily increased membership levels in the plant and extended its domination of the works council, winning its biggest majority ever in the 1987 elections.[36] And the IG Metall has done this without disrupting a labor-management "partnership" that the work force has supported since the early postward period.

Unlike other West German auto firms that bargain collectively with the IG Metall at the regional level as members of an employer association, VW bargains separately with the regional-level union. This difference is rooted in a tradition of public ownership at VW; the firm was handed over to the federal government by the British military authorities in 1949 (Streeck 1984a, p. 40). In 1960, the government moved to "privatize" against the opposition of the union (Koch 1987, pp. 93–94), selling 60 percent of the shares to small owners and leaving 20 percent in the hands of the federal government in Bonn and 20 percent controlled by the state government of Lower Saxony. But even in a minority ownership position, government influence has been important, if only because the government has had a vested interest in industrial peace at this "flagship" West German auto firm.[37]

[36] As of 1988, IG Metall membership at Wolfsburg was 95% (98% hourly, 85% white collar). In the 1987 works council elections, 87% of blue-collar workers voted and 90% of these chose the IG Metall list; 81% of white-collar workers voted and 75% chose IG Metall. In the system of proportional representation that takes effect when alternative lists are presented, IG Metall won 62 of 69 seats (data supplied by the IG Metall Verwaltungsstelle in Wolfsburg and the VW-Wolfsburg works council).

[37] Most important, perhaps, public ownership has made a difference for union–works council participation in supervisory board decisions and access to information from the firm. In this regard, codetermination at VW in the past has been similar in some ways to legislated *Montanmitbestimmung* in the coal, iron, and steel industries, where works councils and unions have stronger codetermination rights than anywhere else in West German industry. Although governed by the more general (and weaker) Codetermination Act of 1976 and lacking parity supervisory board representation, worker board members at VW have better access to information than is usual and nominate the personnel director (*Arbeitsdirektor*). For useful discussions of the firm's supervisory board–level codetermination at VW, see Koch 1987, pp. 177–81; and Streeck 1984a, pp. 43–45, 65.

In the 1980s, the conservative CDU/CSU-FDP government under Kohl moved to sell off its remaining shares. Works council representatives at Wolfsburg are of the opinion that this sale has changed the balance of power on the supervisory board in favor of private investors, increasing the pressure on management to push back works council and union influence.

The growing strength of the IG Metall at Wolfsburg combined with separate bargaining at VW and background government influence have meant that contracts at VW have frequently set patterns for the IG Metall and the metalworking industries as a whole (which in turn often play the role of pattern setters for the entire West German labor movement). Examples of pattern setting at Wolfsburg include the campaign for a forty-hour workweek in 1955–57 (Koch 1987, pp. 96–99); the unwillingness of workers' representatives to make concessions or accept layoffs even in the VW crisis years of 1973–81 (Koch 1987, pp. 158–59; Streeck 1984a, pp. 56–81); bargaining in 1978 for six weeks annual vacation; successful negotiations in 1979–80 for a new pay differentiation scheme (called LODI, or *Lohndifferenzierung*), advocated by the works council, in which temporarily reassigned workers keep their pay levels (Hildebrandt 1981; Brumlop 1986; Brumlop and Jürgens 1986); and a rationalization protection contract in 1987 that assures full pay protection (and increases the prospects for retraining) for workers displaced by new technology or work reorganization, for a virtually unlimited time period.[38]

For many in the German labor movement, industrial relations at VW are a model, a sort of microcorporatism or "concerted action" that is worth striving toward. The key elements of this model are cooperative or "social partnership" relations between labor and management; the virtual identity of union and works council;[39] considerable engagement of the works council in managerial decision-making processes; unity within the works council and union (*Geschlossenheit*) so that differences regarding such critical issues as policy and candidate selection are hammered out internally and a united front is presented in negotiations with management; a high rate of union membership and a strong union presence on the shop floor (more than a thousand shop stewards at Wolfsburg alone); virtual

[38] For workers with over twenty-five years seniority, full pay protection is guaranteed for the worklife at VW; for workers with from one year to twenty-five years seniority, full pay is guaranteed for five years, during which time the worker, according to the intent of the agreement, can find a new position in the firm at the same pay level or receives additional training so that he or she qualifies for such a position ("Tarifvertrag zur sozialen Sicherung der Arbeitnehmer bei technischen und arbeitsorganisatorischen Änderungen," negotiated between Volkswagen AG and IG Metall Bezirk Hannover, March 2, 1987). This is the best such agreement in the German auto industry—other agreements are typically not contractual and can be terminated by either side—and it is considerably better than any such agreement in the U.S. auto industry.

[39] In addition to the dominance of IG Metall members on the works councils (in Wolfsburg as well as at the other five VW plants and on the general works council, where all members are IG Metallers), the IG Metall national president is the vice-president of VW's supervisory board, and the head of the general works council sits on the IG Metall's national executive board.

lifetime pay and employment security for the work force; a management (from top to bottom) that is trained to listen to the concerns of work-force representation and to seek consensus before the implementation of policy; and last but not least, a firm that is highly successful in world markets, whose management and labor representatives at least in the past have regarded "cooperative conflict resolution" at VW as a source of competitive advantage in the marketplace.[40]

The model fared well in the past decade and a half of intensified market pressure. VW survived market crises from 1973 to 1975 (the demise of the Beetle and worldwide economic recession) and 1979–82 (an even deeper recession and a general crisis for automakers in advanced industrial societies) without major union concessions, layoffs (reductions in the work force occurred principally by means of early retirement and voluntary buyouts), or plant closures. Both works council and management have come up with new production and organizational concepts that have been successfully implemented, as the following two examples show. The works council promoted the LODI pay grouping agreement that took effect in 1981 and was designed to trade pay protection for the workers against greater flexibility in allocation of labor for management.[41] Management for its part has rapidly introduced new technology, including the famed Halle 54 (the most automated final automobile assembly line in the world), and has introduced new job design concepts such as the *Anlagenführer* (systems monitor), who supervises the technology and intervenes when necessary, in a production job that reintegrates tasks and has proved popular with workers (Kern and Schumann 1984, pp. 40–100; Jürgens, Malsch, and Dohse 1989, pp. 306–10). All of these organizational and technological changes were preceded by extensive negotiations between

[40] Volkswagen AG's market success is well known in Europe, but this point is worth stressing for readers in the United States, where declining sales make VW look like a market loser. Although VW has largely abandoned the small-car market in the United States to the Japanese and others, the company has more than made up for this loss by success in other markets, particularly in Europe, where VW has led the field in sales volume in recent years (VW was number one in sales in Europe for the combined years 1985–89). European markets, it must be added, are partially protected. French and Italian auto markets, for example, are open to VW and other German firms but virtually closed to the Japanese. And in West Germany, a tacit agreement apparently limited the rate of growth for Japanese auto imports, although Japanese market share exceeded 15% by the late 1980s.

[41] Managers today complain that LODI has benefited the workers more than management, as shop-floor resistance to reassignment has undermined managerial flexibility; but there are no plans to roll back LODI, and works councillors claim that management has failed to develop a unified concept and to organize itself adequately for the proper use of LODI flexibility.

management and works council; implementation was based on prior consensus and was facilitated by both sides.[42]

The model, however, is currently facing new sources of stress. In part the new tension is a result of current and predicted intensified market competition, as Japanese and Korean firms expand market share in the European market and older competitors such as Fiat and Peugeot show new strength, and everyone braces for 1992 and beyond; and in part the new tension is a result of past success, both for VW as a firm and for the VW industrial relations model. The firm's market success has been accompanied by increased employment levels so that VW now finds itself in a position of potentially serious cost disadvantage. From 1978 to 1986, for example, Ford in Europe increased production volume by 17 percent while reducing employment by 20 percent; Fiat increased production by 15 percent and reduced employment by 40 percent; but VW increased production by 5 percent and increased employment by 22 percent (*Der Spiegel*, March 1989, p. 130).

In spite of record sales in the late 1980s, therefore, management is determined to cut costs and employment levels in the coming years. In October 1987, management submitted to the works council a twenty-one-point cost-cutting program. In addition to anticipated steady reductions in the work force through attrition, management proposed significant concessions in such areas as break time. The responses of worker representatives to such initiatives vary: on one hand, they recognize the competitive needs of the firm (as they always have; this is a hallmark of the VW model) and go along with what they think necessary for market success, including gradual work-force reductions; on the other hand, they see such proposals as part of a new managerial aggressiveness, the product of a new breed of younger VW managers (many brought in from outside the VW ''family'') more attentive to market pressures than to VW traditions and the cooperative industrial relations model. Works councillors and shop stewards worry about the increased possibility of future conflict if the new managers push too hard.

For their part, worker representatives have also displayed a new willingness to take initiative and to mobilize the work force when this is

---

[42] The works council, however, had little advance input into managerial decision making regarding new technology and production concepts (Article 90 of the Works Constitution Act requires only that they be informed and consulted); but the works council did agree to the changes and actively negotiated the terms of change, regarding effects on the work force, before implementation. The current trend is toward increased advance input on the part of the works council, as we will see below in the discussion on group work.

considered necessary. The VW model has been based on cooperative relations and engagement between management and works council; for the most part this has not included the work force directly (Koch 1987). But since 1984 and the extensive shop-floor discussions and mobilization around demands for a shorter workweek (although the national IG Metall strike did not include VW), the works council at Wolfsburg has shown an increased propensity to involve the work force, as demonstrated by the community and shop-floor campaign (which included work stoppages) in 1985–86 against the Kohl government's amendments to the Works Promotion Act (AFG article 116; the changes weaken regional and national strike potential); and the spread of works council–promoted discussions among the work force concerning proposed new work organization, in particular group work, beginning in 1989. In part, these changes result from a new generation of works council leaders; both the Wolfsburg and general works councils were led from 1984 to 1990 by Walter Hiller (who officially took office in 1986), a "new breed" counterpart to the younger, tougher managers, apparently more willing than his predecessors to engage in internal union and work-force debate and to take a strong stance toward management if necessary.[43]

The increased willingness of both sides to push in the present period raised talk of a possible strike over contract negotiations in 1990. Although no strike occurred, each side was clearly testing the other in the new climate and jockeying for position as market developments made clear the need for major adjustment and ongoing reorganization of work. In the meantime, both sides moved forward with new teamwork-oriented work organization initiatives. Management initiated quality circles, which the works council accepted in 1986 after a two-year debate and after the inclusion of strong provisions to include union and works council in the implementation; and management set up production teams (*Fertigungszelle*) in the stamping plant and teams of systems monitors (*Anlagenführer*), always after extensive discussion with works councillors. From the union–works council side, the major organizational initiative of the past few years is the campaign for group work.

As is true for all U.S. and West German auto firms, VW management is pressing toward team forms of organization in the search for lower costs, higher productivity and production flexibility, and better product quality (inspired by Japanese success). But company concepts regarding

[43] Hiller resigned his works council posts in May 1990 after his appointment as minister of labor and social policy in the new SPD-led government for the state of Lower Saxony. Klaus Volkert was elected to replace Hiller by the Wolfsburg and general works councils.

the specific shape of teamwork remain vague, as management enters a period of what it perceives to be trial-and-error adjustment, in which new forms of work organization are tried out in various parts of the plant. The works council, however, adopted the well-developed, IG Metall–promoted group work concepts and has bargained with management for their implementation. For the works council, group work appears to be an issue whose time has come; in view of the current competitive, cost-cutting needs of the firm, the works councillors cannot reasonably expect to provide the work force with steadily increasing pay and employment levels as they have done in the past. Rather, the incumbents in works council election campaigns hoped to be able to advertise major gains in working conditions, in part through the coming of group work. Group work proposals also include labor savings (thereby cutting costs and possibly also employment levels for the firm), which gave the works council a strong negotiating position toward a management whose own teamwork concepts were not yet so well defined.

The general works council adopted the IG Metall group work concepts in 1988;[44] as of 1990, the council at Wolfsburg was engaged in active negotiations with management toward both the adoption of a plant-level agreement on group work and the establishment of pilot projects in the plant.[45] At the same time, the Wolfsburg works council was beginning to spread group work discussions down through the ranks of the shop stewards and the work force, to include the workers in the campaign and in the formulation of the precise shape of group work proposals for particular areas of the plant. As one example, the works council held an intensive week-long seminar in January 1989 for shop stewards and works coun-

---

[44] In a remarkable foreword to the twelve principles of group work (the statement is available from the general works council in Wolfsburg and can be found in Riffel and Muster 1989), the general works council makes the following argument for its promotion of union-developed work reorganization (this is a summary translation of the content):

We need to move toward group forms of organization both because Japanese and American auto firms are doing this and to get rid of Taylorism. We are conscious of the particular role of VW (as a model) and of the general position of West Germany as an export nation now facing serious competitive challenges from countries with much weaker social rights (including weaker unions). We need to develop a democratic work culture to show the way for modern democracies; our task is to meet world market risks with our own strengths, those that emerge from a democratic firm culture (as at VW) based on social progress. Good performance and top quality do not come in the long run from pressure or incentives but from interesting work, good teamwork, and appropriate opportunities for input.

[45] In the negotiations for the first Wolfsburg pilot project in 1989, the works council and management could draw on the experience of several ongoing group work pilot projects at other VW auto plants and at Audi, a subsidiary of VW, where group work is perhaps most advanced in the West German auto industry (Muster 1988a).

cillors from the Wolfsburg paint shop to discuss management's plans for new technology (essentially, the building of a new paint shop) and works council plans for group work organization.[46] On the first day, key planning managers attended and presented detailed plans for technology and organization in the new paint shop. The rest of the week was devoted to a discussion of basic group work concepts, organizational and health and safety problems in the paint shop, and detailed proposals by the shop stewards (working in small groups) for the implementation of group work in their particular work areas. The works council's strategy, through such sessions and through in-plant meetings and discussions, is to engage shop stewards and workers in the design and implementation of new group organization. There appears to be an active process now in motion that management will curtail only with great difficulty and that in any case dovetails in important ways with managerial goals for improving productivity, product quality, and workers' responsibility.

Both sides at Wolfsburg recognize that new forms of teamwork are coming in one form or another; both sides appear to agree that the works council has now taken the primary initiative in this regard (so that management is now negotiating changes in the union–works council plan, as opposed to vice versa); and both sides claim to be optimistic that a settlement will be found, based on overlapping interests and a joint learning process as pilot projects are examined. This is a period of great uncertainty for both the VW industrial relations model and the future of work organization; it is also a period when the prospects for work humanization at Wolfsburg and other VW plants look promising and when the odds for successful adjustment and work reorganization at VW look good (especially in comparative perspective), given the past track record and cooperative negotiating processes. The extent to which labor and management can agree on the details of group work organization remains, of course, an open question, given the potential collision course between labor's new assertiveness on the issue and management's cost-cutting campaign.

One cannot claim that the industrial relations model at Volkswagen is the primary determinant of the firm's success in the past decade. In fact, another very successful European auto firm of the 1980s, Fiat, went on the attack against its unions and successfully marginalized much of the past influence of worker representation.[47] At VW the move upmarket

[46] For a lengthy report on this seminar, see Riffel and Muster 1989. The conference took place at the Hustedt conference grounds near Celle in Lower Saxony; I attended for three days as an observer and participant.

[47] Fiat operates in a much more protected domestic market, one that has largely excluded

toward "high quality, diversified production" (Sorge and Streeck 1988) and the development of appropriate designs and good marketing and investment decisions (including the purchase of SEAT in Spain for low-end market production) were all probably necessary for continuing success. But the industrial relations model at VW arguably made all of these possible, as works councillors and managers engaged in ongoing consensus-building negotiations that resulted in smooth implementation of production decisions, including model changes, new technology, and work reorganization. VW and Fiat together, the two current sales leaders in the European market, perhaps show that in a period of work reorganization, representation of workers' interests must either be integrated into managerial decision making or it must be marginalized (the U.S. auto industry is a middle case in this regard, with interest representation that in some cases is being integrated in core plants but in other cases is being marginalized, as in many parts supplier plants and some of the Japanese transplants).

Opel-Bochum: Contention within the Institutions of Collaboration

The big question for management at Opel-Bochum, as at other GM plants in Western Europe and North America, is how to transform a traditionally run GM plant (with authoritarian management practices, fragmented assembly-line work, and adversarial labor-management relations) into some approximation of the NUMMI model without closing the plant down for two years and starting over.[48] At Bochum, there are at least four contending views concerning how to interpret the lessons of NUMMI. On the management side, the traditionalist view is out of official favor these days but still very much present in the attitudes of Opel managers: we cannot learn much from this U.S.-greenfield-Japanese (pick one) special case; our management approach and work organization are just fine, and besides we have a cooperative relationship with our works council and work force already. But the new official view is different: NUMMI is a model we can learn from; we need to be less authoritarian and we need to open up the channels of communication; we need to solicit participation

---

Japanese competition. It is unclear how well Fiat would do vis-à-vis VW in more open markets; the test may come as external markets open up in the drive toward a single European market.

[48] See above, Chapter 1, for a discussion of NUMMI and the attempts to adopt lessons of the NUMMI model at other U.S. plants.

from the workers and spread the team concept throughout the plant. On the union–works council side, the majority view is that we need to reorganize work, both for competitive reasons and to humanize working conditions, but we can do much better than NUMMI (avoiding its work-intensification features) with our own union group work concepts. And a strong minority on the works council argues against any proposals to reorganize work either from management or from the union or works council majority, including the team concept or group work (synonymous in this view), because these proposals reduce manpower levels, intensify work, and cause workers to identify with the firm rather than with the working class. As they negotiate some compromise form of new shop-floor teamwork, the dominant groups in management and labor, representing the second and third viewpoints, face political minefields on their flanks. This makes for a complex set of bargaining options and makes the implementation of union-sponsored group work perhaps more problematic at Bochum than at any other large auto plant in West Germany.

Opel is a subsidiary of General Motors Europe and has three large auto plants in West Germany: assembly plants at Rüsselsheim and Bochum and a motor plant at Kaiserslautern. GM Europe also has plants in several other European countries, a fact that GM managers have increasingly used to extract parallel concessions and innovative agreements at plants competing in the same product markets (just as GM managers in the United States have learned to do).

There are three Opel plants in Bochum, collectively known as Opel-Bochum and served by one elected works council. The first plant is the assembly plant, including a stamping plant, which as of early 1989 employed 11,000 workers; the second plant makes motors, transmissions, and axles and employs 5,500; the third plant produces tools and other parts and employs only a few hundred. Total employment at Opel-Bochum at the start of 1989 was 17,600.

The first and still the largest Bochum plant was built in 1962 on abandoned mining sites in the heavily industrial Ruhr District. Although rarely matching the market success of competing Volkswagen small-car models, the Kadetts produced here (five generations of them so far) have been popular, inexpensive cars that have held a fairly steady market share on the West German and European markets. Although originally enjoying the latest production technology, Bochum management adopted a wait-and-see attitude toward new technology and work organization so that in 1982, when an auto industry specialist from the IG Metall made his first visit to Opel-Bochum, he called it a "museum of auto production technology." The negotiations and conflicts that most concern us here are directly related to management's moves since then to catch up and perhaps move ahead by rationalizing production through the introduction of new technology and work organization.

Bochum provides a useful "laboratory" for examining the interaction of past U.S.-influenced managerial approaches (essentially authoritarian and adversarial toward the work force) with the collaboration-oriented institutions of industrial relations in West Germany. The next three plants we will look at (Opel-Rüsselsheim, Ford-Cologne, and Ford-Saarlouis) have faced the same problematic, but the friction has been most intense at Bochum. The outcome has been a form of industrial relations that is perhaps at the opposite end of the spectrum for the auto industry within West Germany from the VW-Wolfsburg case.

Like the other West German high-volume auto producers, Opel management is deeply concerned about rising competition from Japanese and Korean firms, as well as other European competitors such as Fiat and its own domestic rivals, VW and Ford. Since 1982, management at Bochum has moved to rationalize production on several fronts. Employment levels were cut from 20,000 in 1980 to 17,600 in early 1989, while production volume has risen—giving Bochum a head start on the labor power reduction dilemma now faced at Wolfsburg. New technology has been brought in extensively in such areas as the paint shop, body shop (flexible welding robots), and door and cockpit module assembly (automatic guided vehicles). And work has been reorganized correspondingly, without a great deal of regard, until recently, for works council demands such as group work. Thus for the most part where new technology has been brought in, as in the paint shop, production workers have not been grouped but rather have been polarized into simple-task machine feeders and complex-task systems monitors (*Anlagenführer*). Some jobs have been made richer, as in door and cockpit module assembly, where workers perform an entire set of assembly operations, but the work has been intensified (in opposition to proposals from the works council) to eliminate waiting or buffer time and the chance for a worker to work ahead and then take a breather. A recent team experiment in the body shop (hood, door, and trunk lid installation) adopted some elements of union-concept group work so that workers followed the entire operation down the line and were to some degree self-regulating; but again intensification of the work pace and tight constraints on the group's autonomy made the experiment unpopular with many workers and caused union representatives and works councillors to disown this project as group work.

In its efforts to gain flexibility, especially in the area of working hours, management has played hardball with its works council and work force.

In West Germany, the free weekend is sacred, more so perhaps than in any other industrial society, and it is the product of past union struggles. But in recent years, employers have increasingly leaned on works councils to approve longer regular hours of operation, in part to pay for the costs of expensive new automation technology. Opel management, using the threat of disinvestment, thus secured a round-the-clock work hours agreement at Opel-Kaiserslautern in 1988, opening an important breach in the unity between works councils and IG Metall. With the Kaiserslautern agreement in hand, Opel management then told the works council at Bochum that the planned new stamping plant would not be built unless agreement was reached on 139.5 hours per week potential operation. The works council, this time working with the local IG Metall to secure the best possible terms, gave in; although the agreement applied only to five hundred workers in the stamping plant, it was seen by both sides as an important precedent.

At the same time, contradicting the above developments, there is considerable talk these days within the ranks of Opel management, at Bochum as well as at the other two plants, of a new managerial style that would do away with the old authoritarianism and open up the lines of communication to promote employee morale, input, and commitment to the firm. Although movement in this direction has come considerably later at Opel than at Ford in West Germany and the United States or at GM in some U.S. plants, it appeared in 1989 to be picking up steam, led by a new, young Opel general director (an American named Louis Hughes), who shocked works councillors not only by speaking German but by using first names and addressing them with the familiar ''du'' form. Related to the internal management reform effort was a proposal for the introduction of production teams (*Fertigungsgruppen*) at Bochum (Hölterhoff 1988). Drawing on the experience of NUMMI and GM's Aspern motor plant in Austria, management proposed a five-year plan for Bochum's version of the team concept, resulting in teams for ten thousand of the plant's workers (including almost the entire direct production force) by 1993.

The works council majority at Bochum (IG Metallers who in 1989 occupied twenty-three of thirty-seven seats) has long taken a critical if cooperative stance toward management's rationalization drives. As early as 1982, official union literature adopted an angry tone toward management's deskilling and polarization approach to technological change and work reorganization. The union and works council majority demanded better protection for displaced or downgraded workers and called for alternative forms of organization, including group work. According to works councillors, management bargainers laughed at proposals for group work (a union pipe dream) until 1987–88, when management developed its own interest in teams.

If the works council majority was not able to have much direct influence on work organization, it went along in return for the negotiation in 1984 of an extensive rationalization protection agreement, comparable to the agreements now in force at all major West German auto plants, that in effect gives all currently employed workers virtually full pay and status protection.[49] With this agreement in hand, and with management's obligation to inform and accept input formally fulfilled, the works council majority at Bochum has tolerated management initiatives, including recent teamwork experiments that draw more on management concepts than on union designs. The works council strategy seems to be to push and negotiate the shape of these experiments, and especially the succeeding versions, in a union group work direction; a major focus of works council organizing and bargaining efforts now lies in the promotion of group work. Just as at VW, these group work initiatives, based on the same twelve principles, have been pushed along by information, organizing material, and representatives from the IG Metall national headquarters in Frankfurt.

Works councillors from the majority grouping give different opinions about whether their biggest problem has been a recalcitrant management or a militant works council minority, occupying fourteen of the thirty-seven seats (from 1987 to 1990).[50] The split dates back to intra-workforce conflicts in the 1960s and the first election of radical/oppositional works councillors in 1972. Since then, the official IG Metall list has won a fairly stable 60 to 70 percent of the vote in works council elections every three years, but the minority has solidified its position, won over key defectors from the other side, and gradually increased its number of seats.

From the very start, the split has been bitter, with neither side inclined to compromise. The majority participated in the expulsion from the IG Metall of nine of the fourteen minority councillors on the grounds of anti-union attacks (against the positions or actions of the IG Metall). And the minority has waged a permanent campaign, challenging majority initia-

[49] The Opel agreement was negotiated by the general works council for all three Opel plants, including Bochum. The agreement calls for lifetime pay protection for workers fifty years old with fifteen years of service (or fifty-five years old with ten years service); all others get four years of full pay protection, during which time they are supposed to get new job or training opportunities that allow them to remain at their old pay status (or find a better one). Unlike the VW plan, these provisions are not contractual (the result of formal collective bargaining) but rather exist in the form of an agreement (*Vereinbarung*) that can be withdrawn by either side.

[50] In the 1990 works council elections, the majority retained control, but the margin was narrowed even further.

tives and agreements with management at every turn. In 1987, for example, the minority councillors, accompanied by a group of workers and
shop stewards, burst into a key works council committee meeting at which
reduction of the work force was being discussed, to demand no early
retirements without replacement (Transnationals Information Exchange
1987, p. 16). In the buildup to the 1990 works council elections, the
opposition waged an active campaign against any form of team or group
work, rallying skilled workers, for example, against the notion that they
be integrated into direct production teams and rallying production workers
against the intensification of work and the reduction of size of the work
force.

The bitter split has apparently had little effect on union membership
rates at Bochum, which from 1982 to 1987 ranged steadily between 89
and 92 percent of the blue-collar work force and between 37 and 40 percent
of the white-collar work force.[51] But the split arguably affected the capacity
of the works council to develop, propose, and negotiate plans for work
reorganization. In 1984, for example, when management reconstructed
and reorganized the paint shop for the new model Kadett, the council
majority developed its own proposal for new work organization; but as
the two sides fought it out on the works council and in the work force,
management went ahead and implemented its own plan. There are fears
today among unionists that the same thing could happen with teamwork;
although local IG Metall officials are closer to the majority than to the
minority, they are critical of intransigence on both sides (Hinse 1989). In
the course of my interviews at Bochum, I heard the opinion expressed
several times by IG Metallers that from the point of view of management,
the current works council is perfectly constituted (i.e., bitterly split and
thus at least partially paralyzed).[52]

The Bochum pattern of managerial intransigence and works council

[51] Data supplied by the IG Metall.
[52] In May 1989, during my research investigations in West Germany, I was invited to
address the biannual mass meeting of the six hundred Opel-Bochum shop stewards. They
wanted to hear about NUMMI and other developments in U.S. auto plants, in comparison
to what I had seen in West Germany. After my talk, the microphone was open for general
discussion, and I had the opportunity to witness the most vigorous (and sometimes vitriolic)
debate that I heard during my year in Germany. Representatives for the two sides were
unusually well informed about issues of work reorganization. They debated at great length
how to avoid NUMMI's team concept (in spite of my critically sympathetic portrayal), the
majority by substituting IG Metall group work for the team concept, the minority by waging
a campaign against all team or group reorganization efforts. This incident brought home
to me the importance of NUMMI as a model; the intensity of debate and conflict that work
reorganization regularly arouses; and the uncompromising nature of the split at Bochum.

division meant that when negotiations over the reorganization of team and group work began in earnest in 1988–89, the plant had little history of joint pilot projects on which to build, as did VW and Daimler-Benz (Muster 1988a, pp. 262–66). Given the four contending viewpoints at the plant, pro–team management can make the following arguments (spoken or unspoken) in negotiations with the works council majority: if you don't come to terms with us, you will get the old hard-line managers back; we will impose our own plan, after fulfilling legal requirements to inform you and consult with you, since you and your colleagues are fighting it out; if we make you look weak, you will get voted out at the next election. The works council majority, for its part, can make the following arguments: if you make us look bad, we might lose the election and then you will have to deal with the militants; if you don't come to terms with us, you will lose out to the hard-liners in your own ranks; if you don't make significant concessions in our direction, we cannot possibly, for political reasons, reach agreement; and there is no way your team system will work without support from the works council and shop stewards.

As a result of labor-management negotiation, group work began to spread at Bochum in 1990. The key question is how the teams or groups will be structured in future comprehensive implementation: to what extent they will be based on union concepts such as voluntary participation; the integration of skilled workers into direct production teams without sacrificing the integrity of skilled work; considerable group autonomy; an emphasis on the training of production workers for new tasks and skills to bring them up toward the level of skilled workers; and labor savings without work intensification.[53] Or they could look more like NUMMI teams (the management model), which to West German worker representatives contain several unappealing features such as mandatory participation; tightly regulated work assignments; a constant emphasis on improved productivity; an intense work pace driven by short cycle times; the elimination of waiting and buffer time; an emphasis on job rotation and some job enrichment for production workers in lieu of substantial skills training; and a continuing rigid separation between skilled and unskilled workers.

For management, the big difference between current bargaining for teamwork and past rationalization initiatives is that this time management very much needs the cooperation and participation of shop-floor workers (and soliciting such input is a key part of the rationale for new team structures; see Hölterhoff 1988). Having a majority of works councillors

---

[53] IG Metall estimates that group work, simply as a better form of work organization, can save 12 to 17% in worker hours, without work intensification.

and shop stewards support the new system would help a great deal to win worker support, especially since a sizable minority will be fighting the new project in any case. So management appears to be bending in the union direction, as evidenced by the agreement in 1988 to set up a first union-style group work pilot project for ring-gear fabrication (in the second plant). Although the opposition organized actively against the experiment (including a petition campaign for skilled workers opposed to group work and their own integration into direct production), works councillors from the decision-making majority voiced new optimism in the spring of 1989 about the prospect of successful group work negotiations with Opel's "new management." (And the breakthrough agreement came in 1991; see below, p. 136.)

In some ways, Bochum sounds very much like some GM plants in the United States, where opposing groups in the union slug it out over management's new plans to raise productivity by introducing teams.[54] There are clearly firm-specific similarities in managerial style and strategy, and it may be that these similarities are associated with industrial relations outcomes that are in some ways alike (problematic labor-management relations; intraunion and work-force conflict) and that may have a negative effect on management's ability to introduce innovative work organization. To the extent that management at GM is serious about reforming its own practices, as it claims to be, researchers will have an ideal opportunity to observe changing patterns of industrial relations at GM plants such as Bochum, Hamtramck, and Van Nuys (if all three remain open) over the coming decade.

But the cross-national similarities, though important, should not be overstated. There are important differences between Bochum and the U.S. plants that put the former squarely within the distinctive West German national framework of industrial relations. Opel management, for example, is virtually unable to lay off workers; has had to concede rationalization protection measures to the works council and work force that are unparalleled in the United States; must give much fuller information in advance to worker representatives regarding technological and organizational change and allow for full consultation and input (even if it is then disregarded);[55] must negotiate in advance the terms of change, for all issues (such as pay and reassignment) that affect personnel; can do things such as outsource seat production (as Bochum management has done) but must give the works council extensive time to study and propose alter-

---

[54] See Chapter 1 above, especially the case studies of GM-Van Nuys and Hamtramck.
[55] See Jürgens, Malsch, and Dohse 1989, pp. 291–92.

natives and then to negotiate fully the terms of change, including no layoffs and full pay protection; and has no formal or practical authority to impose teams on a reluctant work force without extensive negotiation and substantive agreement with the works council. The works council, for its part, has what plant-level union representation at U.S. plants lack: an independent, well-articulated vision of the shape of new work organization along with considerable leverage to negotiate for its implementation.

Given the institutional framework, current market imperatives, and the negotiating positions on both sides, it is unsurprising that Opel management and the works council majority reached agreement on the introduction of more group pilot projects and a framework and timetable for fuller implementation. The outstanding questions are political. Will a new framework of teams or groups win the support of the work force? Will the opposition successfully undermine the new project, either by winning control of the works council or by mobilizing shop-floor resistance? Will management carry through on promises of greater participation for workers and a new, more open, less authoritarian managerial approach? The answers to these questions will be very much the product of ongoing intramanagement, intra–works council and shop-floor debate and will determine whether group work succeeds or fails at Opel-Bochum.

Opel-Rüsselsheim: Negotiations Under Way

The Rüsselsheim case is presented here very briefly as a useful counterpoint (with overlapping elements) to the Bochum story. Wolfgang Streeck describes bargaining and conflict between the Rüsselsheim works council and Opel management from 1975 to 1977 concerning management demands for extra shifts and overtime (Streeck 1984a, pp. 118–35). He concludes that a (newly elected) leftist works council, taking a tough stance toward management and making new and imaginative demands, reached the same substantive outcome as a much more conservative and collaborative works council at Volkswagen. The institutional framework of industrial relations turned out to be a more important determinant of bargaining outcomes than the ideologies or strategies of particular works councils (Streeck 1984a, pp. 114, 135). When the Rüsselsheim case is set between the Wolfsburg and Bochum cases (which offer contrasting pictures along important dimensions of management and works council strategy and behavior), Streeck's argument is at least partially supported: all three cases appear to be moving down similar roads in group work negotiations.

The Rüsselsheim plant, Opel's largest factory and the firm "flagship," is 127 years old. It was originally a sewing machine plant, then a bicycle plant, a motorcycle plant, and finally an auto assembly plant since the 1930s. Although Opel lost money in 1980–81 and 1984–86, it bounced back to show good earnings from 1987 to 1989 (and beyond), spurred on in part by the brisk sales of the new upscale models produced at Rüsselsheim, especially the Omega and Vectra (Adam Opel Annual Reports, 1987–88). Rüsselsheim management helped its net earnings position by a considerably sharper reduction in the work force than the one at Bochum, from forty-three thousand employees in 1979 to thirty thousand in 1989.

Opel management at Rüsselsheim is cut very much from the same cloth as at Bochum.[56] As part of general GM developments, Rüsselsheim is undergoing a process of managerial reform, including new training for all managers, peer evaluation, and regular meetings, aimed in part at creating a new managerial style that will promote teamwork and solicit employee cooperation and input. The big difference between Rüsselsheim and Bochum lies in the makeup of the works council.

There is no major split on the Rüsselsheim works council. Richard Heller led the victory in 1975 of an activist group within the IG Metall over an older, conservative works council majority, and he has served as chairman ever since.[57] He has made it a priority to develop and preserve unity in the works council, pulling together election slates and work committees representing a diversity of opinion within the plant.[58] This political strategy has been successful, as Heller's slates have won every election since 1975 by large majorities and as of 1989 held forty of forty-seven works council seats. Support for the IG Metall is also shown by blue-collar work-force membership rates that have fluctuated between 80 and 90 percent, although this rate has gradually dropped since 1982.[59] In

[56] Opel headquarters are at Rüsselsheim, making for considerable back-and-forth flow between Bochum and Rüsselsheim. GM Europe headquarters were also at Rüsselsheim until 1988, when they relocated to Zurich; this is a source of frustration for Opel works councillors, who must now negotiate with a management that is constantly looking to Zurich for direction and permission.

[57] Streeck characterizes the campaign as left versus right, which is not inaccurate. But I avoid the formulation "leftist" here to distinguish Heller's left-SPD orientation from communist, Trostkyist, and other left-sectarian groupings often implied by the term. The opposition leaders at Bochum, by contrast, tend not to identify with Heller but rather belong to or identify with groups to the left of (as opposed to within) the SPD.

[58] This is similar to the *Geschlossenheit* approach discussed above at VW.

[59] Membership rates are lower at Rüsselsheim than at Bochum most likely because the company collects dues automatically for the union at Bochum through payroll deduction, while the company does not at Rüsselsheim. Union membership rates have fallen at Rüsselsheim from 92 percent of the blue-collar workers in 1982 to 81 percent in 1987 and

addition to heading up the Rüsselsheim works council and the Opel general works council, Heller sits on the national executive board of the IG Metall, showing once again the virtual identity of union and works council at the large auto plants.

While Heller and his group have remained hard bargainers, the works council in the past few years has shown a new ability and willingness to engage itself in the firm's decisions in areas such as work reorganization. In part, this reflects a new professionalization of the works council, as younger, well-educated works councillors are brought in and expanded use is made of hired experts (the *Referenten*, who advise the works councils at company expense on issues such as new technology and help develop bargaining positions); and in part, the new engagement is a response to changes in management strategy and the imperatives of world markets and new technologies.

In any case, there appears to be a new, more cooperative tone to labor-management relations at Rüsselsheim. A manager told me that this was because the works council has changed in recent years (coming to terms with market realities); a works councillor told me this was because management was changing (showing a new willingness to work together, led by the young general director, Hughes[60]). I suspect that both are true. But another reason may be that management is over its major personnel reduction initiatives of the past decade; Opel as a whole cut personnel costs from 28 percent of total costs in 1979 to 21 percent in 1987, and the largest share of this reduction came at the Rüsselsheim plant. Qualitative issues such as work reorganization have now been added to quantitative issues such as wages as major areas of concern; and the new overlapping areas of interest (humanization on one side, productivity on the other) afford possibilities for negotiation. This can be seen in the current discussions regarding new forms of teamwork.

As one manager at Rüsselsheim put it, the plant is farther along than

---

from 42 percent of the white-collar work force in 1982 to 37 percent in 1987, for reasons unclear to me (IG Metall data).

[60] In the course of my interviews at Rüsselsheim in the spring of 1989, I happened to be eating lunch in the company cafeteria with three works councillors on the day when Director Hughes made his first appearance there. "You are watching history in the making," one of the works councillors told me, "no general director has ever come and had lunch with us here before." Accompanied by half a dozen other managers, Hughes figured out how to use the token machine and got himself a tray lunch just like everyone else. When he saw the works councillors I was sitting with, he made a beeline for us and shook hands all around; he wanted to make sure that we knew he was doing this. This is unusual behavior in German society; the works councillors were clearly impressed by this brash, young, "new generation" American, who now would be a key bargaining partner for them.

GM plants in the United States in the move toward more cooperative labor-management relations and a team form of shop-floor organization because of the institutions and history of codetermination. Rüsselsheim is not as far along, said the same manager, because negotiations are just beginning in earnest.

Management has reorganized work along with the introduction of new technology such as flexible welding robots in the body shop and automatic carriers for door assembly. And work reorganization has paralleled that at Bochum: work enrichment accompanied by intensification in some areas (module assembly) and the bifurcation of the work force into multitask system monitors and single-task machine feeders in other areas (stamping plant, body, and paint). As everywhere in the auto industry these days, management has moved to cut out "unproductive" jobs such as inspection, integrating quality-control work into direct production jobs. And now management is bargaining for the introduction of production teams similar to those put forward at Bochum, based on GM experience at NUMMI and Aspern.

In a first small pilot project, the works council and management negotiated terms for the establishment of a team at the final assembly "marriage" point.[61] The works council planned to monitor this experiment carefully and demanded written guarantees regarding the number of workers and the amount of work as teamwork is implemented to avoid speedup and the elimination of all waiting and buffer time. The council put forward the IG Metall principles of group work and added one of its own: the concept that expected group work productivity gains are divided equally between company and work force, with one-half going to savings for Opel and one-half going into more break time and training time for the workers. As at other auto plants, the works council demands a general framework agreement before the extensive introduction of group work, something the council claims to have promoted for years with little interest on the other side. The negotiation of this framework agreement, to lay the groundwork for the implementation of groups or teams (depending on who concedes the terminology as a bargaining concession), became a main order of labor-management business at Rüsselsheim by 1989. The breakthrough came in April 1991, when the Opel general works council and management formally agreed on the gradual introduction of comprehensive group work at all Opel plants, including Rüsselsheim and Bochum.[62]

[61] This is where the engine assembly is finally "married" to the body.

[62] Because production workers in the new groups gain both new responsibility and training, they will be better paid—and this was apparently a major consideration for the works council in negotiations for new group organization.

Streeck's picture of a militant works council was confirmed when Rüs-selsheim played an active role in the six-week-long 1984 strike for the shorter workweek. Rüsselsheim was the only auto plant in West Germany to pull both blue and white collar workers out for the extended period (and this active strike role may account for the modest subsequent drop in union membership). As at Bochum, the work force appears to remain ready for conflict. But by 1989, as the two sides moved gradually toward new group or team forms of work organization, both hard-line management and militant worker representation appeared to be softening.

Ford-Cologne: Social Partnership on the Rhine

The Cologne flagship plant was built on the Rhine in 1931 in the days of Model A production; it remains the headquarters for Ford-Werke AG (Ford in Germany) as well as the largest Ford plant in Europe. Of the approximately 38,000 Ford-Werke employees in West Germany, 25,400 work at the Cologne plant, where both the upscale Scorpio and the mass-market Fiesta are produced (*Ford-Werke AG Annual Report* 1987). Ford-Werke cut its total employment from 46,000 to 38,000 from 1979 to 1980 (at the beginning of the period known in Cologne as "after Japan"); total employment has remained stable ever since, although the number of white-collar workers is dropping gradually each year and plans are under way for corresponding cuts in the blue-collar ranks. Union membership was stable from 1982 to 1987, holding steady at 75 percent of the blue-collar work force and rising slightly from 32 to 36 percent of the white-collar workers.[63] Ford-Werke lost money in 1980–81 and 1984–85 but returned to profitability in 1986 and began earning record-breaking profits beginning in 1987.

According to both managers and works councillors, management has undergone a substantial reorientation since 1979 in its approach to both the works council and the work force. Although management and works council at Cologne have collaborated well together under the provisions of the 1952 and 1972 Works Constitution Act, management was histor-ically set very much in the authoritarian auto industry mold, giving the works council the minimum required information and consultation and running the plant in top-down fashion, with drill-sergeant foremen com-pleting the chain of command. But a cooperative tradition and framework

[63] Unlike Wolfsburg and Bochum, union dues at Cologne are not collected automatically through payroll deduction.

existed in relations between works council and personnel (the office of the *Arbeitsdirektor*), so that when Ford in the United States sought organizational reform through Employee Involvement beginning in the late 1970s and Mission Values Guiding Principles (MVGP) in the mid-1980s, Ford managers in West Germany were already one step up.

The process of change, as I heard it described on both sides (and from different points of view within the works council), has been gradual since 1979. EI has been especially important within the ranks of management, as managers began to meet in groups in the early 1980s to talk about greater openness and input from top to bottom of the organization. MVGP, beginning in 1985, extended the process, committing Ford-Werke formally to such "new" ideas as the following: "Our people are the source of our strength. . . . Involvement and teamwork are our core human values. . . . We must treat each other with trust and respect."[64]

Even works councillors on the left side of the political spectrum agree that there is a genuine quality to this process and that managers are not the same today as they were ten years ago. The works council gets a larger and much more regular dose of information and requests for consultation and agreement now than it did throughout most of the postwar period, and workers are drawn into shop-floor production discussions concerning the introduction of new technology, work reorganization, and model changes.[65] The number of foremen was substantially reduced as the span of control was widened to sixty workers; consequently, many of the old-school foremen were given early retirement at age fifty-five. Between foreman and workers, a new level was created called the group leader (*Kolonnenführer*), a position generally filled by a skilled worker who takes on many of the foreman's functions, especially concerning the details of work flow and organization.

As everywhere in the auto industry, Ford-Werke management has moved to integrate quality inspection and some repair into the jobs of direct production workers; and management, although lacking its own well-developed concepts for group work, has been open to proposals from the works council and the start-up of new pilot projects. But management at Ford-Werke is also not an independent entity; Ford-Werke is integrated more closely into Ford-Europe (and consequently into the "mother" in

---

[64] The one-page MVGP statement is now routinely used as the preamble for Ford management manuals.

[65] Workers' suggestions regarding product and process were actively solicited when both the Scorpio and the latest Fiesta were introduced, before the start of mass assembly-line production, and literally thousands of suggestions were accepted. This would have been unheard-of ten years ago.

the United States) than is Opel into GM-Europe, and when Ford-Europe or Ford-U.S. says "cut costs," Ford-Werke management cuts costs. Thus managers plan increased rationalization of the shop floor and reduction in the work force (for example, intensified rationalization in seat production) and expect the works council to fall into line. And as Ford develops its new Centers of Excellence, a modified world-car strategy that will shift and centralize production and development in selected locations, Ford-Werke management in Cologne will press the works council to accept the necessary dislocation. When Ford-Europe, for example, announced in October 1988 that the motor line would be discontinued at Cologne in favor of consolidation at Dagenham in England, Cologne management's role was to accept the decision while the works council led the successful campaign for reversal.

For the works council at Cologne, cooperation with management has always been the main theme, but ten to fifteen years ago this cooperation included a much smaller role in managerial decision making. Today, "modern" managers and works councillors engage in daily processes of discussion and decision making, and no major in-plant decisions (from the strategic to the shop floor) are made without consulting the works council. In part this is a product of new managerial approaches, and in part it reflects an ongoing transformation by the works council of its own role. A concerted and successful campaign for more extended works council influence, based on growing professionalization of the works council and internal political unity, has been orchestrated by the chairman of the works council at Cologne, Wilfred Kuckelkorn (who is also the chairman of the general works council for Ford in West Germany as well as a national executive board member of IG Metall).

The works council at Cologne has maintained a similar unity to the famed *Geschlossenheit* at VW-Wolfsburg. But the unity has developed against a backdrop of conflict, dating back to the 1973 "Turk strike" (as it is still known in the plant), when foreign workers and others joined in a wildcat strike to protest working conditions and the treatment of the *Ausländer* (foreigners).[66] A left-right electoral campaign resulted in a twelve-to-twelve works council in the 1975 elections, and similar outcomes have occurred in every election since. But the big difference to Opel-Bochum is that at Cologne the different views are not consolidated into a split between opposing camps but rather pulled together within a broad IG Metall coalition. A long process of meetings and discussion

[66] This strike also apparently did a great deal to undermine the legitimacy of the old-school managers and foremen.

(similar to processes at Wolfsburg and Rüsselsheim) precedes each election campaign, and so far these negotiations have resulted in an inclusive IG Metall coalition that has dominated the elections (and in 1989 included thirty-seven of forty-one total works councillors). People at the plant credit this successful strategy for the works council's increased clout of the past decade, and most of those I interviewed, from management as well as from diverse positions within the works council, credit Kuckelkorn's political skills for the solid unity that IG Metall works councillors have displayed both in plant elections and in bargaining with management.

As at all the large auto plants, the works council has moved to professionalize its work in the past few years, making increased use of computers as well as the services of experts (both those employed by the works council itself, the *Referenten*, and advisers on new issues such as work organization from the IG Metall). In this effort, the "activists," as at all plants, have come up against entrenched officeholders, those set in their ways and unwilling either to put out more effort or to put their effort in new directions. Nonetheless, the works council has moved effectively to gain new influence, and this can be demonstrated in two campaigns at Ford-Cologne, one against the threat of disinvestment and the other for new work organization.

In October 1988, Ford-Europe announced that a new motor line would be built at Dagenham, England, to centralize engine production. The production of motors at Cologne would be discontinued with the introduction of a new engine model. In defense of the threatened 2,800 jobs, Kuckelkorn and the Cologne works council, from one day to the next, announced that no Cologne workers, from any area of the plant, would work overtime (including special weekend shifts) until management reversed the decision. Although the issue of overtime is technically unrelated to decisions regarding future investment, the Works Constitution Act gives the works council full codetermination for the former (the use of overtime requires works council approval) but not the latter. The works council flexed its muscles where it had clout and in a way that would hurt management at a time of high demand and production. Within two days, Ford-Europe backed down, and on October 6, management and the general works council signed an agreement including the following key points:

> Ford Management in Europe believes that a successful Ford European manufacturing organization must include a strong, efficient and profitable German manufacturing base. . . . Management and employee representatives of the affected plants will have the opportunity before an investment decision is taken to review the related investment figures on the basis of verifiable facts

and data and to present improvements to the planned investments. . . . In turn, the employee representatives are committed to further cooperate in improving the cost structure and competitiveness in the remaining areas. ("Agreement dated 6th October 1988," one-page company document signed by representatives of management and works council)

The commitment to the German manufacturing base undermines management's capacity to play plants off against one another (at least cross-nationally), and the toughened advance information provision gives the works council time and leeway to organize oppositional strategies (such as refusal of overtime) if necessary.

But the threat of disinvestment is not the only problem. Rationalization is reducing future labor requirements in many areas of the plant, for example, in seat production. Here the works council has not been actively involved in work reorganization but has been engaged in discussions at a higher level, concerning the financial rationale for management decisions and the commitment to avoid layoffs and pay loss and to increase the opportunity for retraining for affected workers. In these negotiations, the works council is aided by a rationalization protection agreement (first signed in 1978 and then improved in 1985) that is comparable to the agreements at VW and Opel, although as at Opel this is an agreement and not a contract (in contrast to VW, where the strongest formal protection exists). The practical effect of the agreement has been (and apparently will continue to be, if the intent of both parties is carried forward) that no one is laid off and no one loses pay status because of new technology or work organization.

With its initiatives since 1985 for group work, the works council has taken its interest in work organization to a new level. As at the other plants considered, the works council, with advice from national IG Metall headquarters, has led management in the development of concepts and in the submission of proposals for new shop-floor group organization. After a year or two of discussion and debate, the works council decided that group work could offer both improved working conditions for its constituents and good productivity; in 1987, a working group was established to develop a proposal. Members of this group read the literature on group work, visited other plants to look at pilot projects, and by the summer of 1988 drew up their own proposal, won full works council acceptance, and formally submitted the plan to management. The Cologne plan is not identical to the plans at VW and Opel and is not based formally on the twelve IG Metall principles of group work, but the substance is similar (Kuckelkorn 1988). The basic idea is to replace Taylorism with groups of flexibly skilled, highly paid workers who can integrate tasks much more fully than the existing organization allows for and who to a significant degree are self-regulating. Better working conditions, in this vision, dovetail with the firm's interests in more machine time and higher profits.

Rooted in discussions of the humanization of work that emerged within the Social Democratic party in the 1970s, the new works council initiative is also based on the acknowledgment that informal forms of group work, with foremen often included, have expanded in the past decade and have become a useful and popular part of what still remains an essentially traditional work organization (and this seems to be much more true, for example, at Ford than at Opel-Bochum). But the group work proposal is also based on the perceived success of a multi-year pilot project in the tool-and-die shop at Ford-Cologne, which has drawn the following praise from national union headquarters:

> Experiments with group work are already under way in several plants, above all in the auto industry. Their common goal is a more human work organization through the far-reaching elimination of hierarchy, control and the division of labor. Perhaps the most developed example of teamwork is in die- and mold-making at the Ford plant in Cologne, which has stood the test of practice for two and a half years.[67]

The politics of this pilot project's implementation are revealing. Management had proposed the introduction of a new flexible manufacturing system (FMS), which would require only seven skilled workers spread over three shifts (Roth and Königs 1988). The works council, at the urging of Peter Königs (the works councillor responsible for the tool-and-die plant) and Siegfried Roth (from IG Metall national headquarters), proposed an alternative group work system (with the same advanced automation) using thirty-nine workers on two shifts and produced extensive data and argumentation to show that such a system, based on the integration of machine programming and operation for which all workers would be fully trained, would save the company money (through reduced downtime and more efficient machine operation). The company was reticent and planned to go ahead with its own plan until the works council played hardball, threatening lengthy settlement board or labor court proceedings over the failure of management to provide full and timely information (which even if the works council lost could have considerably delayed the introduction

[67] My translation, from the newspaper *Metall* (published for the membership by IG Metall in Frankfurt), No. 1/13, January 1989, p. 21.

of new technology). Management came to terms and agreed to try the works council's design.

For the first three years of operation, the works council claimed that the experiment proved, with verifiable data, the superiority of group work, not only for working conditions but for productivity. Although the pilot project was somewhat marred by problems with the new technology, no one appeared to blame the innovative work organization. The group work experiment was popular with workers, who trained on and off the job for a good three years until they could do almost anything in the shop; and the great advantage for management is that with the full reintegration of programming and production (the workers actually spend more time at the computers than on the shop floor), traditional communication problems (such as error correction) between the shop floor and the technical centers are overcome. Plans were developed to spread such group concepts to the entire tool-and-die shop, one thousand workers strong, as advanced technology is introduced.

The FMS pilot is held up as a model of new work organization to accompany the introduction of advanced automation. But a crucial question is whether such concepts are appropriate in the "lower-tech" part of the plant, such as final assembly, where workers collectively are less highly skilled and where FMS-type automation remains a future vision. In other words, do pilots like this one represent an alternative to Japanese or NUMMI work organization, one that includes assembly-line production workers in its team concept? Or is this a model for highly skilled workers with little room for unskilled and semiskilled production workers (progressive group work for the skilled, Taylorism for the rest)? This is an important political question as group work negotiation and implementation proceed; proponents of group work argue that the model is widely applicable and can be modified or "layered" to include both production workers and skilled workers in most parts of the plant. A critical part of all group work negotiations (at Ford as at the other plants in West Germany) is works council demands for increased training for the production workers, not just so that they can do a few more tasks and rotate jobs, but so that they can acquire new skills that can be used in a variety of ways in the groups. These demands are facilitated by the overabundance of shop-floor workers who have completed skilled apprenticeship programs and by the already well-developed training programs and traditions that exist at Ford as well as at every other West German auto plant.[68]

[68] That the apprenticeship system (which has contributed to the surplus of skilled labor) is thriving in Germany, compared to its relative demise in the United States, has much to

With many questions unresolved, and with the political repercussions of work reorganization still an unknown entity, the works council has taken a cautious approach in its negotiations with management and in its formulation of a timetable for change. Several new pilot projects (in the motor plant, transmission plant, and assembly line) were in the planning stages in 1989 as prerequisites for the full-scale implementation of group work. The works council envisioned learning lessons from each pilot so as to help refine future implementation, in an eight-to ten-year process resulting in group work throughout the Cologne plant.

Management, for its part, acknowledged the leading role of the union and works council in the drive toward group work. As management continued to study the works council proposal (no framework agreement had been signed as of late 1989, but both sides predicted this was coming), its own concepts of new shop-floor teamwork remained vague. Management negotiators argued that the union vision is utopian, that not all the workers in a group can get the same top pay, that the group itself cannot have the degree of autonomy proposed. At the same time, management was attracted by the promise of a committed work force with high morale, "top fit" (as they say in contemporary German) for high productivity, quality control, and problem-solving flexibility. Managers at Cologne acknowledged that some negotiated version of union group work design will most likely shape future work organization at this crucial Ford plant in ways that would probably amaze that mass-production-line genius Henry Ford.

Ford-Saarlouis: Partnership Follows Works Council Overthrow

Like the Opel plant in Bochum, the Ford plant in Saarlouis is relatively new and was built in an area where traditional mining industries were on the decline. Located in the Saarland near the French border, the plant started production in 1970 with a work force composed largely of displaced miners; since then, a large contingent of young, skilled workers and apprentices has been hired to replace the retiring miners and to fill out a work force of seventy-six hundred at the plant in 1989. Over half the current work force has completed an apprenticeship, and many of these

---

do both with the influence and codetermination rights of the works councils and the role organized labor plays on the tripartite boards that oversee skills training and apprenticeship systems in Germany (Streeck et al. 1987).

skilled workers are positioned in "unskilled" production jobs, which has facilitated the integration of maintenance and quality-control work into direct production work over the past decade. The Saarlouis plant claims to have the highest productivity of any Ford plant in Europe. The plant makes Ford Escorts, which are also produced in England and Spain (thus permitting management to pursue a whipsawing strategy if it so chose), and exports 70 percent of these throughout Europe.[69] The plant has undergone a wave of rationalization since 1980, when it became the first Ford assembly plant in Europe to introduce robots. But rationalization has proceeded surprisingly smoothly, especially considering an electoral upheaval on the works council that took place in 1981.

By 1980, dissatisfaction among the shop stewards, work force, and within the works council itself had begun to grow at Saarlouis as a result of two increasingly widespread perceptions: increased pressure on the work force from a traditional hard-line Ford management as cost-cutting and rationalization plans were formulated; and a conservative do-nothing works council leadership. An opposition group within the IG Metall won the local union elections in 1980 (outside the plant) and proceeded to put forward a new union slate at the Saarlouis plant, without the incumbent (IG Metall) works council chairman, for the 1981 works council election. The new group swept to victory (winning twenty-five of the thirty-one seats) and has maintained its dominant position ever since, adopting a unity strategy in subsequent elections in which a previously hammered-out "consensual" IG Metall slate is put forward.

From management's point of view (and management as well as the Ford general works council at Cologne had opposed the new group), the new works council majority was composed of militants who inhibited labor-management cooperation for a year or so until they learned better. From the current works council point of view, it took a year for management to learn that this group was serious and would stand up for the work force when necessary and that a hard-line approach was counterproductive.[70] Whichever is true, both sides claim that relations improved significantly after the first year, and both sides agree that today's decision-making processes are more collaborative than ever before.

In particular, both sides see substantial managerial change in both structure and approach; these changes reflect broader processes of organizational reform under way in Ford worldwide. Managers at Saarlouis

[69] The plant is important for the Saarland's economy, accounting for 30 percent of the region's exports.

[70] The departure of the personnel manager lends credence to the works council interpretation.

appeared to grasp the situation well: intensified market competition increases the need for productivity, quality, and flexibility, which means that the work force, and especially its elected representatives, need to be drawn in. As one manager told me, formerly management would stand on the law, yielding the information that it had to yield under the Works Constitution Act. Now management has learned both that the law lets the works council block change and that the works council can be a powerful ally in facilitating organizational change. As a result, management now goes over the line, to give more information than required and to engage the works council more in its decision-making process.

Both managers and works councillors were careful to emphasize that management still makes the decisions on new technology and work organization; but the works council is included in discussions and gives input, and management gets works council agreement (with whatever trade-offs are necessary) before implementation. Significantly, both sides acknowledge that a new generation of younger foremen is becoming established in the plant now, a cohort group that is inclined and trained to share information and work out agreements on a daily basis with works councillors. As a result, organizational change brought by steady rationalization since 1980 has been remarkably smooth at Saarlouis.

Formal management structure has also changed. In 1984–85, management eliminated the level above the foreman (*Obermeister*), widened the foreman's span of control, and established the new *Kolonnenführer* (group leader) position between foreman and worker. As an example of new voice to represent workers' interests, works councillors have been invited several times since 1987 to participate in management training programs and to give their opinions on potential new managers as well as *Kolonnenführer*. And for the latter, management submits its selections to the works council for approval.

Part and parcel of the smooth introduction of new technology at Saarlouis (and corresponding organizational innovations such as the *Kolonnenführer* and systems monitors in the stamping plant and body shop) has been rationalization protection. Here the works council claims its biggest victory, as Saarlouis pioneered an unlimited-time protection agreement in 1982, preceding the 1985 agreement at the Cologne flagship plant. "As long as the economic situation permits," workers displaced by new technology and work organization are given full pay protection for an indefinite time period; the only stipulation is that they must accept transfer to a comparable or higher-status job (including shifting from blue collar to white), if required. Works councillors maintain that this agreement was a prerequisite for good labor-management relations and the successful restructuring of the 1980s.

Saarlouis is the one West German plant looked at in this study where negotiations for new group work had not yet taken root by 1989. Management, for its part, claimed that the plant already had groups, in the pay groupings, *Kolonnenführer* groups, and problem-solving groups that have grown out of the Ford Employee Involvement program; management as yet had put forward no general teamworking concepts such as occurred at Opel and VW. The works council awaited the outcome of negotiations for group work at Cologne, in which Saarlouis councillors participate as members of the general works council.

Both sides hesitated at Saarlouis as a result of a failed experiment in the 1970s; and both sides agreed that the early pilot project failed largely as a result of inappropriate, traditional management. The group work experiment was set up in the name of work humanization and to test the idea that participation increases productivity.[71] But the union–works council critique claims that it was run according to management concepts alone and resulted in speedup and self-exploitation, with the weak driven out and no substantial pay or other benefits for those who participated. Worker resistance undermined the experiment and it was soon laid to rest, leaving some bitterness on both sides toward innovative group forms of organization.[72]

But works councillors at Saarlouis, although understandably (and for political reasons) cautious, also support the IG Metall position on group work and see it as coming, especially as the limits of advanced technology are reached. If the earlier experiment failed because of authoritarian management, in the works council's view, then the chances are much better with today's managers and labor-management relations.

Management, for its part, while awaiting developments at Cologne before initiating any broader teamwork organization discussions with the works council, has a policy of encouraging job rotation and sees in current developments (EI problem-solving groups, *Kolonnenführer* groups) an evolution toward increasing group-structured forms of participation. And management at Saarlouis takes a definitely pro-partnership view. As one manager put it, given 15 to 20 percent overcapacity in the European auto industry as 1992 approached, today's better-educated works councillors,

[71] It was apparently inspired by experiments with new work organization at Volvo.

[72] A similar failure occurred at VW-Salzgitter in the same time period, and this legacy has been one that group work advocates at Wolfsburg and elsewhere at VW have had to overcome in current work-force discussions and negotiations with management.

and the fact that partnership works better, plants with the best labor-management relations would be the most successful—and Saarlouis intended to be one of them.[73] The groundwork was clearly laid to overcome the failure of the 1970s and move to negotiate and implement a more extended form of group work when the signal is given at Cologne.

Conclusion

What is remarkable about negotiations for new work organization in the West German auto industry, especially by comparison to parallel developments in the United States, is the narrow range of outcomes so far, both for work reorganization itself and for the stability and extent of workers' interest representation.[74] If VW-Wolfsburg and Opel-Bochum represent the opposite ends of the range, similarities in developments are nonetheless striking: steady rationalization and fairly smooth work reorganization at both plants since the early 1980s; a management that shows an increasing propensity to include the works council in discussions regarding work organization and to negotiate agreement with the works council before implementing new shop-floor arrangements; an increasingly well-informed and "professionalized" works council (as the flow of information from management increases and the works council expands its own use of experts to analyze the information and formulate bargaining positions); an extensive package of rationalization protection for the work force; a stable and high level of union membership and union dominance of the works council; an increasing assertiveness by the works council on questions of work organization, as indicated above all by the well-developed, union-sponsored proposals on group work that are on the bargaining table at both plants; and the current establishment of group work pilot projects and the ongoing negotiations for the spread of group work throughout the plants.

The West German plant cases taken together (within the relatively narrow range of variation) can be characterized as follows, for the three variables that operationalize the stability and extent of workers' interest

[73] This manager also predicted more tripartite government, business, and labor discussions in preparation for 1992 and beyond.

[74] In Chapter 3, I will systematically compare the evidence presented in this chapter on the West German auto industry with the evidence presented in Chapter 1 on the U.S. auto industry. Here, I summarize the evidence briefly, offer an explanation to account for variation within the narrow range of outcomes, and point to some implications for the German political economy, themes I will return to in the concluding chapter.

representation: (1) high and stable union membership density throughout the auto industry, with no incursion of nonunion plants and with stable union membership throughout the industry, including the parts supplier plants and firms; (2) extensive, virtually complete rationalization protection for the current work force in the large plants; and (3) the credible promotion by the IG Metall and works councils of an independent vision of the shape of new work organization (group work).

What accounts for variations within the range of outcomes? VW-Wolfsburg, for example, is farther along on all three of the above dimensions than is Opel-Bochum. It is beyond the scope of this book to work out a full comparative analysis of industrial relations outcomes at the different plants within West Germany; but two variables appear to contribute most directly to an explanation for plant-level variation. The first is the same one identified in Chapter 1 as most critical in explaining the wide range of variation within the U.S. auto industry: managerial behavior, or managerial approach and strategy. VW management, as a product of its fifty-year history of paternalism, evolving into social partnership as the union–works council presence grew in strength and assertiveness, has been most inclined to engage the works council and negotiate consensual solutions. Opel, by contrast, has a more heavy-handed tradition, and this is probably not unrelated to Opel's being part of GM; until very recently, management at both Bochum and Rüsselsheim showed considerably less interest than management at VW in engaging the works councils (although this has begun to change). Ford-Werke is also part of a larger U.S.-based firm, one with a typically hard-line management tradition; but in Ford-Werke's case, this tradition began to change several years before Opel did, as part of an internal managerial process of reform. The expansion of engaged, social-partnership-type relations at Ford in both Cologne and Saarlouis dates, not incidentally, from around the time when management began its own reform movement.

It is not, of course, only the connection with a U.S. firm that accounts for a less compromising management orientation; West Germany has an authoritarian management tradition of its own. Daimler-Benz, for example, the fourth largest West German auto industry employer (after the three mass-market manufacturers considered in this study), also has a contemporary reputation for tough management.[75] Although Daimler-Benz is not considered in this book, the analysis presented here would predict

[75] I heard this in several interviews with auto industry experts in academia and at the IG Metall, and the impression was confirmed in interviews with works councillors at one Mercedes plant.

that contrasting managerial approaches and industrial relations outcomes at VW and Daimler-Benz are rooted at least in part in the particularities of different corporate histories.

The second variable that appears to account for variations within the range of outcomes is the behavior of the works council, both its strategy and its ability to put forward a united front. United but compromise-ready works councils at VW-Wolfsburg and Ford-Cologne have arguably increased the incentives for management to work out consensual bargains. "Revolution" at Ford-Saarlouis followed by a united front on the works council appeared to have the same effect. An earlier similar development at Opel-Rüsselsheim pitted a militant works council against a hard-line management in a predictably more adversarial relationship; but as unity within the works council held, and as management began its own internal reform process relations moved toward a more cooperative engagement. At Opel-Bochum, where a bitter split has plagued the works council since 1972, workers' interest representation appears to have had the least influence on managerial decision making, and relations between labor and management have been the worst of any plant considered here.[76]

What stands out in contrast to the United States, however, is not the variation from plant to plant but the narrow range of outcomes, in spite of very different corporate and works council histories. Even with the influence of U.S. management traditions at Opel and Ford-Werke, industrial relations outcomes at these plants fit well within the narrow West German range. I would argue that the narrow range reflects the fact that management in the West German auto industry simply has less independent discretion than do its counterparts in the United States. This limited discretion results directly from institutional constraints: the integration of the union and works councils into managerial decision-making processes; the legal framework (codetermination laws, especially the Works Constitution Act) that regulates this integration from outside the firm; and the relatively cohesive labor movement led by the IG Metall. The latter two constraints have taken away from management the option of avoiding unionization or the direct challenges to union influence and concession bargaining so prevalent in the United States.

[76] Thelen (1987b, pp. 267–71) identifies a greater incidence of factions within auto industry works councils than within the other industries that IG Metall organizes. What interests me here is that there are factions at some auto plants and not at others; and four of the five plants considered here are marked by unity rather than factionalism. Although Thelen argues that factions are a source of political power for the works council in its relationship with management, that claim is not confirmed here. On the contrary, labor at Opel-Bochum is in some ways paralyzed by factional strife, while the more united works councils seem better able to assert their interests.

This is not to say that the IG Metall and the auto industry works councils do not have problems. Management even at VW has shown a new aggressiveness in the face of intensified market pressure (for example, the cost-cutting program discussed above in the section on Wolfsburg). Works councils at all plants will most likely face continuing reductions in workforce size. Management is learning to play works councils and work forces off against each other, and this presents dangers for what so far has been a united IG Metall approach in the auto industry. As 1992 approached, bringing a predicted intensification of competition, and as overcapacity in the European auto industry magnified the possible serious employment effects of the next recession, managerial strategies favoring one plant over another could drive a wedge between union and entrenched works councils (and make a reality even in the auto industry of Hohn's "plant syndicalism"; Hohn 1988). The opening up of East Germany gives managers a new locus for both investment and whipsawing strategies; and although the IG Metall has expanded quickly into the East, it has encountered a vast array of new problems there.

If the dangers inherent in a dual system of representation are real, especially in a period of economic crisis, West German industrial relations have so far proven adaptable, and perhaps nowhere is this more true than in the auto industry. Just as it first captured the works councils in the 1950s, the IG Metall in the 1980s shifted much of its research and bargaining focus to the works councils to tackle new issues of work organization, technology, and humanization of the workplace. From a strong organizational center, the union moved to make use of decentralized instruments of influence in an era when shop-floor issues took on a critical new importance, and it has done this in an effective and flexible way without sacrificing organizational integrity or unity (Thelen 1987a).

The dominant picture that emerges from the evidence considered here is of institutional stability in the West German political economy. The IG Metall, the works councils, and the essential elements of industrial relations in the West German auto industry have survived economic crisis in the 1970s and early 1980s as well as rather intense shop-floor rationalization since 1982; and these institutions appear to be well on the way to engineering a shift to "new production concepts," the breakdown of Taylorism as we have known it, and the coming of some version of group work. The contrast to turbulent industrial relations in the U.S. auto industry points up the critical importance of the mode of interest representation. Workers in West Germany are organized in a particular way into particular institutions, and these institutions have proved adaptable in the face of dramatic changes in world markets, technology, and work organization.

The stability of workers' interest representation in the auto industry has so far been consistent with successful industrial adjustment, a continuing campaign for work humanization, and the expansion of what has often been called industrial democracy within the plants. In its contributions along these lines, union and works council stability has arguably strengthened political democracy in the Federal Republic. As Peter J. Katzenstein puts it:

> West Germany's industrial relations system is politically perhaps less visible but nonetheless of great importance to the nation's politics. Through the institution of codetermination, joint decision making both at the workplace and in corporate boardrooms, labor is intimately linked to the requirements of capitalist production and international competition; business cannot neglect the consequences of its investment decisions on employment and social welfare. . . . Worker participation in works councils or boardrooms probably has pacified labor by instilling a sense of participation, and it has not interfered with the technical or economic efficiency of West German firms. Conversely, employers have adjusted to the institutional presence and demands of worker representatives. On balance, West Germany's complex industrial relations system has had a stabilizing effect on the political fabric. (1989b, pp. 11–12)

CHAPTER 3

Comparative Industrial Relations in the U.S. and West German Auto Industries

The pictures of adaptation in industrial relations that emerge from the preceding two chapters on the U.S. and West German auto industries are quite different. In the U.S. case, we have seen a wide range of plant-level outcomes, management that offers up both sharp challenges and new cooperation to the union, a union that remains divided and uncertain regarding appropriate responses to managerial initiatives, even as its own influence is called into question, and a patchwork pattern of success and failure for innovations in work organization and industrial relations. In the West German case, we have seen relative stability in the institutions of industrial relations, a narrow range of plant-level outcomes, management that is also newly aggressive in some ways but remains narrowly constrained in its capacity to implement new policies without works council consent, and works councils and a union that have expanded their influence in the plants without yielding traditional bases of strength, while carving out independent strategies for new work organization.

These contrasting pictures are mirrored in broader labor movement developments in the United States and West Germany. Density of union membership in the United States, for example, declined from 31 percent in 1970 to 17 percent in 1986; in the same time period, it rose from 37 to 43 percent in West Germany.[1] In Germany today, scholars worried about the fate of German unions speak not only of a threatened ''Japanization'' of industrial relations (Streeck 1984b) but also of ''Americanization'' (Hoffman 1988), referring both to the exclusion of a large part

[1] These figures are for the nonagricultural, employed work force; Freeman 1989, p. 130.

of the work force from substantial union protections and to the incorporation of the core work force into collaborative, firm-oriented, and management-led relationships.

In Chapter 4, we will look beyond the auto industry to assess how far the findings of the previous two chapters can be generalized into a U.S.-West German cross-national comparison. In this chapter, I compare the findings of the previous two chapters and consider alternative explanations. In this two-country comparison, cases are compared at the industry, firm, and plant levels to test for the standardization of results and to consider the relative importance of various factors, including firm- and plant-specific variations. Methodological problems in comparative analysis are well known. Giovanni Sartori (1970) points out the necessity of making cross-national comparisons at the same level of analysis in different countries; industry, firm, and plant comparisons will allow us to do this in a consistent and appropriate way at three levels of analysis. Following John Walton (1973) and Alexander L. George (1979), the cases will be compared systematically, using parallel evidence based on the same research methods in both countries (intensive interviews with managers and union representatives as well as a reading of company, union, and works council documents).

Multilevel, Bipolar Comparison

The most glaring contrast that stands out from a comparison of these two national industry cases is the vast difference in the interplant range of both industrial relations and work organization outcomes. In the United States, the range of outcomes is very wide, extending from innovative nonunion to traditional (including both adversarial and cooperative variants) to innovative unionized (including both relative successes and failures). The level of influence and the precise roles of the union are very much in a state of flux with future directions uncertain within the current wide range. In West Germany, by contrast, the range of outcomes is narrow, characterized by strong union presence and entrenched works council position, along with growing input into managerial decision making throughout ongoing processes of work reorganization in the 1980s.

I have argued that the wide range of outcomes in the United States is accounted for by the relative absence of constraints on managerial decision making at a time when intensified competition has raised major new challenges, to which auto industry managers are uncertain how to respond. Given adverse market circumstances, the fragmentation of organized labor in the United States as a whole makes the nonunion option or direct and indirect challenges to union influence both viable and tempting. The absence of a tradition of union integration into managerial decision making, or laws encouraging such integration, gives managers considerable leeway both in work reorganization decisions and in setting the terms of proposed new jointness and cooperation. Managers, with and without union collaboration, have been trying out a wide variety of plant-level work organization and industrial relations approaches, with very mixed success. The UAW has not so far been in a position to implement a comprehensive strategy for narrowing the range of outcomes in a direction favorable to both union and shop-floor workers' interests.

In West Germany, the relatively narrow range of outcomes is accounted for by a contrasting state of affairs. The relatively cohesive labor movement, entrenched within the political economy in tripartite parapublic institutions (Katzenstein 1987) and in its influential position within the SPD, ensures that the nonunion option in not viable; nor can managers move directly against established union and works council bases of influence. And the integration of works councils (and the union through the works councils) into various levels of managerial decision making, especially concerning the allocation of labor and other personnel matters, has constrained management in its options for the implementation of new work organization. Managers seek prior works council agreement, which puts the union and works councils, through interplant communications, in a position to pursue parallel arrangements. While the institutions thus facilitate union efforts to ensure a narrow range of favorable outcomes, the IG Metall has made a major effort to use these institutions for common plant-level bargaining strategies. The result so far has been a relatively stable position of influence for union and works council in the auto industry and a narrow range of successful work organization innovations and industrial relations practices.

In spite of the wide range of plant-level variation within the U.S. auto industry, there is nonetheless a consistent set of findings for both countries on the three dimensions I have used to indicate the stability and extent of workers' interest representation in the current period of ongoing work reorganization. The contrasting outcomes can be summarized as follows:

United States	*West Germany*
Declining auto industry membership density (Japanese transplants; growing nonunionism among parts suppliers)	Stable auto industry membership density; nonunion option nonviable, parts unionism stable

Modest protections for the work force against the effects of new technology and work organization; substantial improvements in 1987 and 1990 contracts, with some limitations and loopholes

Extensive protections against the effects of new techonology and work organization; virtually unlimited employment, pay, and status security

No unified union strategy in response to managerial initiatives; a scarcity so far of independent proposals for the shape of new work organization

Consistent union strategy and parallel works council approaches on new work organization; well-developed, independent vision with concrete proposals for new group work

Contrasting outcomes are again clear as the three dimensions co-vary. In the U.S. case, declining union membership density is accompanied by modest reactive and weak proactive capacities; in the West German case, stable union membership density is accompanied by strong reactive and growing proactive capacities. The argument developed here is consistent with an explanation for these findings: the combination in West Germany of integration into managerial decision making by works councils organized through the IG Metall as part of a relatively cohesive labor movement has made it possible to defend membership rates as well as to develop strong reactive and proactive capacities. These capacities, significantly, have so far been consistent with successful auto industry adjustment and the spread of new work organization, the terms and sometimes the shape of which are negotiated between labor and management. In the United States, by contrast, the absence of these institutional constraints on management has so far inhibited a stable industrial relations settlement, weakened union capacities, and given management a relatively free hand, which has arguably failed to serve the interests of U.S. auto industry adjustment very well.

Another level on which to compare U.S. and West German outcomes is that of the firm. If, for example, we take the largest auto firms in each of the two countries, General Motors and Volkswagen, and compare them on the basis of the plant cases presented in the previous two chapters, the findings are consistent with the broader comparison. Work organization and industrial relations outcomes at GM vary widely from plant to plant; union reactive capacities are modest to substantial, but proactive capacities are weak; and management has tried out a number of different strategies for bringing in teamwork as well as several different forms of new work organization, usually on its own terms and often with heavy pressure on the union and work force. There is a widespread trend under way toward labor-management jointness, but it remains to be seen how much real input this process will give the union into managerial decision making and to what extent this process will give the union a new basis for strength and influence.

At VW, by contrast, outcomes are fairly consistent from plant to plant, including contemporary negotiations for the implementation of group work on the basis of pilot projects in the various plants. The general works council and the plant works councils have increased their influence in managerial decision-making processes and are in a position to enforce fairly similar plant-level negotiations for new work organization. Labor-management relations are stable and engaged, work reorganization proceeds fairly smoothly, and union–works council roles remain stable and entrenched.

A particularly fruitful comparison can be made between plants of the same firm in different countries. Jürgens, Malsch, and Dohse (1989) have done this extensively in an important comparative study of the plants of three auto firms in the United States, Great Britain, and West Germany. Although on many dimensions, according to their findings, firm differences took precedence over country differences, for industrial relations and certain new production concepts country differences were more important. This finding is confirmed by the evidence presented here. If we consider GM plants in the United States and West Germany, for example, based on the above plant presentations, Opel-Rüsselsheim and even Opel-Bochum look much more like other West German plants, for industrial relations and negotiations for new work organization, than they look like any GM assembly plants in the United States. Even with the substantial differences between Rüsselsheim and Bochum and between each of them and other plants of VW and Ford-Werke, for example, the contours of labor-management relations, the role of the union and works councils, and new efforts such as the drive toward group work fall very much within the narrow range of West German outcomes. Industrial relations and new work organization at GM plants in the United States, by contrast, exhibit the characteristic wide range of outcomes and the relatively weak position on the dimensions of workers' interest representation.

If the comparison is shifted to the level of the plants, findings continue to fall into the general pattern. Given the consistent findings regarding workers' interest representation within each country, we can compare virtually any two plants, chosen at random, and arrive at similar results. In considering, for example, cases of advanced organizational innovation, we might select Wolfsburg from among the German plants and NUMMI or Lansing from among the U.S. plants. At Wolfsburg, we find high union density among both blue- and white-collar workers; very strong union–works council reactive or protective capacities (virtually full employment, pay, and status security for the work force); and growing proactive capacities, especially as union-promoted group work negotiations proceed. The union–works council position remains strong and deeply entrenched, and after internal discussion and debate, works council views are put forward to management from a basis of strong organizational unity. At NUMMI, we find complete unionization among blue-collar workers but no unionization among white-collar workers; strong union reactive or protective capacities (employment security); and limited proactive capacities (the union is integrated into new levels of managerial decision making but does not seek to develop or promote its own concepts of new work organization). In addition, the changeover to "new unionism" required a two-year plant closure and a humbling and traumatic period of adjustment for the work force and local union; and a good 40 percent of the work force votes consistently against the local union leadership. At Lansing, blue-collar workers are all unionized but again white-collar workers are not; reactive or protective capacities are based on the improved provisions of the 1987 and 1990 national contracts but do not include plant-specific employment security as at NUMMI; and proactive capacities parallel those at NUMMI (extensive joint labor-management discussions, problem solving and to some degree planning, without an independent union vision of new work organization). Although not as strong on the three dimensions of workers' interest representation, Lansing parallels Wolfsburg in some ways: work reorganization and closer labor-management engagement have evolved gradually, without major dislocation, on the basis of a strong and unified union presence and a reformed management willing to bring workers' representation aboard while expanding workers' participation on the shop floor.

In considering plant-level cases where work reorganization has proceeded least smoothly and the union has had the biggest problems, we might choose Opel-Bochum and GM-Van Nuys from among the plants presented in the previous two chapters. But even for the most troublesome case in West Germany, union membership density shows no decline and remains high for both blue- and white-collar workers; reactive/protective capacities are strong (virtually full protections afforded in the 1984 "rationalization protection" agreement); and proactive capacities have grown through union–works council promotion of the current group work negotiations. At GM-Van Nuys, by contrast, hourly workers are organized but salaried employees are not; reactive/protective capacities have improved with the 1987 and 1990 contracts; but proactive capacities remained weak, as the local union basically accepted management's team plan and then had to devote a major share of its energies to pushing management to live up to its own promises. At Bochum, the presence of strong, contending factions in the work force and on the works council has undermined proactive capacities; at Van Nuys, similar factionalism undermined for several years the capacity of the union to play any consistent and constructive role in the new work organization.

A final way to compare the extent of contemporary workers' interest representation in the U.S. and West German auto industries is to look at the shape and direction of new work organization itself. Here we can focus on the major contemporary innovation, teamwork; we must be careful, however, because in the United States teams have been implemented throughout a number of entire plants, while in West Germany teams or groups exist as pilot projects pending current negotiations for fuller deployment. But already we see an important contrast: whereas teams have in some cases literally been forced on reluctant work forces in the United States (Van Nuys, for example), the works councils in West Germany are in a position to control the pace of implementation; they have advocated and proposed group work and are negotiating with management for a smooth process of introduction, on a fairly regularized basis from plant to plant.

As for the substance of new work organization, the contrast is significant. In spite of the tendency of both observers and participants to confuse different organizational forms such as the team concept and group work,[2] there are substantial differences between the two. Peter Unterweger (1986), for example, points out some of the contrasts between Japanese and Swedish team organization and shop-floor participation; he argues that the Swedish model, which offers broader autonomy for the work force, is more appropriate for cultural and historical reasons to a U.S. adaptation. The management-promoted team concept in the United States clearly draws most heavily on Japanese organization while the IG Metall's group work looks more to Sweden.

[2] Kern and Schumann (1984, pp. 86–88), for example, write of "das Teamkonzept" as a shift away from Taylorism and toward shop-floor responsibility, without distinguishing between management's team proposals and union group work concepts which represent a much more substantial shift away from Taylorism. (They can be forgiven, however, because the contours of these substantial differences were less clearly visible in the early 1980s.) Streeck (1989) also misses the difference between West German auto industry management's early yearnings toward Japanese-style (or American-style) teams and the IG Metall's more developed proposals, calling for considerably more shop-floor autonomy. This is also a political issue, as the Bochum opposition, for example, has lumped the two together in order to discredit union-promoted group work and the works council majority that supports it.

Jürgens, Malsch, and Dohse (1989, pp. 330–53) discuss substantial differences in training that accompany innovations in work organization, including teamwork, in the United States and West Germany. In Germany, according to this study, there is a greater emphasis on upgrading skills for both production and skilled workers (and many production workers have prior skills training as apprentices); union group work proposals intend to build on the skills reservoir and the notion of a "qualifications offensive" to raise skill levels across the board, within the context of job rotation, ongoing new training, teamwork, and group responsibility and decision making. In the United States, according to Jürgens et al., training that accompanies innovative work organization focuses on broadening skills for the already skilled workers and on organizational development for the production workers. This analysis is consistent with the findings of Ruth Milkman and Cydney Pullman (1988), at GM's Linden plant, that skilled workers are finding their skills upgraded while production workers face deskilling (in a context that includes new technology and work organization but not teams).

The training issue is important. Because the works councils are in a position in the plants to demand the steady hiring of new apprentices, and because the IG Metall participates in tripartite-run training programs, there is a surplus of skilled workers within West German auto plants. Many young workers who have completed apprenticeships work in production jobs. Union group work proposals aim to build on this reservoir of skills and to expand already extensive training to upgrade the skills and responsibilities of each group member. Overcoming polarization of skills is a long-term goal of group work. In the United States, by contrast, where the union has not been so well placed to promote apprenticeship programs and training, no such reservoir of skills exists; team forms of organization include a continuing rigid separation between skilled and unskilled or semiskilled workers.[3]

Ideally, we should at this point compare the substance of team organization in U.S. and West German plants. This cannot be done cleanly,

[3] When German employers complain about skill shortages, they are talking about specific types of skills (as, for example, in cases where the vocational training system has not yet caught up with the demands of new technology). But the surplus of workers who have completed apprenticeship programs within particular industries is a problem that is widely known in Germany (Kern and Schumann 1989, p. 91, who cite German sources to the effect that fully 60% of young Germans complete apprenticeship programs). While West German unions, through the works councils and through participation in tripartite-led vocational training institutions, have promoted extensive societywide apprenticeship training, U.S. unions have often played a role in restricting apprenticeship enrollment, in the interests of the already skilled.

however, because though teams are in place in entire assembly plants in the United States, they exist as pilot projects in West German plants and await fuller implementation. It is helpful, nonetheless, to contrast the prime U.S. model, NUMMI, with the IG Metall's group work concepts, which are in place to a substantial degree in the pilots and which form the basis for labor-management negotiations for fuller implementation:

IG Metall Principles of Group Work	*NUMMI*
1. Broad assignment of varying tasks for the group; long cycle time	Teams either skilled or unskilled (production); narrow range of tasks for most teams; short cycle time (around one minute)
2. Broad group decision-making competence	Job rotation and division of work, with approval; otherwise limited to ''input''
3. Decentralization of plant decision-making structure	Somewhat, for teams, team and group leaders (who oversee several teams)
4. Decentralized technology and production concepts; trained ''semiskilled'' systems monitors to oversee advanced technology	Traditional technology in most of plant
5. Equal pay for group members	Yes, with extra pay for team leaders
6. Special training for disabled and socially disadvantaged (solidarity as basis for group work)	No
7. Personal and occupational development	Limited, except for team leaders and apprentices hired from within
8. Group meetings, at least one hour per week	One half-hour every two weeks
9. Representation of group interests within system of interest representation	Limited and informal; union represents individual not teams
10. Voluntary participation	Mandatory participation
11. Pilot projects before broad implementation	No
12. Joint steering committee to oversee group activities	No

This comparison shows that only one of the IG Metall's group work concepts exists at NUMMI (5, equal pay for group members), but this is true only because the teams are polarized into skilled and unskilled, which runs counter to IG Metall's demand for broad upskilling within the groups. Five of the concepts (1, 6, 10, 11, 12) are not present at all; the rest are only partly present. It remains to be seen, of course, what the works councils in the West German plants will actually get when negotiations for full implementation are complete. But on the basis of pilot projects and current negotiations, the works councils will most likely gain more of what they seek than exists at NUMMI (or other U.S. team plants). To the extent that these concepts were designed in the first place to support the interests of workers, union, and works council (and also make a positive contribution to production), the differences here say a good deal about the contemporary ability of West German workers' interest representation to deliver more in the way of work organization than its U.S. counterpart.

The drive toward teamwork in the U.S. auto industry is management-led, based on Japanese models, and concerned above all with productivity, product quality, and flexibility of the work force (in the interests of production). The most common, "typical" team would be composed of five or more production workers, performing repetitive tasks in short cycle times (e.g., several tasks that add up to one minute, with the one-minute cycle repeated over and over). Assembly-line monotony is broken by occasional job rotation within the team and by half-hour-long team meetings every two weeks or so during which production problems are discussed and workers have a chance to make suggestions and otherwise "have their say." Team members are especially encouraged to make suggestions for improving productivity, and there is some task integration (moving away from traditional Taylorism) as work within the teams includes inspection, minor maintenance, and repair. As processes of negotiation and transition to new team organization have unfolded, the UAW has intervened to protect workers' interests, to promote the improvement of working conditions, and to use the new teamwork to enrich jobs and expand workers' voice.[4]

The contemporary drive toward group work in West Germany, by contrast, was union-led beginning around 1985. Group work in the German

---

[4] As part of the UAW's strategy in this regard, the union has passed convention resolutions regarding new work organization and has begun to educate within its own ranks. In a telling example, one presentation at the UAW-GM and UAW-Chrysler Paid Educational Leave programs for union officials highlights the union guidelines for group work in West Germany, contrasted unfavorably against "Japanese teamwork" (Unterweger 1990).

auto industry has been synonymous not with a management-led drive for productivity, quality, and flexibility but with a union vision of democratic work culture (one that the IG Metall argues is not inconsistent with current market imperatives). In Germany, it is management that has climbed on the bandwagon and attempted to push the emerging groups in a "Japanese" direction. The typical group work pilot project includes a mix of craft and production workers, cross-training for the skilled and upgrading for the semiskilled, longer cycle times than in the U.S. case and a greater variety of tasks, more responsibility and autonomy for the group to plan, control, and execute work, and full works council participation in establishing and administering the group.[5]

The Institutional Argument and the Evidence

For both the U.S. and West German auto industries, work reorganization moved to the top of the agenda for managerial planning in the 1980s; in both cases, the new imperative to reorganize is driven by the intensification of market competition, new technologies, and the rise of new, innovative Japanese production models. But differences in the institutions of industrial relations in the United States and West Germany have presented labor and management with very different options in the two countries. The way in which the institutions themselves have shaped possibilities for strategic and tactical action on the part of labor, management, and the two together has proven decisive in determining the contrasting outcomes for workers' interest representation.

Two institutional characteristics in particular are most significant. It turns out, first, that in both cases an integration of labor into managerial decision making takes on a new and critical importance. This is true because the politics of work reorganization became a critical issue in labor-management relations in the 1980s. From the management side, requirements for smooth implementation of new technologies and work organization mean that managers need union and works council support

[5] There are also pilot projects that look more like the U.S. version, or more accurately, a mix between the two (e.g., all production workers). As the groups spread in the coming years, we will see to what extent union or management concepts win out. One argument is that market imperatives will make the new forms of work organization similar in all countries. The argument here is that the union and works council are playing a stronger role in design and implementation in Germany than in the United States and that groups in Germany will therefore look different from teams in the United States, along the lines described above. But outcomes remain contingent, dependent on market circumstances and the politics of institutional reform.

(unless they can exclude or marginalize the union);[6] engaging worker representatives in decision-making processes is perhaps the best way to win such support. From the union side, work reorganization changes the bases of organized labor's influence in the plants; if unions leave these decisions solely up to management, the outcomes are not likely to favor strong union presence.

In both countries, therefore, unions have pushed for and managers have drawn unions into new involvement in managerial decision-making processes, especially concerning the planning and implementation of new work organization. In the West German auto industry, however, because the works councils were already integrated to some extent into firms' decision-making processes, the transition has been relatively smooth and workers' interest representation has been stable and effective. The effects of works council–union integration are both direct, as in group work negotiations, and indirect, as, for example, demands for more apprentices that result in a surplus of skilled labor in production, which enhances prospects for union-designed group work. In the U.S. auto industry, by contrast, where management and the UAW had a deeply rooted arm's-length, adversarial tradition, management was in a better position to set the terms of new integration while the union had to begin from scratch in developing approaches to participation. The result has been a very rocky transition and an unstable pattern of workers' interest representation, with a union that is still grappling with its new role (in widely contrasting ways from plant to plant) and fighting against declining membership density.

The second critical variable, I have argued, is the presence or absence of laws and corporatist bargaining arrangements that regulate union integration from outside the firm. Where the legal and political framework encourages such integration by independent unions, labor is pushed to participate while management is pushed to include the union in decision-making processes. Legal participation or codetermination rights deny management the discretionary authority either to exclude the union or to set the terms of participation. Where an appropriate legal and political framework exists, workers' interest representation remains stable and can even expand into new areas of influence such as work reorganization. Where no such laws or bargaining arrangements are present, management's discretion in new work organization is wide, and workers' interest representation grapples with new instability in industrial relations and the real possibility of declining union influence.

[6] This is a major theme in Jürgens, Malsch, and Dohse (1989). See also Kern and Schumann (1984), pp. 115–17.

An important aspect of corporatist bargaining is the relative cohesive-ness of the labor movement. This was an important variable in the 1960s and 1970s, when wage bargaining and incomes policies were at the top of the labor-management agenda (cohesive labor movements in Sweden, Austria, and West Germany, for example, could more effectively negotiate wage restraint); and this institutional characteristic is equally important in a different way now. The relative cohesiveness or fragmentation of the national labor movement as a whole says a great deal about the broader economic and political influence of labor and its ability to withstand the shocks of widespread work reorganization. Labor cohesiveness makes it possible both to participate in corporatist bargaining and to defend the legal and political framework that ensures labor's position.

In West Germany, the legal and political framework—Works Consti-tution Act, codetermination, bipartite and tripartite bargaining at many levels, including broad cohesiveness in the labor movement (as indicated by a small number of centralized, industrial unions belonging to one principal federation, itself centralized to some extent by the IG Metall)—has made at least two major contributions to the stability and extent of workers' interest representation in the auto industry (and in other industries as well, as we will see in Chapter 4). First, it has prevented managers from moving directly against or around the union, in union-avoidance plant location strategies, for example, and in high-pressure ultimatums concerning work reorganization. President Reagan, by firing the PATCO unionists in 1981, could send a highly visible signal to managers to take an aggressive stance toward unions in both private industry and the public sector, but Chancellor Helmut Kohl has had no such opportunity (his *Wende* has been far more muted and less successful in weakening union influence). And second, entrenched legal position and organizational co-hesiveness have given the labor movement, especially the largest union, the IG Metall, a strong base along with the resources and perspective to develop independent positions on the shape of new work organization and the parameters of changing industrial relations. In the United States, by contrast, the absence of a legal and political framework that ensures union participation, combined with decentralization of the labor movement (once thought to be a source of great strength in the United States as in Britain) have opened the doors for union-avoidance and direct challenge strategies on the part of management; and for the same reasons unions have been denied the central perspective and resources from which to develop al-ternative positions on new work organization and the "new industrial relations."

This argument, emphasizing particular institutional variables, is historically specific to the period of intensified competition, industrial re-structuring, and rapid work reorganization that began in the mid- to late 1970s. In earlier periods, these institutional variables, although important, did not operate in the same causal way; in the 1960s, for example, one would not find the same contrasting outcomes for U.S. and West German unions, in spite of similar differences in the institutional variables. This is true for two reasons: because world market forces were not driving union decline (as in the present period) and because the intensity of work reorganization was not driving unions toward a much closer concern with management strategies.

Alternative Explanations Considered

Available alternative explanations fall into three groups: general explanations for contemporary union decline, which emphasize broad economic, social, and political forces at work across advanced industrial societies; country-specific explanations, which usually emphasize government, management, and union behavior; and comparative explanations, which often combine various factors and in some cases share with the present argument an institutional perspective.

General explanations for contemporary union decline recognize broad forces at work, usually from within a liberal or Marxist tradition. Contrasting outcomes for workers' interest representation in the U.S. and West German auto industries, however, contradict the fundamental premises of these analyses. Nonetheless, we can consider several of the explanations offered for applicability to see if stated causal factors may have different effects in the U.S. and West German auto industries.[7]

Changing market circumstances, to begin with, are often cited as a primary cause for union decline (see Lange, Ross, and Vannicelli 1982; Gourevitch et al. 1984); intensified international competition, for example, is driving production reorganization and strengthening the hand of management relative to the union.[8] These arguments dovetail with the expla-

---

[7] See Ross and Fishman (1989, pp. 2–3) for a brief but useful survey of the various general explanations offered for contemporary union decline.

[8] Quinn (1989) gives an excellent analysis of the driving impact of market changes on firm and union behavior in the auto industry. He is not, however, explaining union decline but rather firm strategies; industrial relations, in his analysis, are an independent variable that helps to explain production outcomes and relative market success (an argument not inconsistent with the present one).

nation offered here, but they do not account for contrasting U.S. and West German outcomes. In both countries, auto firms have faced intense and growing competition, and in both cases managers have moved to reorganize work. Japanese firms have cut into national markets in both countries; if this has happened more gradually in West Germany than in the United States, Japanese firms nonetheless have largely displaced West German volume sales in the vast American domestic market. Auto firms in both countries experienced new intense problems with competitiveness, and in both countries unions have had to scramble to respond to new managerial strategies and to counter new managerial aggressiveness. The IG Metall has so far done so more effectively than the UAW, but this is not because of more benign market circumstances.

Another general explanation privileges the shift from manufacturing to services, with corresponding shifts in occupational characteristics and class structure. Although this shift is occurring more slowly in West Germany than in the United States, it is happening in both countries, and it is hard to see why this general trend should have much to do with specific contrasting auto industry outcomes. Related to these changes is a general explanation that emphasizes new social movements and the rise of a "postindustrial" younger generation, more interested in environmental, peace, and women's issues than in labor and the traditional social-democratic agenda (see Dalton, Flanagan, and Beck 1984; Inglehart 1984). These analyses identify important social and political developments that represent major challenges to organized labor as a political and economic force, and one can see the extent to which these issues have become increasingly important concerns within unions in both countries. But one cannot argue that such changes have happened more slowly in West Germany, the home of the original Green party.

Another common explanation for union decline cites the shift toward political conservatism; this is a favorite explanation in Great Britain and in the United States as well. Yet West Germany also had a conservative government from 1982 on, one that was explicitly dedicated to rolling back the influence of labor in the economy. As we have seen, the IG Metall has adapted quite well under the circumstances, holding its influence steady and even expanding it in some areas, such as work organization in the auto industry.

The introduction of advanced microelectronic technologies is also used to explain declining union fortunes, as production workers, the mainstays of traditional industrial unionism, are increasingly displaced. But again, auto firms in both the United States and West Germany have rapidly introduced new technologies in the past decade; this is a reality upon which the IG Metall builds in its campaign for group work (Roth and Kohl 1988; Roth and Königs 1988).

If we turn to country-specific explanations, we find the emphasis most commonly on domestic actors (governments, firms, unions), their behavior, ideologies, and structure. Here again there is a vast mine of insights, but in the absence of a comparative perspective, specific national contexts and institutions are given and the wrong conclusions are sometimes reached regarding the performance of one's own unions and industrial relations systems. In West Germany, for example, Hohn (1988) and Hoffmann (1988) each explain declining union influence by reference to the logic of union behavior in relation to firm strategies. The dual system itself is a big problem; unions have aggravated the situation by handing over too much power to the works councils, which are then ready to cut deals with the management of specific firms and plants.[9] The evidence presented in Chapter 2, however, does not confirm an analysis of union decline; quite the contrary is true, at least for the auto industry. And even if pervasive union decline were the case, it is hardly plausible that unions would coincidentally be in trouble at the same time in West Germany, France, Italy, Britain, and the United States for different national-specific reasons.[10]

Freeman and Medoff (1984) and Kochan, Katz, and McKersie (1986) privilege strategic managerial opposition in the United States as the key variable in explaining union decline, as does Goldfield (1987), who refers to it as a "capitalist offensive." The case remains to be made that managerial opposition is truly strategic (Lewin 1987); in the GM cases presented here the picture is more one of confusion than of strategy. It is clear, nonetheless, that managerial opposition is important; this pattern is apparent among the increasingly nonunion parts suppliers and Japanese transplants, and managerial aggressiveness toward the union was clear at several of our case-study plants (Van Nuys, Hamtramck, NUMMI in the two-year transition before the plant opened). But we have also seen traditions of managerial aggressiveness toward the work force and union–works

---

[9] Thelen (1987a) effectively counters this argument, at least for the IG Metall, showing how the union uses decentralized instruments (the works councils) in a coordinated way to reinforce its broader (and central) influence.

[10] In fairness to authors such as Hohn and Hoffmann, one of their major concerns appears to be "social exclusion"—the extent to which a substantial minority is in effect excluded from the benefits offered by works councils—and the long-term social implications and effects on inclusive unionism. Although beyond the scope of this analysis, these concerns are both legitimate and pressing for German unions and society.

council in West Germany, as at Ford-Werke and Opel (often run from the top by American or American-influenced managers), especially before recent internal managerial reform campaigns. Why has the anti-union ideology been allowed relatively free rein in the United States but not in West Germany? Managerial opposition as an explanatory variable, at least from a comparative perspective, does not explain the differences presented here concerning contrasting union performance in the U.S. and West German auto industries.

The comparative arguments for contrasting union outcomes offer a variety of different perspectives. Katz and Sabel (1985), for example, offer an important comparison of industrial relations in the U.S., Japanese, and West German auto industries (they also look at Britain and Italy). In their argument, the critical variable appears to be job-control unionism in the United States compared to flexible manpower allocation in West Germany and Japan. Because the U.S. system is less appropriate for the needs of flexible automation, rapid product changes, and other requirements of newly competitive world markets, American unions have to cede their bases of influence in job classifications and seniority-based allocation. With such a substantial change required, industrial relations and union influence become destabilized and problematic. In West Germany and Japan, by contrast, where shop-floor flexibility is already traded off against union voice (through works councils or enterprise unions), industrial relations systems require much less change from traditional practices.

When the evidence from Chapters 1 and 2 is applied to this argument, a persuasive explanation for contrasting union performance emerges. Katz and Sabel have pinpointed a critical difference with important implications, not inconsistent with the present analysis. I would argue, however, that the emphasis on shop-floor flexibility in a "German-Japanese model" is overplayed.[11] For one thing, they overstate the contrast; the U.S. and Japan clearly differ sharply along the shop-floor flexibility dimension, but West Germany is a middle case. Although managers have the formal right to assign labor more flexibly in the West German auto industry than in the United States, they are in practice constrained in a number of ways. Workers have carved out important informal rights that often are not so

---

[11] Katz and Sabel distinguish a social-democratic (German) and a company-union (Japanese) variant (1985, p. 300). In this view, the German and Japanese variants are distinguished by the role that German unions play in national and regional bargaining. The mistake is to assume that these two "variants" operate in the same way at the plant level. In fact, Japanese unions are dominated by management, whereas union control of works councils in Germany affords much more independent plant-level representation of workers' interests.

different from job control. Foremen know who their best workers are and seek to keep them; they also know which workers are resistant to being reassigned and likely not to perform as well when moved or complain to the shop steward or works councillor. In practice, even in the most flexible of arrangements, such as the LODI agreement at VW (see Chapter 2), a fairly small number of low-seniority workers (especially women and foreigners) are the same ones repeatedly transferred around (Brumlop 1986). This is not so different from the situation in U.S. plants. At Wolfsburg, I heard complaints from managers that LODI had not given them the flexibility they had hoped for.

In addition, the U.S. auto industry today is full of plant-level cases in which workers, usually under heavy pressure, have given up much of their traditional job control (e.g., large reductions in the number of job classifications, the shift to teamwork and job rotation). At Hamtramck and to some extent at Van Nuys, workers, after initial orientation training, often approach the new, more flexible situation with hopes and expectations centered around increased participation and more interesting work. These hopes are all too often dashed when managers revert to the old ways. It is perhaps not so much the absence of flexibility that is causing the problems as it is the absence of constraints on managerial decision making and practice.

Katz and Sabel, therefore, are right in linking flexibility to the voice of unions and workers. Flexibility itself indicates little, unless it is tied to an integration of labor into managerial decision making, in processes that constrain both management and labor, ensure the reality in practice of formal flexibility, and guarantee protections for the work force including trade-offs such as more interesting work or expanded participation. To the extent that a more flexible allocation of shop-floor labor gives West German workers' interest representation a head start over the UAW in adapting to work reorganization, this is made possible by the linkage of flexibility with processes of integration (which is precisely what Katz and Sabel recommend for the U.S. labor movement).

An argument that is similar to the one I have advanced here was developed by the MIT International Motor Vehicle Program (Altshuler et al. 1984, pp. 205–14). In this view, the responsiveness of industrial relations systems to change is a product of structural differences, in particular workers' participation in decision making at the company level, and multi-industry industrial unions (so that unions are not tied to particular interests). This argument is broadly consistent with the evidence presented here: the participation variable is similar to my integration variable (although I emphasize the union role); and for the second variable, the UAW is mainly an autoworkers union while the IG Metall is a metalworkers union (including large numbers of steelworkers, machinery builders, and electronics industry workers). I would quibble with this argument only on the following grounds: first, autoworkers clearly play the leading role within the IG Metall as they do within the UAW (see Chapter 2); second, as we will see in Chapter 4, the general argument presented here is valid also for single-industry unions in West Germany, as in the apparel industry (and Altshuler et al. developed their argument explicitly to apply to the auto industry); and third, therefore, it is not the formal extent of multi-industry unionism that is critical but the legal and organizational position of the labor movement, and in particular the capacity of unions to work together to develop common positions, to follow patterns, and to constrain management from challenging or excluding unions, thereby destabilizing industrial relations.

It is appropriate to conclude this consideration of alternative explanations by returning to the dominant postwar industrial relations analysis in the United States, John Dunlop's (1958) systems model. In this perpective, the differences across industrial relations systems are largely a product of the environment, especially markets, technologies, and the power relations in society. Since markets and technologies, although the driving forces for change in industrial relations, are not decisively different for the U.S. and West German auto industries, that leaves power relations; and here there is a substantial difference between the two countries. Dunlop's analysis, then, is not disproven by the evidence presented here; in fact, the variables I have identified (union integration into decision making; statutory and political regulation) may be regarded as aspects of the power relationships in society. Quite surprisingly (at least to me), Dunlop's framework, when viewed in this way, is broadly consistent with the evidence and analysis presented here. The weaknesses of the systems model lie in its failure to tie variables together into testable hypotheses; its static nature, which gives little perspective on the dynamic changes under way in industrial relations systems; its assumptions of shared ideology; and its linkage to discredited theories of convergence (Dabscheck 1989, pp. 157–58; Katz 1985, pp. 5–6). But Dunlop does provide a useful conceptual map, which thirty years later still points toward the most significant factors at work for industrial relations systems.

PART TWO

THE ANALYSIS EXTENDED: SECTORAL AND CROSS-NATIONAL COMPARISON

Critics have suggested that the auto industry, at the expense of other industries, has been overstudied and that in particular autoworkers' unions and industrial relations receive a disproportionate amount of attention. In spite of extensive research, however, we have much to learn about the dynamic innovations in production and work organization, advanced technology, and industrial relations in this still pivotal industry. In fact, understanding changing industrial relations at the traditional core of union strength is essential for explaining the contemporary fate of unions. It is nonetheless true that other industries, both manufacturing and service, are critical for processes of industrial restructuring, work reorganization, and changing industrial relations. This section moves beyond the auto industry to a study of contrasting industrial relations outcomes in the U.S. and West German telecommunications and apparel industries; and we move beyond the United States and West Germany to both auto industry and general patterns of industrial relations in Britain, Italy, Sweden, and Japan.

Although Chapter 3 examined the evidence and considered contrasting explanations, the possibility remains that the conclusions reached apply only to industrial relations in the auto industries of West Germany and the United States. It may well be that characteristics of that particular industry, union structure, or market make the results industry- or country-specific. The auto industry, for example, is a core manufacturing industry characterized by a small number of very large firms. Unions tend to be at their strongest here, and this is certainly the case for the IG Metall and the UAW. And a bipolar comparison is not in itself persuasive; one could argue, for example, that there may be cultural, historical, or other nationally specific factors at work that account for particular two-country contrasting outcomes. We need more evidence before the suggested causal explanations become persuasive.

To review the argument once more: intensified competition in world markets since the late 1970s has set up managerial imperatives to reorganize production and work, which in turn have driven processes of change in industrial relations, including widespread union decline. But the stability and extent of workers' interest representation vary considerably cross-nationally; contrasting outcomes are best accounted for by institutional variables: the extent of union integration into managerial decision making, the extent to which such participation is backed up by an appropriate legal and political framework, including a cohesive labor movement. In contrast to the traditional view in the United States (favoring arm's-length unionism), integration and regulation have proven compatible with stable industrial relations and extensive union influence. The opposite attributes, including arm's-length unionism, weak statutory and political regulation, and a decentralized or fragmented labor movement, by contrast, have been associated since the late 1970s with unstable industrial relations and declining union influence.

To broaden the sample and test the argument for wider applicability, we now move to a consideration of evidence from the telecommunications services and apparel industries in West Germany and the United States (Chapter 4), followed by a survey of developments in the auto industry as well as general national industrial relations trends and practices in Britain, Italy, Sweden, and Japan (Chapter 5).

Further Evidence: U.S. and West German Telecommunications and Apparel

*A*lthough the auto industries of every country have long been dominated by a small number of large firms, telecommunications services until the 1980s have been largely noncompetitive and monopolistic, highly regulated by government; and apparel has been characterized by intense competition among a large number of small and medium-sized firms. Based on evidence from these additional industries, I will argue in this chapter that outcomes for workers' interest representation in both the telecommunications and apparel industries show contrasts between the U.S. and West German cases that broadly parallel contrasts in the auto industry, and that the outcomes vary cross-nationally for similar reasons. Workers' interest representation in the telecommunications and apparel industries has adapted more successfully to changing circumstances in West Germany than in the United States, because in Germany unions and works councils are integrated into managerial decision making, they have the legal and political means to enforce such integration, and they belong to a relatively cohesive labor movement.

In the telecommunications industry, we will look at labor-management relations in telephone services, the largest employment sector in this industry. The analysis is based on primary research conducted in the United States from 1986 to 1988 and in West Germany from 1988 to 1989, including intensive interviews with union representatives and managers at American Telephone and Telegraph (AT&T), Pacific Bell, and Communications Workers of America (CWA) in the United States, and with personnel councillors (the equivalent of works councillors), union representatives, and managers at the Deutsche Bundespost and Deutsche

Postgewerkschaft (DPG) in West Germany. In the apparel industry, the analysis is based on interviews conducted with managers and union representatives in the United States from 1986 to 1987 as well as secondary material from both countries, relying especially on an excellent study of comparative union performance in the U.S. and West German apparel industries by Steven Silvia (1987).[1]

Deregulation Breeds Turbulence in U.S. Telecommunications

The telecommunications industry in the United States reached a critical turning point on January 1, 1984, when divestiture, as ordered by a federal court judge, broke previously monolithic AT&T apart into one long-distance carrier (the new AT&T) and seven regional Bell Operating Companies (BOCs). This highly regulated, virtually monopolistic, and highly unionized industry opened up suddenly to new competitive pressures, as newer long-distance firms such as MCI and US Sprint challenged AT&T for market share. Although the BOCs remained less subject to direct competition as the authorized carriers of local phone communications, the holding companies faced both new competition in certain areas of service provision (especially services to business) and the threat of more competition in the future. All firms in the industry experienced unprecedented pressures to cut costs and expand the range and quality of service.

AT&T's divestiture represented a (perhaps de facto) policy choice of the federal government and came about as the result of economic and political developments, with far-reaching domestic consequences (Borrus and Zysman 1984; Borrus, Bar, and Warde 1984). For the dominant union in the industry, the CWA, the context for organizing, bargaining, and other aspects of industrial relations changed dramatically and suddenly.

The CWA traces its roots to company unions set up by a paternalistic AT&T in the 1920s (Brooks 1977). When these local unions were forced into independence by the Wagner Act's prohibition of company-dominated unions in 1935, many of them linked up in a national-level association that consolidated itself as the CWA in 1947. In the stable environment of

---

[1] For the telecommunications industry in West Germany, I conducted these interviews myself. For both the telecommunications and apparel interviews in the United States, I conducted some of these myself and the remainder were conducted by Jana Gold, with whom I collaborated on a research project for the Carnegie Forum on Education and the Economy, organized through the Berkeley Roundtable on the International Economy at the University of California, Berkeley, from 1986 through 1988 (see Turner and Gold 1988).

AT&T's regulated monopoly, the union grew steadily throughout the postwar period and drew on its earlier company tradition to support technological change and sustain a largely cooperative labor-management relationship. By the early 1980s, although union-shop provisions did not apply at AT&T (as in the public sector, union membership remained voluntary), the company was highly unionized and CWA had entrenched itself as the dominant union.[2] Industrial relations at AT&T were generally stable, following the broader U.S. pattern of periodic negotiations (usually every three years, in this case most important at the national level), occasional strikes, steady collective bargaining gains in wages and benefits, well-defined job classifications, and extensive use of grievance and arbitration to resolve shop-floor conflict. In contrast to the auto industry, labor-management relations were generally cooperative, and AT&T's shop floor displayed much less of GM, Ford, and Chrysler's "armed truce" characteristics.

But for the CWA, there are important parallels to the experience of the UAW. Like the UAW, the CWA is a strong national union organized on the principles of industrial unionism and entrenched for the most part in one industry.[3] Of the ninety member unions of the AFL-CIO in 1990, both the UAW and CWA ranked in the top eight in total membership; both are known within the labor movement for organizing vitality, postwar bargaining clout, pattern setting, and innovative responses to new market circumstances and managerial strategies.[4] As did the UAW, the CWA faced a fairly stable environment—in this case, for the "mass production"

[2] By the early 1980s, 85% of the union members at AT&T belonged to CWA (according to data supplied by CWA's Development and Research Department). In addition, the International Brotherhood of Electrical Workers (IBEW) organized some groups of employees, including workers at some Western Electric manufacturing plants (a part of AT&T); and some regional groups of employees were organized by independent local unions.

[3] Industrial unionism here is in contrast to craft unionism, in which specific occupational or skill groups are organized. Both the UAW and CWA organize (or attempt to organize) all groups within the industry or firm. Although many unions in the United States are craft unions, there are also a large number of industrial unions, including the UAW and CWA, and these unions are closer to the postwar West German industrial union model than to older U.S. craft unionism. The important difference is that German industrial unions are usually multi-industry while U.S. industrial unions are generally rooted in one industry. Note the contrast here: while both the UAW and the IG Metall are multi-industry, the UAW counts 70% of its membership in the auto industry; the IG Metall has 40% of its membership in autos. In similar fashion, while the CWA is also multi-industry, its membership is mainly in telecommunications; the West German union Deutsche Postgewerkschaft organizes extensively in all three branches of the Bundespost, telecommunications, postal services, and savings bank.

[4] In the 1970s and early 1980s, for example, both unions pioneered the development of joint labor-management programs such as QWL.

of telephone services in a nationally regulated industry—until the late 1970s and early 1980s. And in parallel ways in both industries, the stable environment, including predictable demand, steady or growing employment and union membership levels, and union institutional security, came apart suddenly in the early 1980s (Batten and Schoonmaker 1987).

For the CWA, deregulation, rapid technological change (especially the digitalization of transmission), and the convergence of computer and telecommunications industries have meant a dramatic change of environment. As Morton Bahr, CWA's national president, put it: ''Prior to deregulation, we were in something called the telecommunications industry, and it was virtually 100% unionized. Now we're in the information industry, which is only about 35% organized.''[5] The CWA in the 1980s has come quickly and directly face-to-face with the overarching and dominating reality of contemporary U.S. industrial relations, nonunionism. IBM and other computer and semiconductor firms, and the new telecommunications services competitors such as MCI and US Sprint, exhibit effective and so far highly successful union-avoidance capacities. The CWA, more active and successful at organizing than most unions in the United States today, has little political or economic leverage to use in providing a wedge into the nonunion firms.

At the same time, in part as a result of competitive pressure from these nonunion firms, the CWA has been buffeted within its strongholds by the necessity at AT&T and the BOCs for cost cutting and rapid technological and organizational change. As a highly innovative union, the CWA, at the national level and within various regions and local areas, has pursued new forms of cooperative labor-management relations and has pushed for union influence on job design, the use of new technology, and the processes of work reorganization. If there is a union in the United States that has actively sought cooperative industrial relations from a position of strength combined with what might be called a ''productivity coalition'' with management, it is the CWA. Yet the CWA's influence in these directions has been significantly limited by the combination of economic and political circumstances.

The range of outcomes for the CWA and for industrial relations in the U.S. telecommunications industry since 1984 has been wide, affording another parallel to the experience of the UAW and the auto industry. The range extends from nonunion firms that use ''human relations'' approaches toward employees in part to keep unions out, to traditional labor-

---

[5] *CWA News* 44 (January 1985): 8. At the time of this statement, Bahr was CWA's District 1 vice-president.

management relations at AT&T and several of the BOCs (in some ways more conflictual since divestiture than before), to a new "social partnership" that held sway at Pacific Bell from 1985 to 1989. Brief presentations of the AT&T and Pacific Bell cases will illustrate the range of possibilities within the unionized segment of this industry.

At AT&T, the CWA has waged a long-term effort at the national level to engage management in a process of joint discussion, decision making, and program implementation (e.g., retraining for new technology, semi-autonomous work groups). It is the stated policy of the CWA, for example, to encourage the introduction of advanced technology and to gain input into its design, implementation, and use (Straw and Fogel 1983). The union worked with management in the setting up of quality-of-working-life circles throughout the AT&T system and encouraged the expansion of responsibility and authority for these groups. In contracts of the 1980s, the CWA bargained successfully for the establishment of joint discussion and decision-making groups, such as the Common Interest Forums, Technology Change Committees, and a joint training program beginning with the 1986 contract and extended in 1989.

But the road to better and more engaged relations has been rocky. Within AT&T there has been considerable disagreement concerning how to respond to such overtures from the union. Policies have vacillated over time and by region; while the union has identified allies within the AT&T hierarchy for a relationship of cooperation and engagement, the dominant response so far to competitive pressures has been to challenge the union (through layoffs, effective pay-scale reductions, and massive unilateral reorganization) rather than to work with the union to negotiate solutions. AT&T suffered a partly successful twenty-six-day strike in 1986, whose passion was fueled by perceived grievances and anxieties on the part of the work force.

AT&T management has found itself in an extraordinary bind. Although it is thoroughly unionized, its main competitors in long-distance and information services are not. Three distinct labor relations strategies seem possible: to challenge the union directly for the purpose of severely curtailing (and perhaps eventually eliminating) union presence, in order to level the playing field with nonunion firms such as MCI and US Sprint; to move around the union wherever possible, challenging the union in smaller ways gradually to decrease union representation and clout within the firm (this strategy could be the predecessor to successful implementation of the former strategy); or to work closely with the union, using cooperative relations, union-promoted employee participation, jointly administered training, and reorganization as a competitive advantage. CWA clearly favors the latter strategy, but the middle one seems to have been dominant at AT&T, with fears in the union camp that it is but a stalking-horse for the first.

Labor-management relations at AT&T, according to most participants with whom I have spoken, went downhill after the 1986 contract and strike, as management responded to the continual competitive need for cost cutting with increased pressure on the work force. Largely female occupational groups in job descriptions such as accounts representatives and customer services were pressed to work harder, with a broader range of responsibility and skill, at the same or in some cases lower pay levels; and telephone operators continue to experience intense production pressure (Turner and Gold 1988; Byrkjeflot 1989). Inside and especially outside technicians have fared better, but here too performance pressure from management has escalated without the union managing to play much of a role in the substance of work reorganization. The constant fear of layoff or relocation has served to enhance the pressure and reduce union leverage.

As a relatively strong national union, the CWA has been able to afford its members important pay, relocation, retraining, and grievance rights at AT&T. These include the Reassignment Pay Protection Plan (RPPP), which protects the pay of displaced workers for a limited time period (depending on seniority); termination pay; Employee Adjustment Income Plans to protect pensions and improve benefits in cases of voluntary termination; and joint training programs. Although employment security and joint training have been high priorities for the CWA since the early 1980s, union representatives admit that what has been accomplished so far has been "to kick open the door" to these concepts rather than to make major strides.

Should AT&T decide to challenge union presence and influence directly, CWA is strong enough to make the battle a protracted one; and this is a well-known fact that dampens the attraction of such a strategy. But the union's ability to put forward its own agenda concerning employment security, expanded jointly administered training, and work reorganization has so far been undermined in a political-economic context that makes large-scale competitive nonunionism viable and union organization of new firms almost impossible.

One high-ranking CWA official in northern California described the difference between labor-management relations at AT&T and Pacific Bell in 1987 as "night and day."[6] Pacific Bell is California's local phone sys-

---

[6] Interview by author.

tem and the major company within the larger Bell Operating Company, Pacific Telesis, created by AT&T divestiture. After a year and a half of testing both new approaches and each other in the post-divestiture environment, top company and union officials reached a mutual understanding that cooperative relations could be advantageous for both parties. Beginning around June of 1985, a series of meetings occurred at which both sides committed themselves to a new "social partnership"; this relationship continued to develop and was reflected in the 1986 contract, signed five days before expiration of the old contract and hailed by some Pacific Bell managers and CWA officials as a path-breaking development in the history of U.S. industrial relations. Through the enhanced activity of labor-management Local Common Interest Forums, company and union would, in this vision, find consensual solutions to the challenges of new technology and work organization, expanded service provision, and the new pressure of the marketplace in U.S. telecommunications services.

To some extent, the partnership agreement worked for both company and union for the three years of the contract. As a concept, employment security was advocated in the 1986 agreement, and for the most part management kept to this, running employment numbers down through attrition and voluntary termination (although there were questions about how voluntary some terminations were; Byrkjeflot 1989, p. 53). Union rights in managerial decision making were largely informal; but considerable discussion and input often preceded work reorganization decisions as the company sought prior union agreement. Reorganization, however, moved in more favorable directions for some employee groups than for others (Byrkjeflot 1989, pp. 53–54); technician groups involved in business services experienced better working conditions and expanded group responsibility, but employees in operator and residential marketing services found their work rationalized in ways that gave rise to extensive complaints from the rank and file.

In part as a product of these complaints, some local union leaders advocating the cooperative strategy were voted out of office during the life of the agreement and replaced by advocates of a tougher, more independent approach (as at the large Oakland CWA local). In 1988–89, management became increasingly aggressive toward the union and work force, spinning off nonunion subsidiaries and pushing for greater reductions in the size of the workforce. By contract expiration in 1989, earlier relations of trust were finally undermined by rising health costs (and contrasting views on whether employees or the company should shoulder the costs) and by additional managerial demands for concessions in collective bargaining. The social partnership came apart in a bitter forty-five-day companywide strike that ended with a compromise on health care and other issues. After the first negotiated contract was rejected by the membership, a second was finally approved, but the partnership appeared dead as Common Interest Forums withered away and management began preparing for layoffs and forced downgrades.

What accounts for contrasting union and industrial relations outcomes at telecommunications firms since divestiture? One possible interpretation of the difference between AT&T and Pacific Bell from 1985 to 1989 is contrasting market circumstances: AT&T experienced much greater competition in long-distance markets and was forced to cut costs drastically by squeezing its employees, whereas Pacific Bell's more protected position made the gradual change that accompanies social partnership more feasible. But the 1989 strike at Pacific Bell along with a range of various industrial relations approaches at the other BOCs (with similarly protected markets) discounts such an argument. As in the auto industry, I think, the best explanation lies with managerial discretion. Nonunion telecommunications firms make an explicit choice and mobilize resources to keep union presence out (Turner and Gold 1988, pp. 85–86). At Pacific Bell (and at another BOC, Bell South) from 1985 to 1989, explicit strategies were pursued by management to incorporate the union in a consensus-building relationship; at other BOCs such as Ameritech and U.S. West, and at AT&T, relations became more conflictual in the years after divestiture. And again I would argue that managers have this wide range of discretion precisely because of the absence of institutional constraints that could be imposed by the widespread integration of unions into managerial decision-making processes and by the statutory and political regulation of such integration.

In spite of the wide range of outcomes, we can nonetheless characterize workers' interest representation in U.S. telecommunications services along the three dimensions used for cross-national comparison. First, density of union membership in the industry is declining as a result of the growth of nonunion firms, the establishment of nonunion subsidiaries for special services by the unionized firms, and the difficulties associated with signing up new members at AT&T and the BOCs at a time of cutbacks, layoffs, displacement, and widespread employee dissatisfaction.[7] Second, the

---

[7] Hard data on the actual size of the decline in union density are not available either from company or union sources. To the extent that data do exist for the second and third sources of such decline, they are confidential. But this point is not controversial; both managers and union officials agree that the CWA remains entrenched at AT&T and the BOCs and that the percentage of the work force at these firms that belongs to the union has declined as a result of firms' hiring and reorganization strategies.

CWA has bargained for and won significant protections (such as RPPP) for employees displaced by new technology or organization. But these protections remain modest; they do not in most cases include employment security or protection against relocation and downgrading of pay and status. Retraining rights remain limited and pay protections expire after a set period, depending on seniority. Third, although the CWA has advocated direct union input into the design, use, and implementation of new technology and has advocated and worked with firms (such as AT&T) for setting up experiments in work organization such as expanded forms of QWL and semiautonomous work teams, it lacks a broader, more clearly developed strategy for new work organization. Union representatives on Local Common Interest Forums, for example, have complained that they lack clear union positions on work organization and are thus limited to the role of listening to and commenting on management's plans.

Most critical for the CWA was its initial inability to find and mobilize the allies necessary to prevent deregulation and the subsequent breakup of national bargaining. This was an especially important defeat in an era in which advanced microelectronic automation has made successful strikes more difficult (because the provision of basic telephone services continues, in management's hands, when the workers walk off the job). Deregulation has opened the door for a wide diversity of industrial relations outcomes, including intense management pressure on the work force and union and the spread of nonunionism. The CWA's main efforts to prevent deregulation included joining with and following AT&T in a losing courtroom battle and political lobbying that fell short, in a growing antiregulatory climate, against the efforts of major telecommunications users and would-be competing firms. The union's inability to mobilize sufficient political clout to prevent the opening up of a new and inhospitable environment for unionism is particularly telling in comparison with the West German case, to which we now turn.

Entrenched Unionism at the Deutsche Bundespost

The Deutsche Bundespost is a large government organization in the classic European Postal Telephone and Telegraph (PTT) mode. The Bundespost includes the postal service, public telecommunications (mainly telephone) services, and a savings bank. Of the total work force (over five hundred thousand strong in 1989), about 60 percent were in postal services, 35 percent in telecommunications, and 5 percent at the bank. Telecommunications is the biggest revenue earner and heavily subsidizes the less efficient postal service. The Bundespost is organized in all three of its sectors by one union, the Deutsche Postgewerkschaft, which is now the fourth largest union in West Germany. The DPG organizes about 75 percent of the total work force[8] and maintains a high rate of organization (varying between 60 and 80 percent) among all major employee groups: workers (*Arbeiter*), white-collar employees (*Angestellte*), and civil servants (*Beamte*).[9] The DPG organizes right up through the ranks of management to the top levels (just under the level of the minister of the Bundespost, who is appointed by the chancellor), and DPG members hold a minority of seats on the Bundespost supervisory board (*Postverwaltungsrat*). Most important, the work force (union members and nonmembers alike) elects "personnel councils" (*Personalräte*) at the local level, whose members elect regional and national-level councils. As in the auto industry, these councils are dominated by union members who engage in a regular and ongoing process of discussion and negotiation with management, with rights formalized in the 1974 Personnel Representation Act (*Personalvertretungsgesetz*).

Until 1984, the Bundespost was not so different from AT&T; one was a public monopoly and the other was private, but both were heavily regulated by the state in the large-scale provision of public services, and both were highly unionized, stable organizations. The contrast since 1984, however, is great: while AT&T has been broken up into many different companies and holding companies, bringing new competition into the industry with problematic consequences for the CWA, the Bundespost has remained what Douglas Webber (1987) calls "the fortress on the Rhine." Although the Kohl administration in 1989 approved a separation of the Bundespost into three distinct organizations, postal services, telecommunications, and bank, this is a very modest step compared to the deregulation and privatization called for by some (and realized in the United States).

Major pressures have been exerted to deregulate the Bundespost in an American-style direction. As in the United States, this pressure has come

[8] According to membership data supplied by the DPG in 1989.

[9] The latter group is the largest one and includes former workers and white-collar employees who have passed a series of tests as well as higher-level employees such as engineers and managers. The civil servants are in some cases doing the same work as those in the other groups, but they have the extra status and protection accorded permanent government employees. The civil servants, by contrast, do not have collective bargaining or strike rights. The usual procedure is for the union to negotiate a contract for the workers and white-collar employees and then for management (with "encouragement" from the union) to issue rules or guidelines applying the terms of the agreement to the civil servants.

both from major business users of telecommunications services and from domestic firms seeking entry into new markets in the services and products made possible by new microelectronic technology (Webber 1987, pp. 20–22). In addition, the Kohl government found itself under pressure from American firms and the U.S. government, which, having deregulated at home (and opened the American telecommunications market to expanded competition from foreign firms), now wanted other large domestic markets to open up in similar fashion. And the U.S. and British models of telecommunications deregulation were attractive in themselves to the conservative Kohl regime, and especially to the FDP, the strongly pro-free-market junior partner in the coalition government that came to power in West Germany in 1982. Under the Kohl regime, the pressures for deregulation and privatization mounted in the 1980s. But the DPG led a highly effective defense of the existing system and limited the changes to only modest deregulation for certain new services and the separation of post from telecommunications.

The DPG has effectively mobilized its allies at the Bundespost itself, the Finance Ministry (which gets 10 percent of Bundepost revenues for the federal budget), in the political parties, especially the SPD, within organized labor as a whole (through the DGB and the national unions such as the IG Metall), and at the traditional equipment suppliers, including large and powerful firms such as Siemens and SEL. Webber discusses the reasons for the great caution with which the Kohl government approached telecommunications deregulation, in spite of the active advocacy of the junior coalition partner (FDP):

> The foremost of these considerations is the high likelihood that such changes would unleash a fierce conflict with the highly-organized DPG. Respect for the DPG's organizational strength and the extent to and effectiveness with which it could mobilize opposition to such a project undoubtedly accounts for the minister's desire, testified by the DPG's representation in the government commission, to secure the union's acquiescence in whatever deregulation or privatization proposals he sponsors. (Webber 1987, p. 30)

The DPG has thus so far effectively organized the coalition opposing deregulation, and it is also deeply entrenched within the decision-making processes of the Bundespost. Union participation on the supervisory board is important, but more important are the influential personnel councils. These elected, union-dominated bodies, at the local, regional, and national levels, meet monthly with management to receive information, discuss new developments, and talk over problems.[10] In a sense, these meetings are analogous to the much newer common interest forums at AT&T and Pacific Bell, with the important difference that the personnel councils have extensive formal rights (based on the Personnel Representation Act) to advance information, consultation, and codetermination.

Changing work organization, especially in telecommunications services, is an important contemporary topic of discussion for both the personnel councils and the union in their negotiations with management. Issues regarding work organization are raised in collective bargaining between the DPG and the Bundespost and at the regular meetings of personnel council and management at all three levels. In addition, there are "rationalization" meetings twice a year at the regional and national levels, at which the use of new technology and the terms of work reorganization are discussed and negotiated. By all accounts, the personnel councils exert significance influence on equipment selection and use, working conditions, and the use of space. Although they have little influence on the number of workers at a particular installation or the work standards, the councils have codetermination rights regarding job design and the use of new technology. In the 1980s (and earlier), the DPG and the councils have used these rights to support the introduction of new technology and to ensure that technological change includes an improved quality of working life for the affected employees.

When new technology is in the planning stages, the personnel councils send their own specially trained representatives to study the equipment and analyze its impact on jobs and working conditions. On the basis of their independent analysis, personnel councils then negotiate with management concerning appropriate technology and job design. When operators are moved from the old microfiche system to computer screens, for example, productivity rises and the number of jobs drops. The personnel council negotiates for relocation for the displaced; improved working conditions and ergonomics, extra break time, and a more pleasant environment; and the selection of monitors, headphones, and seats.[11] For office

---

[10] As for the works councils in the auto industry and elsewhere throughout German industry, the personnel councils at the Bundespost are legally distinct from the union. All employees, union and nonunion, are eligible to vote for personnel councillors at the local level. But as in the auto industry, union members dominate the councils.

[11] At the main telecommunications center for the city of Bonn, for example, I watched this changeover in progress. On one floor, information operators in a large room used the old microfiche technology; on the floor above, a smaller group performed the same work in front of computer screens. Although the work upstairs was more intensive (more calls per hour), these jobs had been "humanized," as the Germans put it, and were in demand. The work was more interesting, the environment was more pleasant (a remodeled office

workers, the increasing use of computer monitors has led to a successful union demand for "mixed work," in which office workers spend half a day at the computer and the other half doing different work such as personal customer service. In Cologne, the Bundespost planned construction of a new facility designed to include six square meters per employee; the personnel council argued that this was not enough and negotiated an increase in size of 50 percent, to nine square meters per employee. In follow-up negotiations, the personnel council also negotiated specific aspects of the use of the space, the design of the rooms, and the selection of equipment and job design.

At telecommunications facilities in the United States, there is also a move toward more pleasant working environments and better ergonomics as the work of operators, inside technicians, and office workers is made more intensive with computerization. But unions in the United States have far less advance influence into the planning process, the design of jobs and space, and the selection of equipment; workers in U.S. telecommunications services are dependent on the goodwill and foresight of particular managers in particular locations who believe that "a happy worker is a good worker" (or the insight of MCI and US Sprint managers that "a happy worker is a nonunion worker"). The DPG and its personnel councils are in a position at the Bundespost to ensure uniform improvements in job design and environment throughout West Germany; and they are in a position as well to prevent the extent of work intensification that has given rise to so many complaints in the United States.

A major employee complaint associated with work intensification in telecommunications services in the United States is the use of anonymous electronic monitoring to check the work of employees such as information operators and customer service representatives at AT&T. At the Bundespost, this practice is forbidden as the result of a major battle between labor and management in the 1970s. Management can use monitoring to check the collective work of a group of employees to see if work standards are being met; but the secret observation of individual employees, considered critical to organizational success by many managers in the United States, is off-limits. The union and works councils consider this a major victory which they will continue to defend in an era of increasing computerization.

Employees of the Bundespost have extensive rationalization protection. The jobs of the civil servants are protected by law; the remaining employee

---

with carpets, plants, comfortable seats, and desks), and each operator received a break of ten minutes per hour.

groups are protected under the terms of a 1974 contract between the Bundespost and the DPG. The agreement provides for no layoffs, new jobs for the displaced, and a gradual reduction of pay for those reassigned to lower-paid jobs. This latter outcome is infrequent because of protected pay levels for the civil servants, the majority of the work force; and the extensive union-promoted training and job upgrade opportunities that exist throughout the Bundespost, and especially in telecommunications. When workers are displaced, for example, by a new digital switching station, the personnel council has codetermination rights concerning transfer and retraining decisions.

Although the DPG lacks a vision of the shape of new work organization that is as well specified and coherent as that of the IG Metall's group work concepts, the union nonetheless puts forward the clear contours of its preferences and bargains successfully for their implementation. These include full employment security, a measured introduction of new technology, new opportunities and training for the displaced, better working conditions, environment, and ergonomics with new technology, improved job design, widespread opportunities for training and retraining throughout the Bundespost, and a union and personnel councils actively engaged in decision making regarding the process and shape of change from the bottom to the top levels of the organization.

But the Bundespost is changing, and along with these changes come new pressures on the union and personnel councils. Along with the separation of post, telecommunications, and bank, the biggest change apart from the steady introduction of new microelectronic technologies is the development of a more entrepreneurially minded management. In the past, the relation between employees and management at the Bundespost was rather cosy. With both groups belonging to the same union and in the absence of heavy competitive pressures from the outside, the basis for collegiality was solid, especially between elected personnel councillors and their counterparts in management. But this relationship is changing. In the face of external political and economic pressure, a new cost-cutting, efficiency-enhancing mentality is being encouraged from the top down within the ranks of management; and the stiffened managerial approach is reinforced by specific demands, such as an across-the-board requirement in 1988 for 3 percent cost reductions in every region and local office. Several personnel councillors in different locations told me that though they have little trouble working things out with the traditional managers, they have more trouble with the younger entrepreneurial ones. These "modern" managers appear to be less forthcoming with information and less eager to seek consensus with the representatives of the work force.

Top managers say that these changes will continue as part of the effort to whip the Bundespost bureaucracy into better competitive shape for the 1990s and beyond.

As management escalates the pressure, the union and personnel councils find themselves in a difficult position. On one hand, their ability to serve the interests of their constituents depends on their integration into managerial decision-making processes (from which managers may now try to exclude them as much as the law permits); on the other hand, the majority of Bundespost employees, the civil servants, have no strike or collective bargaining rights. The future of union strength at the Bundespost may well depend on a developing battle for the hearts and minds of the middle managers, a battle that will determine whether this group breaks the social partnership in the interest of greater efficiency and faster change, or whether the DPG and personnel councils will prevail in their view that middle management needs the cooperation of the work force and its representatives to make the desired changes.

So far, the pressures of technological change, displacement, and work intensification, along with the work force's fears regarding the effects of Bundespost reorganization (separation into three units and greater cost accountability), appear to have encouraged rather than discouraged union membership. The DPG has used these problems and fears as a way to recruit members from among the work force, arguing that a unionized worker is a better-protected worker (whether that worker is a civil servant or not) and that the work force needs its own solid organization more than ever. Union membership grew steadily in the 1980s so that in 1989 the DPG passed IG Bau (the construction workers' union) as the fourth largest union in West Germany. After a rise in union membership density from 62 percent in 1970 to 72 percent in 1978, the rate of organization has held steady in the 1980s at between 71 and 73 percent.[12]

The relationship between union and personnel councils remains even closer here than in the auto industry; everyone I talked to at the Bundespost told me that union and personnel councils were practically identical. And the union and personnel councils follow a general policy of strategic unity: decisions regarding policy, bargaining positions, and council candidate selection are hammered out at union meetings where consensus is sought so that one united position can be put forward (and this is similar to the *Geschlossenheit* at VW-Wolfsburg and Ford-Cologne).

In spite of new market, organizational, and political pressures, the picture that emerges from a study of West German telecommunications

---

[12] According to data supplied by the DPG.

at the Bundespost is one of relative stability, and this includes the shape and substance of industrial relations and the role of workers' interest representation. The range of outcomes is narrow, as uniform Bundespost policies are implemented by management throughout the country and a unified set of union responses is put forward in personnel councils and union offices everywhere. Preserving this stability and organizational cohesiveness has been the major goal, and so far the major political victory, of the DPG in the current period.

Along the three dimensions of workers' interest representation in an era of work reorganization, the above findings can be summarized as follows: (1) stable and high union membership density; (2) extensive protections against the effects of new technology and work organization; and (3) clear and engaged union positions, if not a well-developed vision, on the shape of new work organization.

Industrial Relations in Telecommunications Compared

As is the case for the auto industry, the first striking observation is the vast difference in the ranges of outcomes between U.S. and West German telecommunications industrial relations. In the United States, the range is extremely wide, from deliberate and successful nonunionism to traditional, conflictual labor-management relations to attempts at union-incorporated social partnership. In West Germany, by contrast, the range is narrow and stable, as patterns of industrial relations and work reorganization are regulated by the interplay between a Bundespost bureaucracy and its deeply entrenched, union-dominated personnel councils. The difference in ranges was closely linked to the inability of the CWA to find the allies and political clout necessary to prevent the divestiture of AT&T, contrasted to the DPG's successful defense of its Bundespost bastion.

Comparing the three dimensions of workers' interest representation cross-nationally, the differences can be summarized as follows:

United States: CWA	*West Germany: DPG*
Declining union membership density	Stable union membership density
Modest protections for the work force against the effects of new technology and work organization, some retraining opportunities	Extensive "rationalization protections," including full employment security and many training opportunities

| Limited union promotion of independent proposals for the shape of new work organization | Consistent influence of union and personnel councils on job design and the use of new technology |

What accounts for these cross-national differences? Here one could argue that the critical difference was divestiture in the United States versus Bundespost integrity in West Germany, and indeed these contrasting political and legal outcomes have had a major impact on the divergence in patterns of industrial relations in telecommunications services between the two countries. But this divergence is largely accounted for by the much greater political and institutional capacities of the DPG when faced with pressures for deregulation. Although AT&T fought diverstiture in the courts (with union backing), its work force and its political, business, and labor allies were never mobilized to nearly the extent to which their counterparts were in West Germany in the 1980s. The DPG, by contrast, has used its entrenched position within the Bundespost to mobilize the work force against deregulation; and the union has used its position within a cohesive labor movement to build a successful defending coalition.

Can we explain the differences by reference to the greater concentration to begin with of the Bundespost compared to AT&T? This idea is plausible on the surface; yet in the auto case it is the U.S. auto industry which is more concentrated, and the outcomes still contrast in the same way. And even if the Bundespost were less concentrated (and this will be the case to some degree with the separation of post from telecommunications and the opening up of modest new opportunities for competition), it is impossible to imagine the rapid rise of a militantly nonunion MCI or US Sprint in West Germany.

Can we explain the difference by noting that the Bundespost is in the public sector (with employees who enjoy civil servant status) while AT&T is not? This is certainly an important difference, but it is not causal: what is public can be made private, as the experience of British Telecom demonstrates; and as a regulated monopoly, AT&T in any case functioned in a way that was very much like the public sector Bundespost in the provision of telecommunications services.

The CWA has certainly made a major effort to exert influence on issues of new technology and work organization; and one could reasonably argue that this initiative, which has taken shape in Technology Change Committees, Common Interest Forums, and other joint labor-management processes at AT&T and the BOCs, is based on a farsighted view of the role that unions could play. But the CWA, in spite of the joint processes, has so far been largely excluded by a management intent on unilateral cost cutting. Why has the union been thwarted in this effort? The answer offered here is that because the attempted integration into managerial decision making lacked an established, institutional basis, management alone could decide how far to allow such participation. At the same time, the door was open in the United States for the rise of competing nonunion firms, in a national climate of adversarial or union-avoidance management, which emboldened managers even at highly unionized telecommunications firms to take an aggressive (although at times also cooperative) approach toward labor.

Contrasting outcomes for contemporary industrial relations in U.S. and West German telecommunications services are consistent with the general argument presented here for both predicted outcomes and explanations. But now one could argue that we have looked precisely where unions are strongest in West Germany so that the comparison is skewed.[13] Historically, unionism is generally strongest in concentrated industries such as those considered here and weakest in industries characterized by a large number of smaller firms (with certain exceptions, such as the construction industry). In West Germany this is certainly true, as unionism has fared much better in autos and at the Bundespost than it has in less concentrated industries such as machinery and apparel; union decline theorists in West Germany find a much greater resonance for their arguments in the less concentrated industries. We now turn to the experiences of a sector characterized by a large number of small to medium-sized firms, one that has suffered much sharper market difficulties than either autos or telecommunications and in which unionism has been much less monolithic and entrenched, in both West Germany and the United States.

Contrasting Industrial Relations in Apparel

The clothing industries of most advanced industrial societies were battered in the 1970s and 1980s by steadily rising imports from low-wage countries; the resulting widespread crisis in these industries gave rise beginning in 1974 to a regular succession of Multifiber Arrangements (MFAs), which allowed import restraint agreements between developed and developing countries as an exception to the General Agreement on

---

[13] Ironically, I first became interested in studying the UAW and the CWA because these were two of the strongest, most innovative, and influential of American unions. From this perspective, the comparison with the IG Metall and the DPG is telling, pitting as it does two of the best cases (for unions) in the two countries against each other.

Tariffs and Trade (GATT; see Aggarwal 1985). In spite of the MFAs, imports have risen steadily in both the United States and West Germany, forcing employers to adopt new strategies to rationalize production, cut costs, and find new market niches. In both countries, the apparel industry has known employment cutbacks, widespread layoffs, firm failures, declining market shares for domestic firms, aggressive managerial strategies to increase production levels from the remaining work force, and major pressures of crisis dimensions on unions and established patterns of industrial relations.

As a percentage of the domestic market, imports grew in market share in the United States from 7 to 28 percent in the period from 1970 to 1986 and from 11 to 45 percent in West Germany in the same time period (Silvia 1987, pp. 3, 7, 35–36). Because West German firms were more successful at exporting to compensate in part for lost domestic sales, the two countries had a roughly similar trade deficit in apparel by 1985 (the deficit equaled about one-fourth of domestic sales in both countries; Silvia, pp. 8–9). But because apparel consumption rose faster in the United States, West Germany experienced more severe cutbacks in domestic production (Silvia 1987, pp. 10–11). The effects on employment in the apparel industry in both countries were severe: a total employment decline in the United States of 24 percent from 1973 to 1985 and a parallel decline of 50 percent in West Germany from 1970 to 1985 (Silvia 1987, pp. 11–13).

These were clearly crisis circumstances for the unions. In West Germany, firms laid off workers, streamlined production, and sped up assembly lines; in the United States, firms laid off workers and moved production to Sunbelt states where a weaker union presence gave them a freer hand. The major unions in the industry, Gewerkschaft Textil-Bekleidung (GTB) in West Germany and the International Ladies Garment Workers Union (ILGWU) and the Amalgamated Clothing and Textile Workers Union (ACTWU) in the United States, scurried to develop strategies to respond to the crisis and to protect both the members and the unions as institutions.

In these efforts, however, the GTB in West Germany fared considerably better than the ILGWU and ACTWU in the United States. In the United States, union membership totals and density declined precipitously for both unions; for the ILGWU, for example, union density in the women's and children's apparel segment (which the ILGWU organizes) dropped from 53 percent in 1975 to 34 percent in 1985 (Silvia 1987, p. 17). In West Germany, by contrast, though total membership declined along with the substantial drop in total employment, the GTB used the crisis to build up its rate of organization; union density in the West German apparel industry grew significantly from 22 percent in 1971 to 40 percent in 1983.

Why such a large cross-national difference in this regard? In the United States, apparel firms, through relocation strategies and new start-ups, successfully transferred production from union to nonunion shops; apparel unions were unable to organize most of the new plants, reflecting a widespread pattern in American industry and the general weakness in this period of the U.S. labor movement (although the rate of decline in apparel was more substantial than the general rate of decline for organized labor). In West Germany, by contrast, the union was able to use its position on the works councils to build up membership as workers faced uncertain future prospects and sought new protections. In part this occurred as a result of Works Constitution Act provisions under which firms are required to negotiate "social plans" with the works council, providing compensation payments for the displaced; the union used this leverage to facilitate the spread of works councils to previously unrepresented firms and to increase the visibility of previously inactive works councils. Active works councils were then able to assist local unions in building up the rate of membership as workers turned to the union and works councils for protection.

Although none of the apparel industry unions has put forward its own proposals for the shape of new work organization in the same comprehensive and innovative way as has the IG Metall in the West German auto industry, in this case it is the American unions that have a tradition of engagement in issues of technology use. Because the industry has always included many small and resource-poor firms, the unions early on developed their own engineering departments to help bring the latest technology to employers, to keep firms competitive, and to preserve jobs. As David Dubinsky, president of the ILGWU from 1932 to 1966, puts it in his engaging autobiography:

The New York dress agreement of 1941 imposed a contractual obligation on employers to operate their shops efficiently. Imagine, a union telling the boss he had to be efficient or he would be hauled up before the impartial chairman and made to pay damages for not running his plant right. That was certainly a new twist in industrial relations, a big switch from the idea that unions are enemies of efficiency, always plotting to help their members goof off or to keep people in jobs that long ago became superfluous, if they ever were needed at all. . . .

The idea was to assist the employers in improving their operating methods, on the theory that the more efficient they were, the more likely they were to prosper and the higher the standards we could ask for our members. (Dubinsky and Raskin 1977, pp. 126–28)

This tradition continued in the 1980s when the ACTWU joined with large apparel manufacturers to develop advanced process technology at Draper Labs in an effort to keep apparel manufacturing in the United States.

But encouraging efficiency is not the same as developing innovative proposals for the shape of new work organization. In this regard, American unions, like the West German GTB, have been able to do little because they have directed their resources into the battle for survival in adverse circumstances. In the United States, major union efforts since the early 1970s have concentrated on holding established bases of organization (especially in the Northeast) and joining with employers to promote protectionist legislation for the apparel and textile industries. For the most part, work organization has changed little in the U.S. apparel industry in the 1980s.[14]

In West Germany, the GTB is considered a conservative union within the German Labor Federation (DGB), one that takes a cooperative social partnership position toward employers. Regarding new work organization, the union has supported employers' drives to rationalize production and speed up assembly lines (Silvia 1987, p. 26; Wasserman 1985, p. 75). The union rationale has been similar to the traditional ILGWU position expressed above by Dubinsky: rising productivity keeps the firms in business and incidentally raises wages (which are predominantly based on piecework and thus go up with rising productivity).

American unions have been unable to protect workers against the effects of new technology and work organization in a period of substantial deunionization of the industry. Real wages have declined for the employed since 1968 (Silvia 1987, p. 23), and for those threatened with displacement, employment protections and compensation (apart from government-sponsored unemployment benefits) are scarce.

In West Germany, by contrast, though employment protections are also scarce, works councils by law can negotiate social plans for the displaced, the primary purpose of which is to provide substantial monetary compensation for those who lose their jobs. For workers who continue to be employed in the industry and whose work has been intensified in the rationalization drives of the past two decades, real wages have risen stead-

[14] Although computers have moved into the design rooms and automation of processes such as cutting has become widespread, the labor-intensive sewing stages of production have changed little. As one apparel manager told me, "There is only so much you can do with a sewing machine."

ily (by an average of 1.8 percent per year from 1970 to 1985; Silvia 1987, p. 24). Both the rising wages and the strong union position in social plan negotiations (which must be agreed upon by management and the works councils, on which union members generally dominate) have contributed to the growing density of union membership in the West German apparel industry. But this social partner union has encountered increasing internal complaints about the effects of production rationalization on jobs; and on this issue the union has begun the process of revising its accommodative position to demand, from a position of new potential strength (based on its higher membership density), more significant rationalization protections.

This comparison of the accomplishments of contemporary workers' interest representation in the U.S. and West German apparel industries can be summarized along the same three dimensions used for the auto and telecommunications industries:

U.S. Apparel	*West German Apparel*
Seriously declining union membership density	Rising union membership density
Minimal protections against the effects of new technology and work organization	Substantial protections, in the form of rising wages and social plans
Minimal independent union proposals for the shape of new work organization	Minimal independent union proposals for the shape of new work organization

On the third, proactive, dimension, unions in neither country are strong; but on the first two, the West German GTB comes out significantly better. In an industry marked similarly in the two countries by adverse and increasingly competitive market circumstances, many small and medium-sized firms, and unions under intense pressure, representation of workers' interests has fared significantly better in West Germany than in the United States. Silvia, upon whose data much of this section is based, argues that the differing impact of sectoral decline on unions in the two countries is a product of differences in the respective industrial relations systems. Although Silvia enumerates a longer list of causally important differences between industrial relations systems in the two countries, his argument is broadly consistent with the analysis presented here: that the institutions of industrial relations are critical in accounting for contrasting contemporary outcomes for unions.

Through the legally protected works councils, the West German GTB is integrated to some extent into processes of managerial decision making that afford a stability to union representation even in extremely difficult market and industry circumstances; and the position and influence of the works councils, especially regarding work-force protections such as the social plan, make union membership more desirable as conditions deteriorate. At the same time, the GTB's position as part of a relatively cohesive labor movement has made it possible to secure steady real wage gains by following IG Metall patterns as much as possible and at the same time defend the union's position in the industry from potential attack (through either avoiding unions or a legal challenge to the entrenched position of the works councils and their dominance by the union). The absence of these institutional constraints on management in the United States has made it possible for firms to use the crisis in the apparel sector to deunionize the industry significantly.

Conclusion

Having looked at contemporary industrial relations in the auto, telecommunications, and apparel industries in the United States and West Germany, we are now in a position to argue that the outcomes and explanations presented here can be widely applied in a general comparison of industrial relations in these two countries. The outcomes differ cross-nationally in similar ways for each industry, and the institutional explanation makes sense in each case in spite of specific market circumstances as well as industry structures and characteristics that are different for each industry. In each case, West German unions do considerably better than unions in the United States; workers' interest representation is at once more stable, adaptive, and extensive in West Germany in the recent period of ongoing production and work reorganization. The comparative argument developed here, based on national institutional differences, predicts that these contrasting outcomes will hold for a preponderance of U.S. and West German industries.

If industry-specific explanations are ruled out, causality must reside in broader national characteristics. The argument advanced here privileges institutions of industrial relations, and in particular the extent of union integration into managerial decision making and its statutory and political regulation. These factors appear to be at work in each of the sectors considered here for the United States and West Germany. But it is also possible that other national characteristics are at work and are more im-

198 Democracy at Work

portant causally. Aspects of national culture is one argument that is advanced (Lipset 1986b); unique tapestries of social and economic structures is another (Maurice, Sellier, and Silvestre 1986).

To test the argument beyond the particular circumstances of U.S. and West German society, we now turn to a consideration of contemporary industrial relations in Britain, Sweden, Italy, and Japan.

CHAPTER 5

The Broad Scope of Conflict
and Partnership:
Britain, Italy, Sweden, and Japan

*I*n the preceding chapters, I have developed an argument to explain
the contemporary fate of unions, or more precisely, the stability and extent
of workers' interest representation, from a comparative, cross-national
perspective. Having tested the argument by looking at three industries in
two countries, we can now broaden the scope of analysis to determine
whether the argument has more general validity for advanced industrial
societies in the current period. In this chapter, to the consideration of
evidence from West Germany and the United States is added a survey of
industrial relations outcomes in Britain, Italy, Sweden, and Japan, with
a focus both on the auto industry and on general national patterns of
industrial relations.

The countries are selected to represent a range of variation in the structures of interest representation, especially for the explanatory variables
developed here: union integration into managerial decision making; laws
and corporatist bargaining arrangements to back up such integration; and
labor movement cohesiveness. Britain and Italy, like the United States,
are countries with traditions of arm's-length labor-management relations
and decentralized or fragmented labor movements. Sweden is a country
with broad corporatist bargaining and, for most of the postwar period, a
cohesive labor movement, but with little union integration into firms'
decision making until the early 1980s. And Japan is a country in which
unions are integrated into managerial processes at the plant level, without
the benefit of laws or national bargaining arrangements to regulate this
integration, and within the broader context of a highly decentralized labor
movement.

To determine whether outcomes for unions in the current era of work reorganization match the predictions of this argument (as spelled out in the hypotheses presented in the Introduction) we now turn to a brief examination of the country cases.

Great Britain: Union Influence under Attack

The years between the election of Labour's Harold Wilson as prime minister in 1964 and Thatcher's victory in 1979 saw growth and expanded influence for trade unions in Great Britain. With Wilson in power from 1964 to 1970, the TUC (Trades Union Congress, Britain's labor federation, which is linked closely to the Labour party) participated in a range of policy deliberations, including industrial policy (through the National Economic Development Corporation) and incomes policies. After a national miners' strike played the key role in bringing down Edward Heath's 1970–74 Tory regime, unions again played a pivotal role in the Labour governments of Wilson and James Callaghan between 1974 and 1979. During these years, an attempt was made to expand peak bargaining between unions, firms, and government and to develop a British version of democratic corporatism (including a "social contract"), with organized labor in a central role. Union membership density grew throughout the economy in this period, and union shop stewards became famous for their power in the workplaces. But the economy in these years experienced persistent economic crisis, including inflation, balance of payments crises, and stagnation. Under these circumstances, it became increasingly difficult for a highly decentralized labor movement to deliver wage restraint and labor peace; a strike wave in 1978–79, known as the "Winter of Discontent," contributed greatly to the Labour regime's fall and the sweeping Conservative victory in 1979. Thatcher came to power determined to cut back union influence in politics and industry; through a combination of economic policies and industrial relations legislation she succeeded to a significant degree (Bamber and Snape 1987, pp. 46–51). As one reflection of her success, union membership density for the country as a whole declined steadily after 1979.

In the auto industry, unions took a major beating around the turn of the decade.[1] In the wake of the virtual collapse of British Leyland (BL)

---

[1] Before the coming of the Japanese transplants beginning in the mid-1980s, there were four major British auto producers: British Leyland, Ford, Vauxhall (owned by GM), and Peugeot/Talbot (formerly Chrysler/Talbot). There are many unions, some craft, some industrial, which work sometimes together and sometimes at cross-purposes; the two largest

in the 1970s and the mounting competitive challenge posed by Japanese firms, British auto industry managers moved to assert control over the shop floor beginning in 1979. Especially at BL and Ford, the two largest British producers, managers mounted sustained challenges to the entrenched shop-floor power of shop stewards and unions and to the principle of "mutuality," whereby the stewards could negotiate (and effectively block) new work organization (Marsden et al. 1985; Wood 1988). In this effort, management was largely successful; after 1979 firms introduced new technology and reorganized work largely on their own terms, and the influence of the stewards declined (as indicated by their numbers, facilities, and ability to bargain at the plant level; Marsden et al. 1985, pp. 184–87). Management succeeded in the campaign against union influence by direct confrontation that included defeating union-organized strikes. At the Longbridge plant, for example, BL laid the groundwork for rapid productivity increases in the production of its new Metro by announcing in 1980 its unilateral right to change work practices; the company then defeated a strike against the new work rules and the elimination of mutuality by threatening to fire all striking workers. In the ensuing years, BL management reorganized work to a significant degree on its own terms, including the introduction of Japanese-style work teams, in a process that Jonas Pontusson calls "industrial innovation without the participation of organized labor" (1990, p. 319).[2]

The firms' industrial relations strategies after 1979 were two-pronged: to remove union influence and to encourage employee involvement (Marsden et al. 1985, pp. 191–92). By the mid–1980s, the second prong of this strategy had expanded to include bringing in the unions and stewards for consultation to build more cooperative relations now that management had reclaimed the shop floor (Wood 1988, pp. 231–39). Although there is diversity of opinion regarding the extent to which stewards' power was permanently weakened, the new union participation was limited and in the short term, at least, offered little hope for a resurgence of union influence or bargaining strength.

Unionism in the British auto industry, in any case, was far from dead, as indicated by a spirited strike in 1988 by the thirty-two thousand workers at Ford's twenty-two British plants. The key victory for the unions in this

---

unions in the auto industry are the Transport and General Workers' Union and the Amalgamated Engineering Union. Total employment in the British auto industry plummeted from 472,000 in 1978 to 252,000 in 1986 (Willman 1988, p. 215).

[2] Or as Jürgens, Malsch, and Dohse (1989) put it, "Reorganization occurred unilaterally through management" (p. 111). See ibid., pp. 107–11, for a useful discussion of the "we will manage" strategy to regain control of the shop floor in the British auto industry.

dispute was the defeat of a company proposal that would have given management a free hand in the introduction of team organization; the unions agreed to the idea of teams "in principle" but won the right to negotiate the terms of implementation on a plant-by-plant basis.[3] The coming of team organization to the British auto industry was driven in part by the successful example of a new Nissan plant in the Northeast, where the company negotiated a cooperative labor-management relationship with one inclusive union, the Amalgamated Engineering Union (AEU). Ominously for British trade unionism, however, union membership at the new Japanese-run plant was extremely low.[4]

This brief discussion of industrial relations in the British auto industry can be summarized by looking at our three indicators of the stability and extent of workers' interest representation. For membership density, unions at the major British auto plants have maintained high levels of unionization, although of a vastly reduced total work force. With the coming of additional Japanese transplants, however, low union density at the Nissan plant not only reduces total density for the industry but presages difficult times for the unions in organizing new workers to maintain the high rate of unionization. For rationalization protection, the unions have been able to offer their members only minimal support against the displacement effects of new work organization and technology. In the years after 1979, the unions were unable to prevent either steady and substantial employment losses or declining real wages (Marsden et al. 1985, p. 184); and with the stewards' shop-floor power weakened, the unions could offer little protection against displacement for those who did remain employed. And for the final indicator, the unions have not developed coherent alternatives or promoted proposals for the shape of new work organization on any regularized basis.

The findings for these indicators of the stability and extent of workers' interest representation can be generalized beyond the auto industry to the broader patterns of industrial relations in Britain from 1979 to 1989. In the Thatcher years, a once powerful British labor movement was severely challenged. Union membership density for the British work force as a whole dropped from 54 percent in 1979 to 42 percent in 1987 (Towers 1989, p. 175),[5] and the ability of unions to offer new protections for their

---

[3] See articles by Steve Lohr in the *New York Times*, February 14, 1988, pp. F1, F7, February 18, 1988, p. 27, and February 19, 1988, p. 28.

[4] According to Wood (1988, p. 242), membership was in the 15 to 25% range, compared to virtually 100% at traditional British plants. According to Towers (1989, p. 184), the AEU's estimates run as low as 7%.

[5] The figures vary according to the data source. Richard Freeman, for example, cites

members in an era of rapid work reorganization or to influence the shape of new organization has been minimal.[6] Waging losing battles on the industrial front, unions pursued a political strategy, focusing major efforts on electoral campaigns to defeat Thatcher and replace her with a more friendly Labour government. In the 1980s, however, this strategy failed, and the Conservatives swept back into office twice.[7]

Although Thatcher's anti-union campaign contributed to managerial initiatives that resulted in union decline in Britain, political and managerial opposition do not add up to a sufficient explanation. From 1970 to 1972, the Heath government also challenged union influence but was defeated; and the Kohl government in West Germany challenged union influence in the 1980s with much less success. But in an era of rapid market-driven production and work reorganization, labor in Britain was vulnerable to attack. Because unions were not integrated into managerial decision making, they were in a position neither to influence work reorganization strategies directly nor to negotiate trade-offs before reorganization that could have ensured a more secure and influential role for the representation of workers' interests. On the contrary, because union power was entrenched on the shop floor in the person of the shop stewards (at least in manufacturing industries), who could use the tradition of mutuality to block rapid organizational change, management had a strong incentive to challenge stewards' power when market and political circumstances weakened labor's hand. The absence of a legal framework ensuring union participation both allowed managers to reorganize unilaterally and made it difficult for unions to organize in new workplaces as employment shifted out of declining manufacturing industries. And the absence of stable corporatist bargaining arrangements along with the organizational fragmentation of labor prevented unions from presenting a united front in particular firms and industries, making it possible for management to play groups of workers off against each other in a divide-and-conquer strategy. Most

---

these figures for the nonagricultural work force: from 58 percent unionized in 1979 to 51 percent in 1986 (1989, p. 130). Towers's figures are for the total labor force, including the unemployed. Crouch (1990, p. 346) presents data showing a decline for the employed work force from 56 percent unionized in 1980 to 48 percent in 1987.

[6] Some unions negotiated "new technology agreements" in the early 1980s to protect members and gain influence in the introduction of new technology. But these agreements by and large had little effect, as most employers pursued unilateral strategies, either refusing to negotiate such agreements or bypassing them where they existed (Bamber and Snape 1987, p. 47).

[7] The unions were unable to convince even their own members to vote Labour. Compared to a high of 73 percent of union members voting Labour in 1964, 39 percent voted Labour in 1983, and 43 percent voted Labour in 1987 (Towers 1989, p. 185).

unions in Britain belong to one labor federation, the TUC; but power resides in the member unions, which are large in number and composed of a vast amalgam of craft unions, mixed unions, and industrial unions that sometimes compete against each other in the same workplaces.[8]

At Longbridge, for example, the strike led by the Transport and General Workers' Union (TGWU) in 1980 failed in part because the other large union, the AEU, did not support it (Pontusson 1990). In the auto industry, multi-unionism both permitted management to divide the rank and file from the stewards and reinforced the differing interests of occupational groups when new microelectronic technologies were introduced (Marsden et al. 1985, pp. 170–73). And Nissan's strategy, to find a "friendly" union to incorporate on management's terms with exclusive organizational rights, was possible only because of the highly decentralized organizational structure of British unionism.

In an interview with the editors of the *Reader's Digest*, Margaret Thatcher remarked, "I say to people on the Continent: 'Stop talking about worker participation in business management. You are back in the Marxist era!' "[9] Against the backdrop of the Thatcher regime's prolonged campaign against union political and industrial influence, it is nonetheless important to emphasize two points. First, although Conservative partisans argue that one of Thatcher's great contributions, for both political stability and economic growth, has been to "tame" the unions, the extent to which there has actually been a transformation of British industrial relations is debatable. The Conservative government that came to power in 1979 rejected the postwar consensus regarding compromise and went on the offensive against the unions (Crouch 1990; Jenkins 1987). But the institutions of labor, industry, and industrial relations in Britain are old and entrenched, the products of early and prolonged industrialization; they are highly resistant to reform (Hobsbawm 1969; Bornstein and Gourevitch 1984; Towers 1989). There is considerable evidence that though employers have gone on the offensive in some cases and unions and stewards have laid low, the old institutions, for better or worse, remain essentially intact (Rose and Jones 1985; MacInnes 1987; Batstone 1988). Labor's entrenched fragmentation has made unions vulnerable; but managers have also suffered from a fragmented institutional legacy and have lacked the

---

[8] Writing of the effects of this disjuncture between shop-floor power and labor movement fragmentation, Bornstein and Gourevitch aptly argue: "Taken together, this combination of power and impotence produced a union movement much better suited to good economic times than to bad" (1984, p. 71).

[9] First published in a newspaper advertisement, *International Herald Tribune*, April 19, 1989, p. 13.

capacity to develop dynamic strategies for reform either of industry structures and work organization or of industrial relations. As Michael Rose and Bryan Jones argue: "Our claims and evidence suggest that much management policy making and execution... is piecemeal, uncoordinated and empiricist" (1985, p. 99). According to many, this is where the real causality lies for the decline of British industry, both before and under Thatcher (MacInnes 1987; Batstone 1988); and in this view, the system of industrial relations has not fundamentally changed.

The second point to emphasize is that the extent of union decline in Britain since 1979 may well be generally overstated. Although membership density has declined significantly, it has done so from a high base so that the decline has brought density down approximately to the German level; the rate does not appear to be in free-fall toward the much lower U.S. levels. Although employers in general have supported Thatcher's legislative and political efforts to weaken the unions and some have themselves taken on the unions, the majority of employers appear not to have taken a strongly aggressive approach. This is widely explained as reasonable caution, in the face of anticipated future union revival (Crouch 1990, pp. 342–43). What stands out, according to one view, is "the overall survival capacity of British unions at plant level during a catastrophic period" (Rose and Jones 1985, p. 101). As Crouch (1990, p. 354) maintains: "As an inchoate group of organizations, British unions will retain a power and a presence in the British economy: uneven, illogically structured and excessively decentralized as always, rather weaker than before but of continuing importance."

Italy: Labor in Trouble in Hard Times

Italy's labor movement is divided into three contending labor federations, CGIL (linked to the Italian Communist party and by far the largest of the three), CISL (linked to the Christian Democrats), and the UIL (the smallest, linked to the Socialist party). In part because of this organizational fragmentation, Italian unions were generally perceived to be weak and ineffectual in the first two postwar decades. But the position of unions in Italian society was transformed in the wake of the Hot Autumn strike wave of 1969. Although the unions did not lead the strikes and plant actions of this period and at first opposed shop-floor demands such as the election of shop stewards (*delegati*) for factory councils, they quickly came to terms with the mass uprisings and used the events to consolidate new power inside the factories (Salvati 1981; Sabel 1982, pp. 145–67).

The three labor federations worked more closely together in this period and in 1972 agreed to form a "confederation of the confederations" and to move gradually toward merger (Pellegrini 1987, p. 128). From their new bases in the factory councils and spurred on by growing labor unity, the unions increased their clout in collective bargaining and in 1975 won agreement from organized employers (*Confindustria*) for automatic wage indexing. Under this *scala mobile*, wages rose quarterly along with inflation, adjusted so that lower-paid workers received the largest proportional raises (thus institutionalizing a process of income redistribution). Union industrial and political influence grew significantly for most of the 1970s and consolidated itself from 1974 to 1979 in the "era of accommodation" between unions, employers, and government (Brandini 1983, pp. 94–99).

But economic crisis and the collapse of the national unity government of 1977–79 (based on the Italian Communist party's "historic compromise") opened the door for a renewed and successful employer offensive against the unions. The reversal in union fortunes was punctuated by the defeat of a union strike against management reorganization plans at Fiat in 1980 and a weakening, after acrimonious negotiations, of the *scala mobile* in 1984. That same year, the confederation of the three union confederations, in effect since 1972, dissolved, largely as a result of differences regarding strategies toward wage indexation reform.

Fiat, the dominant Italian auto firm, second only to Volkswagen in combined European market share from 1985 to 1989, has played a leading role in setting the tone of Italian industrial relations; events at Fiat demonstrate vividly the changing fortunes of Italian unions. Fiat factories in northern Italy were a major focus for the Hot Autumn strike wave in 1969 and the ensuing new shop-floor power for workers and unions. Sabel shows how skilled worker and communist traditions intersected with the rising militance of migrant workers from southern Italy to set off the strikes, demonstrations, and plant demands of this period; for Sabel Fiat is the paradigmatic case (Sabel 1982, pp. 160–67). The unions, FIOM (CGIL), FIM (CISL), and UILM (UIL), used the events to build up strength in the auto industry and in particular at Fiat, as union activists became factory stewards and vice versa. Although a free-rider problem persisted and Fiat plants never achieved the high rates of union membership found in Britain's closed shops and corresponding union shops in the United States, the stewards and workers themselves achieved unprecedented bargaining power at the shop-floor level. For most of the 1970s, managers at Fiat could do very little to discipline workers, and changes in work organization had to be bargained out not only with work-force representatives but often with individual workers themselves. Union influence was based not on formal work rules, as in the United States, but on the balance of power in the plant (Katz and Sabel 1985); during this period, the stewards were powerful indeed.

Beginning in 1974, the employers' association, under the leadership of a new president, Giovanni Agnelli of Fiat, took a "realistic" attitude, negotiating at the top with the confederation of confederations in the interest of accommodation (Brandini 1983, p. 96). But as the decade wore on, two problems arose that would threaten both Fiat and the unions: like British Leyland, Fiat encountered increasingly serious productivity and financial problems as the years of economic crisis persisted and competition in the auto industry intensified; and local unions grew restive under the accommodative yoke of a grand confederation playing for power at the national level (Locke 1990b). By 1980, Fiat management had decided, in the interest of saving the firm from bankruptcy, to abandon accommodation in favor of a direct challenge to the union, to regain control over production and the work force, and to lay the groundwork for an advanced automation strategy. Richard M. Locke, Thomas A. Kochan, and Chris R. Heye describe the critical conflict of that year:

> In the Fall of 1980, Fiat proposed to place 24,000 workers in *Cassa Integrazione*, a state-financed redundancy fund. The unions rejected this proposal and broke off relations with the firm. Fiat, in turn, declared its intention to fire 15,000 workers, beginning October 6. Things heated up as the unions blockaded the factories and Fiat sent out letters of dismissal. The strike lasted 35 days. Finally, on October 14, Fiat foremen and supervisors organized a successful demonstration calling for a return to work. 40,000 people marched silently through the streets of Turin in protest against the union, many of them blue collar workers as well. That very night an agreement was signed which represented a major defeat for the union. (1988, p. 13)

As a consequence of this defeat, unions at Fiat have seen their influence marginalized as the firm has pursued successful (in market terms) production reorganization, which includes advanced technology, new supplier relations, rather rigid assembly lines for the production of modules that can then be "flexibly" combined in many ways, and participatory programs for the workers that largely bypass the unions (Locke, Kochan, and Heye 1988).[10]

[10] Especially important was the linkage between Fiat's automation strategy and its effort to marginalize union influence and exert control over the workplace. As a top Fiat executive put it in 1987: "Automatic equipment guarantees steady product quality, continuity of the working process, and therefore its best utilization. They can be easily checked. They don't go on strike" (A. S. Plotkin, "Ghidella Explains Fiat Recovery, Says It Was 'No Miracle,'" *Automotive News*, November 30, 1987, p. 34).

Union membership density at Fiat, for the three unions combined, dropped from 32.5 percent in 1980 to 20.5 percent in 1986 (Locke, Kochan, and Heye 1988, p. 43). Union capacity to provide protections for the work force against the effects of work reorganization and new technology dropped way off from the peak years of bargained shop-floor power following 1969. And the ability of the unions to promote new work organization proposals, after instances in which the stewards helped design innovative work islands in the 1970s, was marginalized.

The decline of union influence in the auto industry spearheaded a general decline of unions in Italy in the early 1980s. Freeman shows a decline in total union membership density (for the nonagricultural work force) of 51 percent in 1979 to 45 percent in 1986 (1989, p. 130). Internal union data show an overall decline from 48.4 percent in 1980 to 39.5 percent in 1986 and for the nonagricultural work force from 44.3 percent in 1980 to 36.6 percent in 1986 (Negrelli and Santi 1990, p. 190).[11] Union capacities to protect the work force and to promote work organization proposals arguably showed a parallel decline.

The reversal of union fortunes in an era of work reorganization is understandable in terms of the argument advanced here. Although local unions achieved considerable shop-floor bargaining power in the early 1970s, they were never integrated into managerial decision-making processes in any regularized and stable way. As Katz and Sabel (1985) have argued, union influence in the plants was based not on work rules but on the balance of power; when the balance shifted under pressure from market circumstances (economic crisis, intensification of competition) and political developments (the breakup of the national unity government in 1979, the growing distance between national and local unions), local unions were vulnerable to attack and national unions and confederations could do very little to help them. No formal mechanism for codetermination stood in the way of managerial offensives against union influence in the effort to reassert control over production.

The 1972–84 confederation of confederations was an attempt to build a cohesive labor movement and embark on a corporatist bargaining strategy at national political and industrial levels. As late as 1983, unions, employers, and the government signed a compromise agreement that was supposed to pave the way for an Italian social contract, or democratic

---

[11] Much of this decline is a product of the unions' inability to organized the newly unorganized in growing nonunion sectors (Negrelli and Santi 1990, p. 155). The argument here is that stable corporatist bargaining arrangements or a legal framework to regulate and encourage union participation in management would have greatly facilitated union organizing efforts.

corporatism (Contini 1986, p. 215). But the agreement soon unraveled, and again Fiat led the employers' charge against organized labor. The following year, against bitter opposition from the CGIL (and the Italian Communist party or PCI) and against a backdrop of debate among the union confederations, employers' demands were satisfied when new ceilings were placed, by government decree, on *scala mobile* wage indexation, and the confederation of confederations fell apart under the strain (Pellegrini 1987, pp. 135–36). In spite of the grand confederation, Italian labor had remained essentially fragmented: the confederations were always voluntarily affiliated; major ideological differences persisted between the different communist-, Catholic-, and socialist-affiliated groups; and although the CGIL had in some ways played the role of centralizing agent, its capacity to fulfill this function declined when it found itself under pressure from the Italian Communist party for being too accommodative, beginning in 1979 when the PCI left the government.

It would be inaccurate, however, to paint only a picture of union decline, as many observers have done. Joseph La Palombara, for example, portrays the situation as follows:

> Today the trade unions are in decline, the victims of recent transformations in the West that caught labor organizations flat-footed everywhere. Statements of Italian union leaders ooze defensiveness and false confidence; brave words about a rosier future in the "postindustrial society" barely mask the underlying sense of anger and despair many of these leaders must feel. It is understandable; in the space of a decade, the trade union movement has gone from a condition of unimagined power to one of precipitous degeneration. (1987, p. 38)

Events since the mid-1980s, however, suggest that "precipitous degeneration" is too strong a term. Italian industrial relations at the end of the decade presented a complex, diversified picture, which included influential unions in many sectors, especially at the local level. And the confederations, although no longer moving toward merger and now weakened in the national political arena (where their hopes had previously been high), began once again to collaborate in industry bargaining.

As it turned out, the decline of the labor movement in Italy was cushioned in several ways. Labor continued to play an important role in tripartite institutions, especially at the local level, concerned with industrial restructuring, training programs, displacement of workers, and the like (Negrelli and Santi 1990, p. 183). The union confederations continued to bargain jointly with employers, even after the breakup of the grand confederation; and at the national industry level, labor-employer agreements often included a backup government role (engineering trade-offs in fiscal, economic, and social policy). Finally, labor maintained its influence at the local level in a period of the decentralization of industrial relations, not only through tripartite bodies but also through strong union footholds on the shop floor. These positions of de facto union participation, built up in the years after the Hot Autumn in 1969, gave local unions leverage for new rights to information and consultation and for bargaining over new work organization. If national unions declined in influence, the 1980s was in some areas and industries a period of "the resurgence of local unions" (Locke 1990a).

Employers, for their part, have been far from unified. They have taken divergent approaches to industrial relations, reflected in considerable conflict within Confindustria over appropriate strategies toward unions and work forces (Pellegrini 1987, pp. 129–30). Fiat was a leader in the unilateral approach aimed at marginalizing union influence, but other employers (in the chemical and textile industries, for example) have taken a more participatory approach. And at IRI (a group of state-run industries), an agreement signed with the unions in 1984 offered new rights to information and set up joint committees for consultation and discussion in a number of areas (Negrelli and Santi 1990, pp. 180–81, 186–87).

A critical problem facing unions in Italy in the 1980s, which made them vulnerable to Fiat-type strategies, was not only conflict among unions and union confederations but conflict within unions and confederations, especially between national levels and the base. Federations and national unions in the 1980s faced considerable and widespread opposition to nationally negotiated agreements from the rank and file at local levels, and such opposition undermined the capacity of national unions and confederations to bargain jointly and effectively (Locke 1990a).

As in the British case, Italy offers a picture of overall union decline that is nonetheless mixed and includes not only particular examples of union strength but a continuing substantial role for unions in the political economy, at both local and national levels. Although industrial relations have been generally decentralized, there is less evidence for a thorough transformation. As Serafino Negrelli and Ettore Santi (1990, pp. 192–93) conclude:

> First, like all or nearly all of Europe, Italy has witnessed far-reaching changes in the industrial relations system. More than a profound, decisive "turning point," however, the changes constitute an adaptation to new conditions. Though diminished, concertation practices have remained, after their thor-

ough establishment in the early 1980s. The unions have not lost their "political citizenship," although their practical influence in the political and industrial sphere has diminished. Their bargaining power has declined, but this has not engendered substantial innovations with respect to the earlier period. The national, industry-wide contract continues to be viewed as essential by employers. Decentralization has thus been controlled. Management strategies are designed to decrease the scope and impact of union action, but not as a rule to eliminate it entirely.

Sweden: Economic Ups and Downs, Persistent Union Strength

After decades of industrial conflict, the dominant labor federation (LO) and the employers' association (SAF) signed the Saltsjöbaden Basic Agreement in 1938, committing both sides to free and good-faith collective bargaining with a "peace obligation" during contractual periods. The employers' willingness to establish regular centralized bargaining procedures and to accept the unions, in effect as partners, was based in part on the political strength of the labor-linked Social Democratic party (SAP) (Korpi 1980; Luebbert 1987). The agreement laid the groundwork for a stable "Swedish model" of democratic corporatism that persisted well into the 1970s. The arrangements included Keynesian economic policies; "wage solidarity" (to reduce differentials between occupational groups and drive firms unable to pay good wages out of business); active labor market policies (as high as 2.4 percent of GNP) to retrain and relocate the displaced and preserve full employment; SAP dominance of government (the party has been in power since 1932 except for the years 1976–82); a vast network of welfare state services; and highly inclusive, centralized employer and labor organizations that engaged in peak bargaining, both formally and informally and often in collaboration with top government officials, who arranged state-financed trade-offs for concessions such as wage restraint (Wilensky 1976, pp. 21–30; Martin 1979; von Otter 1983; Rehn 1985). The dominant labor federation is the LO (mostly but not exclusively blue collar), although the TCO (for white-collar employees) and SACO (for higher-level professionals) have grown considerably in size and influence since the 1960s. In 1984, LO had about 2 million members, TCO about 1 million, and SACO 260,000 (Auer 1985, p. 18; Hammerström 1987, pp. 191–92).

The LO has encountered new problems since the early 1970s. The expansion of white-collar work facilitated the rise of TCO and SACO, each opposed in varying degrees to LO's policy of wage solidarity; rising TCO and SACO militance threatened to undermine LO's hold on pattern-setting, centralized peak bargaining. In addition, LO's centralized power included little influence within the plants on issues such as the organization of work; increasing dissatisfaction among the rank and file with working conditions, rationalization, and speedup contributed to rising industrial conflict, including wildcat strikes, which peaked in the years 1970 and 1974 (von Otter 1983, pp. 202–8).

At the same time, growing "wage drift," in part a product of interunion competition (as opposed to wage solidarity), contributed to inflationary problems in the Swedish economy.[12] Economic problems and other issues in the mid–1970s led to the first postwar political loss for the Social Democrats in 1976, followed by six years of governance by a conservative coalition. Although the economy recovered after 1982 under a new SAP regime, serious economic problems reappeared by the late 1980s, once again threatening the viability of Social Democratic rule and the Swedish model (which included the LO's close involvement in government policy making).

Economic, political, and rival union problems posed long-term challenges to LO's hegemony, but none of them appeared to threaten high rates of union membership or a strong, influential place in Swedish society for the representation of workers' interests.[13] The problem of a lack of influence inside the plants gave rise to an "industrial democracy" movement within both the LO and the government in the 1970s, resulting in new legislation for investment funds for wage earners and for codetermination in the workplace. A 1976 law, the Codetermination Act, established a framework for information and consultation rights for unions and employees regarding any proposed changes in the employer-employee relationship (including work organization). Although the early effects of this legislation were disappointing to union advocates, the Agreement on Efficiency and Participation, based on the 1976 law, was negotiated and signed in 1982 by LO, PTK (including both TCO and SACO), and SAF. The intent of the agreement was to accelerate the pace of codetermination

---

[12] A major additional cause of wage drift has been the desire of employers, especially in profitable export industries, to attract labor in a full employment economy. See Martin 1984 for an insightful and thorough analysis of wage drift, LO-TCO relations, the development of LO and government economic policy, and growing economic difficulties of the 1970s and early 1980s.

[13] Some observers, however, predict that current economic problems and especially rival bargaining between labor federations could in time lead to declining union influence (Ahlen 1989, p. 330).

by linking company needs for higher productivity and better product quality with union and work-force demands for better working conditions and for more voice, especially concerning work organization.

Volvo is the dominant auto firm, with a share of the Swedish economy that is far greater than GM's share of the U.S. economy (von Otter 1983, p. 218). Although Volvo is a large, diversified corporation, car, truck, and engine production remain the core activities, employing 60 percent of all Volvo workers (Auer 1985, p. 1). The company has long taken a cooperative approach to industrial relations (contrasted to Saab's more aggressive approach toward the work force and union). Nonetheless, Volvo was no exception to the general employer strategy toward the work force in the years of increasing labor-management conflict beginning around 1970. While the union (the Swedish Metalworkers' Union) joined LO in a strategy that focused on politics, peak bargaining, and new legislation, Volvo decentralized its own approach, directing its attention toward the shop floor and work group in an effort to raise efficiency and at the same time speak to the demands of dissatisfied workers (Auer 1985; Auer and Riegler 1988). Beginning at the Kalmar plant in 1974, Volvo experimented with innovative forms of work organization and earned a reputation for its "human-centered" approach to production.

Kalmar and subsequent organizational designs at other plants have used job rotation, enlargement, and enrichment and have attempted to build team spirit by the designation of work groups. Basic assembly-line concepts have continued to dominate, however, including short cycle times, machine-paced work, a preponderance of narrow, repetitive work, and limited autonomy for workers and groups. As Berggren puts it: "Flexible Taylorism in production design combined with group work in rather restricted forms is the dominant trend" (1988, p. 152). Until the mid-1980s, the union's role in new work organization was limited.

In 1984, Volvo and the LO signed their own codetermination agreement, based on the 1982 Agreement on Efficiency and Participation. The result has been a greatly expanded role for the union in discussions concerning new work organization; the local union itself, rather than works councils as in Germany, is the agent of codetermination. Drawing on past experiences at Volvo, a critical analysis of Japanese work organization, and the work of external researchers such as those based at the LO-linked Swedish Center for Working Life, the union began to advance proposals for group work that greatly extended workers' and groups' autonomy and responsibility. As Auer and Riegler put it: "New codetermination instruments allow trade unions today to support the demand for more autonomy without endangering their representation rights" (1988, p. 1).

The new Uddevalla plant demonstrates the most substantial union success so far in this regard. In the wake of the 1984 Volvo codetermination agreement, the union entered extensively into the planning of this new plant, on the site of a closed shipyard. After prolonged discussion and debate, management and labor finally agreed on a new assembly concept, based on extensive and ongoing training for all workers, assembly stations (as opposed to an assembly line), and long cycle times of two hours or more for groups of workers who put together whole sections of the car (Berggren 1988; Auer and Riegler 1988, pp. 47–50). As Pontusson argues, union influence in the plants is limited because it is missing at the corporate board level and remains secondary to union influence over the "external environment" in which the company operates (through LO's broader political and economic clout). The basic Uddevalla concepts originated not with the union but with management planners; the union successfully threw its weight on one side of an intramanagement debate. Nonetheless, it is clear both at Uddevalla and at other plants that the union has improved its capacity to make independent proposals and is exerting increasing influence regarding new work organization (Pontusson 1990).

Union membership remains close to 100 percent throughout the Swedish auto industry. Rationalization protections for the work force are extensive, enshrined in law (the union-promoted Security of Employment Act; von Otter, pp. 216–17) as well as in collective bargaining agreements and the Volvo Codetermination Agreement (which guarantees new training for displaced workers). Contractual and legal protections are backed up by the world's most extensive (union-promoted) active labor market policies, directed toward training, retraining, and job creation (Rehn 1985). In a period of six to eight years the union moved from having very little influence inside the plants to playing an important role in the promotion of new concepts of work organization.

In Swedish society as a whole, union membership is high and stable; according to Freeman's data, membership density for the nonagricultural work force rose from 89 percent in 1979 to 96 percent in 1986 (1989, p. 130). Protections against the effects of new technology and work organization are extensive throughout the Swedish economy, backed by legislation, collective bargaining agreements, and government policy. And unions in many sectors of the Swedish economy have begun to promote new concepts for work organization, often in collusion with social-democratic-minded managers.

Up until the early 1980s Swedish unions maintained an arm's-length relationship with management in matters concerning production and work organization. When in the 1970s work organization became an important issue because of workers' dissatisfaction, increasingly competitive markets, and employers' strategies, the unions saw their influence in society potentially undermined as managers turned attention to the shop floor. In the face of this new threat, the unions adopted first a legal strategy and then a collective bargaining strategy to develop new processes of codetermination. Union interest in new firm-level participation was driven both by employers' (decentralizing) shop-floor strategies and by rank-and-file protests of the 1960s and 1970s (when workers reacted against the centralization of union bargaining and power; Ahlen 1989, pp. 332–33).

The union-sponsored codetermination law of 1976 was followed by peak collective bargaining agreements for implementation in 1982 so that the law is now implemented at the firm level by local unions and the central organizations play a monitoring role. Because management has the ultimate authority, after respecting union rights to information, consultation, independent research, and proposals, industrial democracy activists have in some cases continued to be disappointed by progress (Hammerström 1987, pp. 198–201). Swedish unions by the late 1980s, nonetheless, found themselves increasingly integrated into managerial decision making at the firm level, especially on issues of new work organization.

Swedish unions could engineer a change in this direction because of the political and economic strength afforded by a cohesive labor movement, situated as a key actor within corporatist bargaining arrangements.[14] Still dominated by LO unions and still powerful throughout society, Swedish labor in the 1980s retained its capacity both to claim new arenas for voice when economic circumstances required and to preclude the Italian, British, and American managerial strategies of direct challenge to union influence.

It has become fashionable, and to some extent accurate, to proclaim the demise of the Swedish model (Lash 1985; Peterson 1987; Ahlen 1989).[15] Since the early 1980s, there has been widespread decentralization of bargaining, encouraged by employers; individual unions (such as the metalworkers) have in various years conducted their own separate negotiations to replace former peak bargaining (Lash 1985; Rehn and Viklund 1990, pp. 318–30). Employers have been motivated in this direction by a desire to curb central union federation strength; by the need to raise wages in particular industries to attract workers; and by the desire for

[14] For an insightful discussion of the development and capacities of Sweden's centralized unions, see Swenson 1989, pp. 31–34, 42–60.
[15] For a contrasting view that sees not the demise but rather changes in the Swedish model, see Rehn and Viklund 1990.

greater flexibility at the firm and plant levels as world markets have changed. Unions have responded to the demands of their members for greater wage drift, as workers with certain skills and in certain industries have sought better deals than they could get under the established principles of wage solidarity. When employers began to push for decentralized bargaining around 1983, intralabor divisions grew in importance.

In addition to the decentralization of bargaining, new outbreaks of industrial conflict along with economic crises beginning in the mid–1970s have indicated if not the demise at least major problems for the Swedish model. There has even been recent talk of Sweden succumbing to the "British disease" (low growth, high inflation, too many interest group demands, and so on). Interunion conflict has escalated, especially between blue- and white-collar unions, presenting new problems both for the Swedish economy and for the development of unified union strategy (Ahlen 1989, p. 338; Rehn and Viklund 1990). By 1989–90, Sweden faced a major economic crisis, Social Democratic political power appeared shaky, and the government prepared major reforms of fiscal and economic policy (especially taxation).

Although Sweden, under these circumstances, may no longer qualify as a "best-case" model combining social progress, prosperity, economic growth, and industrial peace, the extent of union influence in society does not yet appear to be in question (as reflected in high membership rates, bargaining power at national and local levels, strong protections for members, and expanded voice at local and firm levels). And to the extent that future union influence may be successfully attacked, it may find itself vulnerable precisely because of the breakdown of labor movement cohesiveness and the stable corporatist bargaining arrangements of the past. As Gösta Rehn and Birger Viklund (1990, pp. 320–21) conclude:

> Structural change, changes in trade union membership (a shift from unions in private manufacturing to public service) and changes in employer strategy do not in the Swedish case lead to a decreased role for the trade union movement or any weakening in its bargaining position. On the contrary increased overall trade union membership and a new role for the unions in production questions rather indicate an increased union role. The only development which could limit this would be internal division and a decentralization, which could go further than is really in the union interest.

Japan: Weak Unions, Stable Industrial Relations

After World War II, U.S. Occupation Forces promoted labor legislation and the growth of trade unions as a counterforce to Japan's large business conglomerates implicated in the war effort; in part as a result, union membership jumped from zero to 56 percent of the work force from 1945 to 1949 (Cusumano 1985, p. 138).[16] The unions were at once enterprise-based and ideological, including active communist and socialist participation. The efforts of unionists to build an independent labor movement on the U.S. model (based on the new laws, which were similar to American labor laws) failed because of ideological splits within the unions and among contending rival federations and a vigorous employer counterattack when the occupation authorities released their hold in the early 1950s.

As a result of the successful offensive against organized labor in the private sector, activist unions were for the most part either replaced by compliant, company-oriented unions or were subdued into playing a similar cooperative and subordinate role.[17] Employers' success in this period was based not only on superior strength but on the incorporation of important past union demands such as employment security and enhanced union voice at the firm level (Kenney and Florida 1988, pp. 127–29). Union membership dropped off to about a third of the work force and remained fairly stable at that level until the mid-1970s (Kuwahara 1987, p. 219). Since the defeat of independent private sector unionism in the mid-1950s, the hallmarks of Japanese industrial relations have been stability, enterprise unionism, management dominance, and cooperative union-management relations that include the integration of the union into managerial processes, especially at the lower levels of the management structure.

The two main labor federations are the left-leaning Sohyo and the more conservative Domei. Linked to the fragmented political opposition in Japan, the Socialist and Democratic Socialist parties respectively, they have had limited political influence, expressed mainly through the annual spring wage offensive (Shunto) and meetings with the prime minister. Public sector unions have been the most independent and at times militant; but lacking ties to a strong labor movement, they have been isolated and have seen their influence decline (especially after a major defeat of the railroad workers union in a ten-day strike in the mid-1970s). Conservative dominance of private sector enterprise unionism increased after 1973, when firms intensified the pressure on both work force and unions in response to economic crisis and the global export offensive of Japanese

[16] For an introduction to the prewar history of Japanese unions and the historical precursors of the postwar Japanese employment system and industrial relations, see Kuwahara 1987, pp. 212–23; and Garon 1987.

[17] As Cusumano puts it: "Industrial unions might well have survived had managers and white-collar workers headed for managerial posts not united during the 1950s to break up labor federations and replace them with pro-management, company unions" (1985, p. 139).

industry. Although union membership density has declined gradually since 1975, membership remains high at the large firms, and the basic elements of industrial relations remain stable (Taira and Levine 1985, pp. 283–84). Many observers see the engaged labor-management relationship, in which unions serve to facilitate work reorganization and to mobilize the work force for positive contributions to productivity, as a major contributor to Japanese industrial success (Altshuler et al. 1984; Marshall 1987; Kenney and Florida 1988).

The auto industry has been a pattern setter for Japanese industrial relations, and it was the large auto firms, especially Toyota and Nissan, that won path-breaking victories against independent unionism in the early 1950s (Cusumano 1985, pp. 137–64; Halberstam 1986, pp. 131–87). Eishi Fujita argues that enterprise unionism has been central to Toyota's success (and Toyota is not only the largest auto firm but the largest Japanese manufacturing firm as well):

> The most important factor in practising the Toyota system has been industrial relations based on mutual trust between management and labor. Without such industrial relations, the Toyota production system would have been impossible. It was not after the completion of the Toyota production system but after the virtual destruction of a militant and independent trade union that the cooperative industrial relations were established. The independent trade union of Toyota changed into a compliant company union, with its defeat a turning point in the industrial strife of the early 1950s. (1988, pp. 9–10)

Critical to the success of work organization and reorganization in Japanese auto plants has been the role of the foreman, who both mobilizes the work force and makes workers' needs and suggestions known higher up in the management structure (Fujita 1988, p. 11). And this is where the importance of enterprise unionism comes into play: the union leadership is usually drawn from the ranks of the foremen and the supervisors at the next level up. According to Dohse, Jürgens, and Malsch, "The Japanese automobile firms were even able in the past to have the same persons who, as supervisors, had to organize the pressure for work effort and job flexibility be, as well, the labor-union-interest representatives of the employees" (1985, p. 139). It is at this level that we find the union integrated into managerial decision-making processes; the union functions as an arm of management, and union leaders often go on to careers in management. The union is integrated into management because the union leadership *is* management. The foreman and his supervisor have considerable discretion in matters of personnel use, pay levels, promotions, and shop-floor work organization; and these lower-level managers make their decisions often in their capacity as representatives of both management and union.

Workers in Japanese auto plants are organized into teams. The teams serve several purposes: they make possible a more flexible use of manpower; they facilitate job rotation and enlargement, which give workers a broader set of task abilities and make assembly-line work more interesting; and they encourage group and individual efforts to improve production practices (called *kaizen*, or constant improvement) and the raising of work standards. The foreman, who is often a union representative, plays a leadership role for the team.

The extraordinary production success of Japanese auto firms is evidenced by their dominant contemporary position in world markets. But in spite of teamwork, worker participation, and cooperative union-management relations, life on the shop floor is harsh in many ways for Japanese autoworkers. Both within and across teams, workers are thrown into intensely competitive relations with each other because of management's unconstrained prerogative in assigning merit pay and promotions (Dohse, Jürgens, and Malsch 1985). Satoshi Kamata (1973) gives a compelling firsthand account of the intense pressure, rapid work pace, long working hours, and absence of individual or group rights in a large Toyota plant. And Hikari Nohara (1988) writes of the physical and spiritual exhaustion of Japanese autoworkers, in the face of work intensification, long daily, weekly, and yearly working hours, and the absence of an independent personal and social life outside the company. If the blending of management and union has facilitated the world-class productivity, flexibility, and product quality of Japanese auto production, it has also created intense pressure and the conditions of "permanent emergency" faced by Japanese autoworkers.

Japanese industrial success, however, in the auto and other industries, cannot be explained solely by the intense mobilization of the work force made possible by the system of engaged labor-management relations. Comparable pressure on industrial workers has been common in mass production industry everywhere, in developed and developing countries, without yielding comparable results. Clearly the state in Japan played an important role in orchestrating industrial development and preparing industry for massive and successful export drives (Johnson 1982). But perhaps the critical component of contemporary Japanese industrial success is the integrated approach to flexible production and work organization. The engaged labor-management relationship allows the integration of elements that together produce a highly motivated, flexible, and productive work force. These factors include employment security for the core work force, work teams, cross-training, job rotation, task integration, just-in-time parts delivery, and shop-floor voice through individual suggestions and team efforts.[18] As in the NUMMI case, production organization of this type can be exported for use in other countries (see above, Chapter 1). So successful and compelling have been the results of Japanese production organization that many have predicted its rapid spread and eventual dominance everywhere over traditionally organized (and "worker-alienated") mass production. James P. Womack, Daniel T. Jones, and Daniel Roos, for example, see in the Japanese auto industry's "lean production" (as they call it) a new paradigm that will replace mass production and "change the world" (1990, p. 21).

Japanese industrial relations have functioned in a stable way since the mid-1950s; unions in the auto industry and elsewhere occupy a middle ground on the three indicators of workers' interest representation. Although union membership remains high at the large auto plants (where core workers are required to join the enterprise union), subcontractors have made increasing use of nonunion female and part-time workers. In Japanese society as a whole, unionization remains high at large firms, 66 percent in 1986;[19] but for all workers, union membership density dropped from 32 percent in 1979 to 28 percent in 1986 (Freeman 1989, p. 130).[20] Rationalization protection for displaced workers consists almost exclusively of employment security for the core work force at large plants. Enterprise unions have made the preservation of this security a major focus of their efforts, with considerable success (Ishikawa 1984, pp. 280–81; Taira and Levine 1985, pp. 277–82), but the effects of this policy have been to shift the costs of adjustment to the unprotected secondary labor market (Deutschmann 1987b, p. 472). And although enterprise unions are engaged in joint consultation with management, these unions have not been in a position to promote independent proposals regarding work organization. As Christoph Deutschmann puts it: "Union representatives as a rule are lacking information and competence to contradict the proposals of management effectively. Consequently, union involvement mainly has the function of preparing acceptance for the new technology

[18] See Kenney and Florida (1988), who call this "structured flexibility," for a presentation and analysis of the major elements of this system of work organization.
[19] International Labour Organization, *Social and Labour Bulletin*, no. 3 (September 1987), p. 447.
[20] Union membership density, following a long period of relative stability after 1956, peaked in 1970 at 35.4%. It then declined to 33.1% but rose again to 34.4% in 1975. Since then, the decline has been slow but steady (Kuwahara 1987, p. 219).

and an atmosphere of smooth cooperation for its implementation; there is no bargaining on equal footing'' (1987b, p. 470).

Enterprise unionism, which integrates unions into managerial command and decision-making processes, accounts for the relative stability of Japanese industrial relations and the unchanged role of workers' interest representation, even in the past fifteen years of ''permanent reorganization'' in Japanese industry. Because union and management work hand in hand, there was no incentive for firms to challenge the position of the unions, as managers have done in Britain, Italy, and the United States. Not only are union representatives and lower-level managers often the same people, there are also committees for joint consultation from low to high levels of the firm (Dyer, Salter, and Webber 1987, pp. 115–18; Taira and Levine 1985, pp. 295–96); the result has been smooth work reorganization and stable industrial relations.

But because these are enterprise unions, they lack fundamental independence from management. They do not as a rule go out looking for new plants or businesses to organize, nor do they generally present ideas that challenge those of management. In 1988, unionists established Rengo, a new labor federation, in the hopes of pulling together a new organizational center for all unions. After the breakup of the independent and at times militant railroad workers' union, Japanese unions appeared more ideologically united than at any time in the postwar period. But the basis for this unity was the firm-oriented enterprise union. Fragmentation remained at the heart of Japanese labor's lack of independence.

The Politics of Work Reorganization: Summary and Implications

The past decade has witnessed intense pressure on established systems of industrial relations in advanced societies. Driven by economic crisis, intensified competition, and the imperatives of industrial restructuring, firms have embarked on new strategies toward work forces and the representation of workers' interests. Innovation is the order of the day; strategies range from newly adversarial management to genuinely participatory approaches designed to use cooperation for competitive advantage. Unions have responded hesitantly, defensively, and occasionally with enthusiasm, dependent both on managerial strategies and on union capacities to pursue new forms of relations. Governments have helped managers challenge union influence, and (sometimes at the same time) they have encouraged the spread of participation. Established postwar systems of industrial relations in Western societies have eroded under the strain and in some cases have been transformed.

Even in a period of intense economic pressure, even as institutions are being transformed, the established structure and characteristics of the institutions have an important bearing on outcomes. My argument develops the perspective that specific attributes of the institutions of industrial relations shape industrial relations outcomes.[1]

---

[1] This perspective fits well with the "new institutionalism" in political science, which is based on the notion that political institutions shape political discourse (Steinmo 1989 provides a clear formulation). The observation, of course, that organizational structures in the economy and polity count is nothing new in the social sciences. The trick is to specify the circumstances under which specific attributes of structure explain specific outcomes. Steinmo attempts to do this for tax policy; I make a parallel effort for industrial relations.

222

The Argument Tested and Elaborated

In the past decade, changing world market circumstances and accompanying rapid technological change have driven processes of union decline and change and adaptation in industrial relations. But cross-national outcomes have varied substantially, and on the basis of broad national patterns (rather than sectoral or firm differences alone). Contrasting cross-national variations in the stability and extent of workers' interest representation are accounted for by variations in the institutions of industrial relations.

Where unions were integrated into processes of managerial decision making, as in West Germany and Japan, industrial relations practices were relatively stable in the 1980s. When this integration, as a broad national pattern, was backed by law and corporatist bargaining, as in West Germany, union influence remained stable from a position that was independent of management and in some cases extended its scope proactively into processes of work reorganization. Where integrated unions had no such legal and political backing and belonged to a fragmented labor movement, as did the enterprise unions of Japan, workers' interest representation had no basis for independence from management in issues such as work organization; unions remained weak and if anything experienced a modest decline in influence within a stable industrial relations system.

Where labor-management relations were adversarial and arm's-length at the onset of major efforts at industrial restructuring and work reorganization, unions had little leverage from which to influence processes of change; at the same time managers had strong incentives to challenge union influence on the shop floor. When arm's-length relations were combined with organizationally decentralized or fragmented labor movements, as in the United States, Britain, and Italy, unions proved vulnerable to attack by adversarial management, and union influence declined as the pace of reorganization escalated. Where unions with arm's-length traditions were backed up by corporatist bargaining and a cohesive labor movement, however, as in Sweden, they were able to use broad economic and political clout to get integrated in new ways into managerial decision making on issues such as work reorganization; the outcome was continued and perhaps even growing union strength and influence.

In Chapters 1, 2, and 3, I submitted this argument to the test of detailed primary research in the U.S. and West German auto industries. In Chapter 4, I added evidence from the U.S. and West German telephone services and apparel industries; and in Chapter 6, I broadened the scope to include auto industry and general national patterns of industrial relations in Britain, Italy, Sweden, and Japan. The argument stands up well to the comparative evidence presented from selected sectors and countries.

At the minimum, relationships of correlation have been established among the variables; it is possible, nonetheless, that another set of causal factors is acting on both sides of the equation so that the relationships specified here covary but are not causally related. It is important to emphasize, therefore, that this is a causal argument rather than simply a sorting device or a set of correlations. I have looked at a range of possible alternative arguments and explanations (see the Introduction and Chapter 3 and see below); none of them are confirmed by the evidence presented here.

The causal linkage between the variables specified (union integration into managerial decision making; the backing of law or corporatist bargaining) and the perceived outcomes (stable or extensive representation of workers' interests versus unstable and declining union influence) lies in the prevention or facilitation of union decline. Institutional considerations aside, predicted outcomes in a context of intensified world market competition, rapid technological change, and reorganization of work might reasonably include instability in industrial relations and union decline. Such predicted outcomes are confirmed in many cases. What is interesting, however, is that such outcomes do not occur in all cases; institutions condition the effects of intensified economic competition.

Where unions are integrated into managerial decision-making processes regarding issues such as personnel use and work organization, they acquire, in competitive markets, a conscious vested interest in the productivity, product quality, and profitability of the firm or plant. Because they receive substantive information from management and are in a position to consult, veto, or propose alternatives, unions have both a perspective from which to view managerial efforts to reorganize and leverage with which to ensure union institutional security in the new arrangements. They are, in short, in a position to prevent the destabilization of industrial relations and union decline in a situation (intensified market competition; managerial imperatives to reorganize) in which those outcomes would appear likely. Unions in West Germany, for example, through their entrenched positions on the works councils, have been able to play such a role, participating (or at least acquiescing) in managerial decisions to rationalize and reorganize while at the same time defending, and sometimes extending, union position and influence. We have seen this dynamic at work, in different ways, in the West German auto, telephone services, and apparel industries.

Integration by itself, however, is not enough to ensure stable and expanding union influence, especially that which offers a perspective in-dependent of management. In the United States, some employers have offered unions new voice in discussions of work reorganization, but others have used worker participation programs to help keep unions out. And even many employers from the former group have opened new plants and kept them nonunion; the labor movement in the United States has continued to decline. In Japan, enterprise unions are integrated into but also dom-inated by management. Although industrial relations remain stable, unions are weak and lack an independent perspective from which to expand their influence.

Where integration is backed up by law and corporatist bargaining, how-ever, managerial discretion concerning workers' and union participation and deunionization is regulated. Union integration is based on rights exter-nal to the firm; the law, in other words, attributes public status to unions (Offe 1981). Possessing a right to participate, unions are able to maintain and even expand influence in an era of work reorganization, at precisely the time when one might reasonably predict their decline. In the face of world market forces that, by creating managerial imperatives to reorganize, could and often do contribute to union decline, institutions of law and politics in-tervene to permit continued and even expanded union influence. Where the shift away from traditional manufacturing undercuts union membership, the legal and political framework is especially important for new union or-ganizing. In Germany, the Works Constitution Act has in effect required employers in old plants and new to bargain seriously with unions. And in Sweden, corporatist bargaining arrangements gave unions leverage to es-tablish, through both law and collective bargaining, new firm-level union involvement in work organization decisions.

The dynamic element within corporatist bargaining for this analysis is cohesiveness in the labor movement. Where labor movements are cohe-sive, unions have both resources and leverage unavailable to unions in a fragmented labor movement. One defining feature of cohesiveness (see the Introduction for a full definition) is the relatively small number of unions; by definition, then, unions are more comprehensive, and this accounts in part for their success. In Germany, the IG Metall, DPG, and GTB are all more inclusive within an industry or across industries than are their American counterparts. The broader organizational scope of these unions lends them a broader perspective, more extensive resources, and more varied strategic options; at the same time they are less constrained by the demands of particular craft or occupational groups.[2] But this is not

---

[2] See Barnett 1969 (1926), and Slichter, Healy, and Livernash 1960, for classical accounts

the whole story. Cohesive labor movements also have broad political and economic strength that allows them to defend codetermination or to establish it where it was previously absent (as in Sweden since 1976); to defend other labor legislation along with labor's bargaining strength and conflict potential;[3] to counter management's attempts to avoid unions (the Swedish work force is virtually fully unionized; and in Germany, even ideologically nonunion IBM has a significant union presence to contend with); and to put extensive resources into research centers, for the purpose of developing independent views and bargaining positions in rapidly changing circumstances.

By contrast, in contemporary world markets, it is precisely the absence of union integration into management decision making backed up by an appropriate legal and political framework that makes possible instability in industrial relations and the decline of unions. Where unions do not benefit from these positions of leverage, the field, at least in the 1980s, was relatively open for successful challenges to union influence on the part of firms and governments. In the United States, Britain, and Italy, governments have moved against union strength in important ways; at the same time, firms have set up new shops to avoid unions, taken unions on directly in bargaining demands and strikes, and reorganized work in ways that challenge traditional bases of union influence. In spite of new processes of worker and union participation, the overall outcome in all three countries, at the sectoral and national levels, has been instability in industrial relations and the decline of unions.

This argument emphasizes the institutions of industrial relations and the behavior of both management and union within them. Management's actions, as firms respond to changing world markets, are decisive in shaping both changing industrial relations and the success or failure of restructuring. We have seen the effects of company offensives against labor in Britain and Italy, as well as the wide range of outcomes in the United States resulting from the wide scope of managerial discretion, or "strategic choice" (Kochan, Katz, and McKersie 1986). But managers

---

of the differences between craft and industrial unions and the effects of these differences on industrial relations outcomes. See Altshuler et al. (1984, pp. 205–14) for a discussion, pertinent to the auto industry, of the advantages of multi-industry versus single-industry unions.

[3] West German labor lost the battle against the Kohl regime's 1985 legislative reform to weaken union strike potential (Silvia 1988). But major mobilization against the legislation arguably limited the Kohl regime's future initiatives to weaken labor; and the SPD, a credible contender for power, has promised immediate repeal when it next runs the government.

are more or less constrained in their actions, or perhaps it is more accurate to say that they are constrained in contrasting ways in different societies. In Germany and Sweden, constraints resulting from union integration into firms' decision making, law, and corporatist bargaining arrangements have forced managers to consider union interests in processes of work reorganization and prevented firms from either directly challenging or avoiding unions. These particular constraints imposed by unions have both preserved the stability of industrial relations and ensured a position of considerable influence for unions.

There is a paradox in this discussion of constraints. It is commonplace in the literature to note that managers in Britain, Italy, and the United States were more constrained in questions of work organization because of contractual work rules in the United States and union power on the shop floor in Britain and Italy than managers in West Germany, where works councils granted more flexibility on the shop floor in return for involvement in decision making (Katz and Sabel 1985). But under pressure from intensified market competition and the success of alternative production models, management turned out to be less constrained precisely where it had appeared more constrained (Britain, Italy, and the United States). The range of strategic options available to managers in the latter countries (from avoiding unions to attacks on union influence to initiatives for new labor-management cooperation) turned out to be considerably more narrow in West Germany and Sweden, where managers supposedly had more discretion.

One could argue that managers, possessing more shop-floor flexibility to begin with, had less reason to go on the offensive against unions in West Germany and Sweden. This is probably true, although as was demonstrated in Chapters 2 and 5, management's flexibility in these societies has been exaggerated. In Sweden, managers took charge of the plants in the 1970s and moved to reorganize work in the face of labor's broad political strength (Auer 1985); in West Germany, employers fought for flexibility in working hours in the face of the IG Metall's proven conflict potential and successful 1984 strike for a shorter workweek. But whatever the incentives, managers in West Germany and Sweden simply did not have the option of attacking union influence, as managers in other countries did.

In this analysis, I emphasize the structures of representation for workers' interests, the particular constraints that such structures impose on management, and the relations between labor and mangement that such institutional attributes make likely. But although this is admittedly an ambitious attempt to account for cross-national variations in industrial relations trends by reference to a small number of institutional variables, I do not deny the role of strategic actors and their choices. There is a range of outcomes in each country; and domestic variations are to a significant degree a product of discretion within the range of choice. At the plant level in the United States, for example, in the auto and in other industries, managers pursue a wide range of strategies toward their work forces as the pace of work reorganization escalates, and national institutional variables do not explain specific local decisions. Unions integrated into management decision making and backed up by a cohesive labor movement, to cite another example, may or may not develop and promote independent proposals for the shape of new work organization; but this option is within the range of choice, whereas it may not be for unions in other countries, no matter how much they might wish to take such an approach. There is, therefore, a range of strategic choice for both management and labor in questions of industrial relations and work reorganization, a range that is defined by institutional possibilities. Contrasting cross-national outcomes can be understood as the products of contrasting ranges of choice, themselves the products of particular institutional variations. As Kochan, Katz, and McKersie (1986) have argued in setting up their strategic choice model, firms and unions do have decision-making discretion (whether broad or narrow), and the choices they make do matter. And last but not least, under certain historical circumstances, actors can and do change institutions (a point I return to in the final section).

The question of choice properly brings up the limits of the present argument. In an effort to account for widely varying contemporary cross-national outcomes for industrial relations and for unions, I have weeded out from among the myriad of possible explanations a small number of institutional variables that together appear to offer the best predictive power for the past decade. This argument cannot, however, account for decisions made within national ranges of choice. Nor can this model predict the outcomes of political battles (especially in crisis circumstances) over institutional change, which in turn could lead to different outcomes. In the attempt at parsimonious explanation, I have crafted this argument in as determinist a way as possible; the extent to which it (and the real world) falls short of determinism is the extent to which the predictive powers of this model are limited.

The Literature Reconsidered

Since the 1920s, the politics of work reorganization has been studied by industrial relations analysts in the United States under the general heading "unions and technological change." Traditional studies have examined specific instances of technological change within a narrow framework, looking for various forms of union resistance or accommodation. Typically, such U.S.-based analyses have used a typology of union strategies toward technological change first developed by George Barnett in the 1920s (Barnett 1926), adapted by Sumner Slichter in the 1940s, and further systematized by Slichter, Healy, and Livernash (1960). This typology includes five categories of union response: encouragement, willing acceptance, adjustment, competition, and opposition. In addition, a substantial number of explanatory variables are suggested as clues for why one response is chosen as opposed to another (Slichter, Healy, and Livernash 1960, pp. 342–71).

In the most recent major study using the Barnett/Slichter typology and framework, Doris McLaughlin (1979) develops a long list of variables that influence union strategies toward technological change. She lists the variables in order of importance (the seven most important, the five next most important, and so on) but gives no theoretical framework to organize the causal analysis, to show how combinations of variables may act, or to demonstrate sufficient conditions leading to specific outcomes.

Research using this framework typically finds that unions generally accept or adjust to change; infrequent opposition is usually followed quickly by adjustment as the terms of change are negotiated. Patterns of industrial relations change very little, and productivity outcomes are generally favorable because union presence forces managers to plan technological change and incremental work reorganization carefully and rationally. Specific findings include, for example, the empirical observation that industrial unions are more accepting of technological change than craft unions.

Although this may have been an adequate framework for understanding industrial relations and technological change in the United States in an earlier period (in spite of theoretical limitations), the world has changed. The traditional model implicitly assumed steady economic growth, U.S. industrial strength in the world economy, incremental technological change along with markets that appear static in comparison to those of today, and stable patterns of industrial relations. These assumptions have collapsed; the critical questions today no longer center around union acceptance of new technology (unions have little choice in this regard, if they ever had) but rather the stability of industrial relations, the persistence of union strength, and the prospects for union influence regarding new technology and work organization (Streeck 1985b; Raskin 1986; Marshall 1987).

Two recent important works on changing industrial relations and work organization in the United States, by Katz (1985) and Kochan, Katz, and McKersie (1986), do not use the above framework but rather begin with critiques of the traditional static "subsystem" view of industrial relations (from Dunlop 1958). In the previous section, I referred to the strategic choice model of these theorists from the perspective of the findings and analysis of the present study. In setting up the strategic choice framework, Kochan, Katz, and McKersie provide an accurate portrayal of the fate of unionism in the United States, carefully analyzing the growth of managerial opposition, the rise of nonunionism, and the spread of new participatory programs and cooperative relations in firms that remain unionized. The authors provide rich empirical description as well as a useful conceptual map of the many factors that combine to shape contemporary industrial relations outcomes.

But like any major new contribution, the framework has limitations. First, there are too many variables, and too little theoretical coherence is provided to sort out the relative importance of the variables (Kochan, Katz, and McKersie 1986, p. 11). Second, managerial values, especially for avoiding or opposing unions, are given great weight in the analysis, but the values are taken as given rather than linked to the political opportunity for their expression. And finally, perhaps because the framework is U.S.-specific, it contains little about the place of organized labor or management in society, the organizational cohesiveness of the labor movement, or the structure of the political economy. But comparative analysis does make readily apparent the key role these political and structural attributes, which vary considerably from country to country, play in defining the range of strategic choice.

A substantial number of recent studies have emphasized managerial opposition and anti-union values in constructing explanations for the decline of the labor movement in the United States (Freeman and Medoff 1984; Dickens and Leonard 1985; Kochan, Katz, and McKersie 1986; Goldfield 1987). There is an "American exceptionalist" flavor to these perspectives, in which the depth of managerial anti-unionism appears unrivaled elsewhere. But as was demonstrated in Chapter 5, unions have also declined in influence in Britain and Italy since 1980 in the face of heavy anti-union campaigns by employers. Perhaps managerial values in the United States are not so distinct after all; when changing market circumstances make challenges to union influence possible, managers in other countries as well, in the absence of particular constraints (such as the integration of unions into firms' decision making, law, and the cohesiveness of the labor movement), have waged successful anti-union campaigns. Only where management is institutionally constrained, as in

Germany and Sweden, have the outcomes been different. Contemporary
theorists are thus correct to point to managerial opposition as central to
an explanation for declining union fortunes; but the timing and success
of such opposition can be fully understood only in a broader institutional
and comparative context.[4]

A great virtue of the literature on democratic corporatism has been that
it looks broadly at the position of labor and business in different political
economies (Schmitter 1974; Wilensky 1976; Katzenstein 1985). Much has
been written about the strengths and weaknesses of this literature. For
purposes of the present analysis, of greatest importance is the conceptual
breakthrough represented by the link between structures of political economy and the behavior of actors within those structures on one hand and
specific industrial and political outcomes on the other. By insisting on
such links, the corporatist framework adds a new dimension to comparative
analysis that moves beyond the insights of neoclassical economists, traditional industrial relations institutionalists, and more recent strategic
choice theorists. The perception that economic and political institutions
vary greatly across advanced industrial societies and that these differences
matter a great deal for specific economic and political outcomes should
be the starting point for contemporary analyses of comparative industrial
relations (see Lange, Ross, and Vannicelli 1982; Bamber and Lansbury
1983; Gourevitch et al. 1984; Swenson 1989).

Although the present study has not focused either on the tripartite peak
bargains or the pluralist fragmentation that most characterize the perspective of the literature on democratic corporatism, the findings do provide a lens through which to assess certain claims of the literature. Most
important, the evidence presented in Chapters 1 through 5 indicates that
there are predominant national patterns for the stability and extent of
workers' interest representation. As the corporatist literature would predict, these contrasting cross-national outcomes are linked not to specific
market or industry characteristics but to attributes of the broader political
economy. Much of the original "corporatist league" has shifted focus to
sectoral-level studies of "meso-corporatism," arguing that organized capitalism can best be understood at this level rather than at the national level
(Cawson 1985; Schmitter 1988). Although I agree that issues such as
industrial restructuring, work reorganization, and industrial relations must
be studied at the sectoral level, my findings nonetheless indicate that at

[4] This perspective is consistent with that advanced by Lloyd Ulman (1987), who argues
against considerable dissenting opinion that what is distinctive about managers in the United
States is not their values but the constraints, or rather absence of constraints, that they have
historically faced.

least in these areas national patterns and broad cross-national differences continue to demonstrate overriding significance.

As Pontusson has argued, we need linkages between micro and macro levels of analysis, between the micro and macro politics of industrial restructuring (Pontusson 1990). The variables tested in the preceding analysis provide precisely such a linkage: union integration into firms' decision making is a micro-level variable; law, corporatist bargaining, and labor movement cohesiveness are macro-level variables. The latter are well-established concerns of the literature on democratic corporatism, but union integration into firms' decision making represents a downward extension, which I would argue is consistent with the general framework of that literature.

Perhaps the most useful contribution to the contemporary study of comparative industrial relations is that of a "neo-corporatist," Wolfgang Streeck. In a wide-ranging series of studies, Streeck explores the connections between market changes, institutional structures, work reorganization, union and managerial strategies, and industrial relations processes and outcomes. Streeck argues, for example, that external labor market rigidities imposed by unions in West Germany (at central collective bargaining levels and in the unions' entrenched bases in the works councils) have forced firms to keep and retrain workers, use labor flexibly, and move upmarket into "diversified, quality, high-volume production" (Streeck 1985a; Sorge and Streeck 1988). Competitive success resulting from complementary product-market and internal labor-market strategies has further consolidated the position of unions and works councils.

Streeck's work is perhaps most useful for the close examination of the shape and consequences of national institutions (especially the position of organized labor) for production and industrial relations outcomes (Streeck 1984a, 1987b). Streeck's arguments, especially his emphasis on the role of strong, engaged unions in West Germany contrasted to the fate of unions elsewhere, are generally confirmed by the comparative evidence gathered for this study (in opposition to the "decline of the unions" theorists within Germany). What is missing in Streeck's work is systematic cross-national comparison to sort out the key variables and move toward more widely applicable explanation.

But such explanation must be carefully constructed and differentiated to allow for contrasting cross-national outcomes. The contemporary literature on comparative political economy (which includes but is by no means limited to the literature on democratic corporatism) helps clarify the continuing importance of national institutions and politics, along with the limitations of general explanations for widespread phenomena such as union decline.[5] In Chapter 3, I considered several such general explanations and found them wanting, given the evidence produced in the U.S. and West German auto industry case studies. Now that other sectors as well as evidence from several additional countries have been examined, the explanatory power of broad general explanations alone in accounting for industrial relations outcomes appears even more limited. Pervasive economic, political, and social trends present throughout the advanced industrial world cannot account for the consistent patterns of cross-national variation apparent in the evidence presented here.

In the comparative literature, the innovative work of Piore and Sabel has been important in analyzing major changes in world markets and the driving influence of these changes on firms' strategies, organization of production and industrial relations; and they have stressed the importance of plant-level research to uncover the processes and politics of change (Sabel 1982; Piore and Sabel 1984). My research has confirmed the critical importance of both of these emphases, at least for understanding the politics of work reorganization and changing industrial relations.

Piore and Sabel's model combines both a potential general convergence toward flexible specialization as a production model and decentralized industrial relations with a set of plant- and firm-level outcomes rooted in corporate histories and local political and economic particularities. These local dynamics are clearly important for understanding the specifics of individual plants and regions, and there is always variation both within and across sectors in any given country. But the evidence and analysis presented here demonstrate that there are persistent national patterns that remain essential for the explanation of contemporary industrial relations outcomes; cross-national divergence remains important. The variations within a country help to explain cross-national contrasts and can best be understood within a national, rather than a converging international, framework.[6]

The comparative arguments for contrasting union outcomes offer a variety of different perspectives. Wallerstein (1989), for example, argues that cross-national differences in union membership density can be ac-

---

[5] For a sampling of some of the best of this literature as it has developed, see Katzenstein 1978; Berger 1981; and Goldthorpe 1984a.

[6] Piore and Sabel, of course, do not ignore the role of national institutions. In their model, contrasting patterns of labor-management relations (or patterns of shop-floor control) are understood with reference to the technological paradigm, national regulatory institutions, and particularities of corporate histories (Piore and Sabel 1984, pp. 111–12). Although this approach is theoretically somewhat loose, it is nonetheless richly suggestive of the causal connections between changes in national politics, production organization, and industrial relations outcomes.

counted for in large part by the size of a country and by the cumulative history of left-party governance. Wallerstein's study is interesting, especially over the long run, but it does not help us very much here. Neither West Germany nor Britain, for example, changed appreciably in size in the 1980s, and both had conservative governments; yet dynamic changes were under way, with contrasting union outcomes in the auto industries of the two countries as well as in societywide patterns of industrial relations, including union density. The assumptions governing Wallerstein's analysis, based on the logic of wage bargaining, may have lost their robust quality in the contemporary period of intense work reorganization; contrasting outcomes for unions in the 1980s can be explained by reference neither to size nor to party governance.

Freeman uses regression analysis to argue that "the institutions that govern labor relations rather than broad-based economic forces determine the changing cross-country pattern of unionism" (Freeman 1989, p. 120). In this view, managerial opposition is the reason for union decline in the United States; but when such opposition is muted by the centralized wage bargaining of corporatist industrial relations (as in Scandinavia), union density increases. These findings are generally consistent with the evidence produced here, provided one recognizes the essentially "corporatist" nature of West German industrial relations.

I have now examined the argument, tested it against the evidence produced, and considered the claims of other analyses in light of the facts and interpretations presented here. Although the argument could not be expected to apply to every sector in every advanced industrial society (there are special circumstances that fall outside the bounds of any attempt at theoretical explanation), it should apply as a general rule, if the analysis is correct. Further testing would look at the politics of work reorganization and the stability and extent of workers' interest representation in additional sectors and countries. Sectoral studies in Norway and Austria, for example, with cohesive labor movements, increasing union integration into managerial decision-making processes, and strong, stable representation of workers' interests would be expected to confirm the present argument (in a way similar to Sweden and West Germany for industrial relations outcomes). France, with a fragmented labor movement, adversarial tradition, and unions in decline, would also be expected to confirm (in a way similar to the Italian case).

Canada presents a problem for this analysis. The fragmented labor movement and adversarial tradition would suggest that unions in Canada should be experiencing declining influence as the pace of work reorganization accelerates. But at least in membership, Canadian unions have done considerably better than unions in the United States in the past fifteen years.[7] Future studies of the politics of work reorganization in Canada should clarify whether it is a question of timing, and as pressure for work reorganization escalates, Canadian industrial relations may become increasingly unstable, with declining union influence; there are legal and political differences that are critical (labor legislation; perhaps a de facto cohesiveness in the labor movement, through Canadian nationalism vis à vis the United States and ties to the New Democratic party); or the present argument is flawed or at least in need of modification.

Implications and Prospects for Institutional Change

Except in Japan, where managerial hegemony is firmly entrenched in a system of enterprise unionism, employers have two options if they seek successful work reorganization in the contemporary period: to challenge, weaken, marginalize, avoid, or exclude union influence, or to work with and incorporate unions in processes of managerial decision making.[8] Managers constrained by some form of codetermination backed by law and by the political and economic strength of cohesive labor movements, as in West Germany and Sweden, have increasingly pursued the latter option. Managers who are not so constrained, as in the United States, Britain, and Italy, appear to have chosen the former option (although the latter exists here and there as well). It is by now an old observation that managers in the United States (and elsewhere) do not want to give up the right to make unilateral decisions (Bendix 1956). Managerial opposition has been a proximate cause (if not a sufficient condition) for union decline in countries with adversarial traditions and fragmented labor movements; the decline in union density in these countries is one indicator that such opposition has been successful to a significant degree.

What seems clear is that the old unrevised adversarial, arm's-length tradition does not work in market conditions that demand major work reorganization and new commitment and participation from workers. The great advantage of engaged unions for employers is that management has a powerful ally to help facilitate technological and organizational change. Where this is not the case, including nonunionism in the United States

[7] A considerable body of literature attempts to explain the U.S.-Canadian contrast in cultural, historical, legal, and political terms (Huxley, Kettler, and Struthers 1986; Lipset 1986b; Adams 1989).
[8] They may pursue both strategies in different parts of the same country, industry, or firm.

and the (temporarily?) weakened union position in the British and Italian auto industries, industrial relations may be unstable in the long run. Persistent authoritarian practices by management undermine the trust necessary for new levels of commitment on the part of workers, a highly sought-after attribute conducive both to the successful implementation of advanced technology and the high productivity, product quality, and flexibility required to compete successfully in today's markets. For this reason, managers who have avoided or attacked unions have also introduced new programs for work-force participation and, where unions remain present, new union-management cooperation.

But one cannot have it both ways. Combined adversarial and cooperative approaches from the same management breed plant-level stalemate and unstable industrial relations, as occurred in the U.S. auto industry at Hamtramck and Van Nuys, in the U.S. telephone services industry at AT&T and Pacific Bell, and in the British and Italian auto industries. West German engagement, by contrast, offers both successful and ongoing work reorganization and stable industrial relations. Policy implications of this analysis for management are that it is now possible and perhaps imperative to move beyond stalemate at the plant level, not to defeat or marginalize the union but to incorporate it, not to use new technologies and market-based bargaining strength to subdue and control workers but to draw out their participation, not to offer up merely the trappings of humanization but to move decisively away from the authoritarian managerial tradition.

For unions, the push toward some form of codetermination, at least in questions of technological change and work reorganization, is increasingly on the agenda. As Katz and Sabel (1985) have argued, unions may need to trade off rights to enforce uniform working conditions and work rules in return for new decision-making rights. If subordinate unionism can be avoided, the trade-off is worth it, as was demonstrated by the comparative strength of West German unions in the 1980s. But avoiding subordination, even given an appropriate legal framework to regulate participation, is the tricky part; the best insurance may be a cohesive labor movement, but this is very difficult to build (note the failed Italian attempt) where one does not exist. Nonetheless, institutions can change. The transformation of the Italian Communist party in the direction of democratic socialism may lay the groundwork for new unity on the left in Italy along with new possibilities for labor cohesiveness. As another example, the continuing centralized strength of the UAW, reflected in national collective bargaining, makes increasing collaboration with other unions possible, especially in the current crisis period for unions in the United States. Such collaboration could bring with it both concerted campaigns for new participation rights (building on current jointness and other cooperative and participatory programs; promoting legislation to formalize and extend new rights to participation) as well as more vigorous efforts by unions to promote new concepts of work organization (building, for example, on relevant UAW resolutions adopted at conventions in 1987 and 1989).

If unions face the prospect (and to some degree the choice) of exclusion or integration, the latter is certainly preferable. But there are very different ways in which labor can be integrated. One way, enterprise unionism, means the subordination of union influence and also appears to mean intense pressure on the shop floor to work faster and harder; the other way, based on independent unionism, means a new and broader scope for workers' representation at the plant level. The critical problem for unions in countries with fragmented labor movements (such as the United States, Britain, France, and Italy) is that the second way has so far emerged as a general pattern only in countries with more cohesive labor movements. Unionists in the United States, Britain, France, and Italy, therefore, are right to have reservations about new cooperation proposed by firms—but if enterprise unionism threatens as an outcome, the empirical alternative to greater integration so far appears to be continued decline and exclusion.

Union leaders in the present period, therefore, must be ready to brave internal political obstacles, in the interest of organizational survival, to move toward a closer engagement with management. If unions can do this and at the same time make their labor movements more cohesive, perhaps through national labor campaigns for "new industrial relations" and strategies for union-promoted work reorganization, then union decline may well prove reversible even where it now appears most entrenched. The fundamentally new circumstance facing unions appears to be that in the current era of intense international competition and widespread work reorganization, unions, in the interest of their own survival, are called on to make a positive contribution, not just a passive one, to firms' performance in such areas as productivity, product quality, and process flexibility. This is the substantive meaning, in current world markets, of integration into managerial decision making.

Policy implications of this analysis for unions are to continue to push management for more say in decision making; to collaborate actively with productivity-enhancing work reorganization, while at the same time promoting an independent and viable vision of the shape of new work organization that includes a substantial commitment to union and worker participation; to promote interplant and intraunion communication and coordination of strategy to keep current changes from further fragmenting labor and as a way to increase pressure on management to live up to the human promises of reorganization; to build new organizing campaigns not only on the basis of a challenge to adversarial management but on the basis of the above positive humanization-cooperation themes; and to work actively within national labor federations both for a more cohesive labor movement and to promote new legislation to institutionalize union integration and engagement efforts at the firm level. In the present period, it appears that unions must either participate in managerial decision making or continue to decline in influence (to end up as the representative of a small, entrenched core work force or die out altogether). This turns the traditional union logic on its head; that logic claimed that if unions did get drawn into managerial decision making, they would lose independence, lose credibility with the rank and file, and decline in numbers and influence. Several unions in the United States today, including the UAW and CWA, are actively pursuing efforts aimed at expanding participation.[9]

For government policy, there are also implications, depending on the commitment of governing political coalitions to successful industrial adjustment or the preservation of independent labor unions. Although it has not been proven in this study, stable industrial relations settlements that include integrated unions (as, in different ways, in Japan and Germany) appear conducive to successful industrial restructuring and the reorganization of work (Marshall 1987). There is clearly a public interest in industrial competitiveness in contemporary world markets, one that governments can and do reflect in more or less systematic ways. Even in the most noninterventionist political climates, governments could do more to spread education about work reorganization and labor-management cooperation into managerial and union ranks (building, for example, in the United States on the efforts of the Bureau of Labor-Management Cooperation at the Department of Labor). Short of full-blown industrial policies, governments could promote active tripartite discussions at national and sectoral levels. National, state, and local governments could continue to expand funding and incentives for training and retraining, including intrafirm training for work reorganization, and could expand the safety net

---

[9] Here we are dealing in the realm of realistic policy alternatives for national and local labor unions and federations under current circumstances. The resurgence of union influence has in the past, however, often been linked to other social movements (in "cycles of protest"; Tarrow 1990) or workers' mobilization that began outside established union frameworks (as in the United States in the 1930s and in Italy in 1969). In unpredictable periods of crisis or social upheaval in the future, therefore, declining unions could find new life. My argument in this regard is that new union influence would most likely be unstable unless unions use their leverage to expand influence into management decision-making processes and to formalize these relations in law.

for displaced workers (most usefully to include guaranteed retraining). National governments could develop, adopt, and implement legislation and policies to encourage and regulate union and worker participation in management decision making.[10] Finally, and most controversial perhaps, governments could use their own incentives and influence to promote more cohesive labor movements, to turn the tide against union decline and begin to rebuild a countervailing force against management's reluctance to turn decisively away from an increasingly inappropriate authoritarianism in the modern workplace.

Just as the study of interest groups is at the core of the field of political science (Berger 1981, p. 2), the "mode of interest representation" and the relative power relations among contending interest groups are matters of deepest concern to modern democratic governments. The extent of union integration in managerial decision making, legal and political frameworks, and labor movement cohesiveness are aspects of the mode of interest representation. One way to express the findings of this study is therefore to say that the mode of interest representation itself accounts for contrasting union fortunes in the 1980s, or more precisely, variations in the stability and extent of workers' interest representation. Some modes of interest representation are more appropriate than others for contemporary circumstances.

Where the forms of interest representation are inappropriate, that is, where arm's-length relations, weak legal and political frameworks for participation, and fragmentation within the labor movement persist, governments have a choice: to remain neutral and thereby allow the continuing decline of unions; to encourage employers in their challenges to union influence (while secondarily supporting new forms of industrial relations); or to promote reform in industrial relations to bring the mode of interest representation in line with contemporary needs, encouraging both a new stability in industrial relations and a halt to the sliding fortunes of unions. In the United States and Britain in the 1980s, governments arguably adopted the second strategy to encourage employers in their challenges to unions (e.g., Reagan's firing of the PATCO workers; Thatcher's labor legislation). An alternative and viable strategy would be the third one: to

---

[10] The European Community is currently discussing, as part of its Social Charter debate, directives to encourage worker-union information, consultation, and participation rights throughout Western Europe. Unions tend to favor participation rights "with teeth," while employers favor more watered-down versions. Outcomes of the debate remain uncertain. It is beyond the scope of this study to spell out possible legislation or policy for any given country (the United States included); in every case such initiatives would have to be adapted to particular national, political, and institutional circumstances.

promote industrial relations reform in the interest of both successful industrial adjustment and a reversal of union decline.

The continuing decline of unions should be neither a matter of indifference for governments nor a desirable policy outcome. The pursuit of stable industrial relations and industrial restructuring arguably makes the case for positive, as opposed to anti-union, industrial relations reform. But quite apart from those questions, although not unrelated, are issues of industrial and political democracy.

In the industrial arena, unions have attempted to resolve what T. H. Marshall called the "war" between citizenship and class by the extension of citizenship rights into the workplace (Marshall 1950; Goldthorpe 1984b, pp. 320–21). But recurrent shop-floor conflict over the extent of managerial authority has led to recurrent and often counterproductive labor-management tension and low worker morale. The integration of unions into management decision making combined with the spread of substantive worker participation offers a way to redirect the tension in a more constructive direction, raise employee morale, and at the same time further extend citizenship rights in the workplace. In the absence of countervailing unions, it is difficult to see what force might stand in the way of a future reversion to traditional authoritarian management ways.[11]

In the broader political arena, unions have played a prominent role in the development of democracy, from the efforts of early British unions to extend voting rights in the nineteenth century to the Solidarity-led transformation of Polish political institutions in the contemporary period. Through their ties to political parties, unions have broadened the aggregation of interests, bringing political participation and representation to many who would otherwise have no realistic channels (Bok and Dunlop 1970; Greenstone 1977).[12] To the extent that unions decline in numbers and influence, their integrative political function is weakened; again it is difficult to see where large numbers of rank-and-file employees in manufacturing and service industries alike would find new, direct channels for interest group representation.

In the end, then, union decline is not just an industrial or economic issue but a political issue as well. If union decline has undesirable ram-

---

[11] This is true even for the most enlightened managements in firms with participatory cultures. As one executive of a large nonunion telecommunications firm in the United States put it in an interview: "We keep the union out by treating our people decently and fairly."

[12] In this regard, the contemporary relations between unions and parties, and the effects of changing union fortunes in the workplace on broader political representation, are important subjects for future research.

ifications for broader political representation, public policy can and should help reverse the process through the politics of institutional reform.

Based on the findings in this study, I am arguing both for unions that are integrated into managerial decision making and for more cohesive labor movements. Somewhat paradoxically, therefore, I am arguing at once for stronger unions and for more collaborationist unions; this is what contemporary world markets appear to demand if unions are to continue playing an important economic, social, and political role.

But what are the prospects for institutional reform? This is a critical yet uncertain question, a fitting one on which to conclude this study. In Britain, for example, Labour government attempts from 1964 to 1970 and 1974 to 1979 to promote state-led economic growth on the French model or bargained growth on the Swedish model floundered because the established institutions were inappropriate (Zysman 1983, pp. 171–232; Regini 1984). Is it realistic to suppose that industrial relations institutions can be reformed, to promote at once successful industrial restructuring, stable industrial relations, and renewed union influence (where unions are in decline)? Or is this a study of comparative union success and decline that for many will have an unhappy ending?

With the reader, I can only speculate on these questions. Institutions are products of history, shaped either gradually or at critical junctures in periods of crisis and reconsolidation. As such, they defy easy transformation; an argument rooted in institutional structures, therefore, may appear as a determinist construct that does not allow for change in the foreseeable future. I have in fact structured the analysis in as determinist a way as possible to comprehend how things reached this point. Nonetheless, institutions can and do change. They change as a result of crisis, learning, incremental change, politics, and the coalitions and choices of actors, whose decisions are constrained but not fully determined by the institutional contexts in which they operate. At certain points in history, institutions can change suddenly and in surprising ways. The events in Eastern Europe since 1989 have at the very least taught us this lesson, shaking us vigorously from our institution-bound complacency.

Especially at times of historical crisis, institutions can be transformed. Such a crisis may be approaching for industrial relations in many advanced societies. As new models of work organization and labor-management relations are tried out at plant and firm levels, elements of institutional reform could be developing.[13] And as new political coalitions take shape,

[13] For a stimulating discussion of the transformation of industrial relations in Italy and elsewhere, from a perspective that differs on certain points from this one, see Locke 1990a.

the prospects for legislation to broaden and entrench the reforms may grow.

In the United States, for example, there is active experimentation with new participatory programs within the union sector. Adrienne Eaton and Paula Voos (1991) have studied the entire range of these programs, which they argue are probably on the road to institutionalization; the prospects, in other words, for a new union role in processes of innovation and managerial decision making may be promising. Whether such new roles could become encouraged and regulated by law and could contribute to a reversal of union decline remains problematic, the outcome of future political struggles.

In Germany as well, incremental change is pushing industrial relations in new directions. We have looked closely at growing union engagement in work organization decisions in the West German auto industry; and from a comparative perspective the German industrial relations model has been celebrated in this study. But there are problems as well. Critics have pointed out the process of social exclusion in the "two-thirds society," in which many (especially foreign workers, women, and the unskilled) are excluded from the favorable employment relationship that includes works councils and integrated unions. Exclusion may breed new instability, a problematic that increased with the massive migration from East to West in 1989–90 and the coming of open labor markets in the East. Incremental change may well become more dramatic as the institutions of the Federal Republic spread to East Germany in the process of German unification. While the institutions of industrial relations in the East are clearly at a historically "critical juncture," the heretofore stable institutions of West Germany (now united Germany) will also creak under the strain in unpredictable ways.[14]

For the European countries looked at in this study, the coming single European market adds another dimension of considerable uncertainty. In this business and government-led drive for far-reaching national deregulation (Sandholtz and Zysman 1989), labor has been pulled along and has so far fought, without great success, rear-guard actions to protect workers' and union rights on the "social dimension." The subject of European-

---

[14] As German unification proceeds, the transformation of political and industrial relations institutions in the East as well as the effects of unification on West German institutions will afford an exciting opportunity for researchers in the coming years, one that may shed new light on our ideas of institution building and transformation. Although the outcome will undoubtedly be the expansion of West German institutions, including unions, works councils, and industrial relations practices, into the East, the actual functioning of these institutions in the new environment is arguably contingent.

wide regulations for worker and union participation in managerial decision making, in particular, is hotly contested within the institutions of the European Community. The outcome in the years ahead of this and related political debates will have a considerable bearing on future union influence and the prospects for institutional reform at the national level, as well as on union influence and possible new institutional forms (such as multi-national bargaining) at the European level.

Although institutions in advanced societies are entrenched and resistant to pressures for reform, they and the people in them can and do change. This is what makes the study of comparative political economy and industrial relations interesting.

References

Abernathy, William J., Kim B. Clark, and Alan M. Kantrow. 1983. *Industrial Renaissance: Producing a Competitive Future for America*. New York: Basic Books.

Adam Opel AG. Annual Reports. Various issues.

Adams, Roy J. 1989. "North American Industrial Relations: Divergent Trends in Canada and the United States." *International Labour Review* 128: 47–64.

Adams, Roy J., and C. H. Rummel 1977. "Workers' Participation in Management in West Germany: Impact on the Worker, the Enterprise, and the Trade Union: A Research Report." *Industrial Relations Journal* 8 (Spring): 4–22.

AFL-CIO Committee on the Evolution of Work. 1983. *The Future of Work*. August.

———. 1985. *The Changing Situation of Workers and Their Unions*. February.

AFL-CIO News. Various issues.

Aggarwal, Vinod K. 1985. *Liberal Protectionism: The International Politics of the Organized Textile Trade*. Berkeley: University of California Press.

Ahlen, Kristina. 1989. "Swedish Collective Bargaining under Pressure: Inter-Union Rivalry and Incomes Policies." *British Journal of Industrial Relations* 27 (November): 330–46.

Almond, Gabriel A. 1983. "Corporatism, Pluralism, and Professional Memory." *World Politics* 35 (January): 245–60.

Altmann, Norbert. 1987. "New Technologies, Design of Work and the Unions in the Federal Republic of Germany." Manuscript, Institut für sozialwissenschaftliche Forschung, Munich.

Altmann, Norbert, and Klaus Düll. 1990. "Rationalization and Participation: Implementation of New Technologies and Problems of the Works Councils in the FRG." *Economic and Industrial Democracy* 11 (February): 111–27.

Altshuler, Alan, Martin Anderson, Daniel Jones, Daniel Roos, and James Womack. 1984. *The Future of the Automobile*. Report of MIT's International Automobile Program. Cambridge: MIT Press.

Apitzsch, Wolfgang, Thomas Klebe, and Manfred Schumann, eds. 1988. *BetrVG '90: Der Konflikt um eine andere Betriebsverfassung*. Cologne: Bund-Verlag.

245

Armer, Michael, and Allen D. Grimshaw, eds. 1973. *Comparative Social Research: Methodological Problems and Strategies.* New York: John Wiley.

Aronowitz, Stanley. 1973. *False Promises: The Shaping of American Working Class Consciousness.* New York: McGraw-Hill.

——. 1983. *Working Class Hero: A New Strategy for Labor.* New York: Pilgrim Press.

AT&T Annual Reports. Various issues.

Atkinson, Michael M., and William D. Coleman. 1985. "Corporatism and Industrial Policy." In Alan Cawson, ed., 1985, pp. 22–44.

Atzert, Lutz. 1987. "Die Automobildatenbank: Betriebsdaten und Länderdaten." IIVG paper dp87–221, Wissenschaftszentrum Berlin.

Auer, Peter. 1985. "Industrial Relations, Work Organisation and New Technology: The Volvo case." Discussion paper, IIM/LMP 85–10, Wissenschaftszentrum Berlin.

Auer, Peter, and Claudius H. Riegler. 1988. *Gruppenarbeit bei Volvo: Aktuelle Tendenzen and Hintergründe.* Stockholm: Arbetsmiljöfonden and Wissenschaftszentrum Berlin.

Automotive Industries. Monthly. Various issues, 1983–89.

Automotive News. Weekly. Various issues, 1983–89.

Baglioni, Guido, and Colin Crouch, eds. 1990. *European Industrial Relations: The Challenge of Flexibility.* London: Sage.

Bamber, Greg J., and Russell D. Lansbury. 1983. "A Comparative Perspective on Technological Change and Industrial Relations." *Proceedings of the 36th Conference of the Industrial Relations Research Association.* Madison, Wisc.: IRRA, pp. 92–99.

——, eds. 1987. *International and Comparative Industrial Relations: A Study of Developed Market Economies.* London: Unwin Hyman.

Bamber, Greg, and Ed Snape. 1987. "British Industrial Relations." In Bamber and Lansbury, eds. 1987, pp. 33–56.

Banks, Andy, and Jack Metzgar. 1989. "Participating in Management: Union Organizing on a New Terrain." *Labor Research Review* 14, vol. 8, no. 2, (Fall): 1–55.

Barbash, Jack. 1967. "Technology and Labor in the Twentieth Century." In Kranzberg and Pursell, eds., 1967, pp. 64–76.

Barbash, Jack, and Kate Barbash, eds. 1989. *Theories and Concepts in Comparative Industrial Relations.* Columbia: University of South Carolina Press.

Barkin, Solomon, ed. 1983. *Worker Militancy and its Consequences: The Changing Climate of Western Industrial Relations*, 2d ed. New York: Praeger.

Barnett, George E. 1969 (first published 1926). *Chapters on Machinery and Labor.* Carbondale: Southern Illinois University Press.

Batstone, Eric. 1988. *The Reform of Workplace Industrial Relations: Theory, Myth and Evidence.* Oxford: Clarendon Press.

Batten, Dick, and Sara Schoonmaker. 1987. "Deregulation, Technological Change, and Labor Relations in Telecommunications." In Cornfield, ed., 1987, pp. 311–30.

Bean, Ron. 1985. *Comparative Industrial Relations: An Introduction to Cross-National Perspectives.* New York: St. Martin's Press.

Bendix, Reinhard. 1956. *Work and Authority in Industry.* Berkeley: University of California Press.

——. 1964. *Nation-Building and Citizenship.* Berkeley: University of California Press.

Berger, Suzanne, ed. 1981. *Organizing Interests in Western Europe.* Cambridge: Cambridge University Press.

Berggren, Christian. 1988. " 'New Production Concepts' in Final Assembly— The Swedish Experiences." In Dankbaar, Jürgens, and Malsch eds., 1988, pp. 133–66.

Berghahn, Volker R., and Detlev Karsten. 1987. *Industrial Relations in West Germany.* Oxford: Berg.

Bergmann, Joachim, and Walter Müller-Jentsch. 1983. "The Federal Republic of Germany: Cooperative Unionism and Dual Bargaining System Challenged." In Barkin, ed., 1983, pp. 229–77.

Berry, Bryan H. 1986. "State-of-the-Art Automaking: GM's Detroit/Hamtramck Plant." *Iron Age*, February 21, pp. 25–30.

Bok, Derek C., and John T. Dunlop. 1970. *Labor and the American Community.* New York: Simon and Schuster.

Bornstein, Stephen, and Peter Gourevitch. 1984. "Unions in a Declining Economy: The Case of the British TUC." In Gourevitch et al., 1984, pp. 13–88.

Borrus, Michael, François Bar, and Ibrahim Warde. 1984. "The Impacts of Divestiture and Deregulation: Infrastructural Changes, Manufacturing Transition, and Competition in the United States Telecommunications Industry." BRIE Working Paper 12, Berkeley Roundtable on the International Economy, University of California.

Borrus, Michael, and John Zysman. 1984. "The New Media, Telecommunications, and Development: The Choices for the United States and Japan." BRIE Working Paper 7, Berkeley Roundtable on the International Economy, University of California.

Brandini, Pietro Merli. 1983. "Italy: A New Industrial Relations System Moving from Accommodation to Edge of Confrontation." In Barkin, ed., 1983, pp. 81–110.

Brody, David. 1980. *Workers in Industrial America: Essays on the 20th Century Struggle.* New York: Oxford University Press.

Brooks, Thomas R. 1977. *Communication Workers of America: The Story of a Union.* New York: Mason/Charter.

Brown, Clair, and Michael Reich. 1989. "When Does Union-Management Cooperation Work? A Look at NUMMI and GM-Van Nuys." *California Management Review* 31, no. 4, pp. 26–44.

Brumlop, Eva. 1986. *Arbeitsbewertung bei flexiblem Personaleinsatz: Das Beispiel Volkswagen.* Frankfurt/Main: Campus Verlag.

Brumlop, Eva, and Ulrich Jürgens. 1986. "Rationalisation and Industrial Relations: A Case Study of Volkswagen." In Jacobi et al., eds., 1986, pp. 73–94.

Burawoy, Michael. 1979. *Manufacturing Consent: Changes in the Labor Process under Monopoly Capitalism.* Chicago: University of Chicago Press.

——. 1985. *The Politics of Production: Factory Regimes under Capitalism and Socialism.* London: Verso (New Left Books).

Bureau of National Affairs. 1985. *Unions Today: New Tactics to Tackle Tough Times.* Washington, D.C.: BNA.

Business Week. Various issues.

Byrkjeflot, Haldor. 1989. *From Telephone Operators to "Work Station Professionals"? Technological Change, Markets, and Dilemmas of Control in the United States Telecommunications Industry.* Bergen, Norway: AHS.

Cameron, David R. 1984. "Social Democracy, Corporatism, Labour Quiescence, and the Representation of Economic Interest in Advanced Capitalist Society." In Goldthorpe, ed., 1984a, pp. 143–78.

Cawson, Alan, ed. 1985. *Organized Interests and the State: Studies in Meso-Corporatism.* London: Sage.

Chinoy, Ely. 1955. *Automobile Workers and the American Dream.* Boston: Beacon Press.

Chrysler Corporation Report to Shareholders. Various years.

Cohen, Stephen S., and John Zysman. 1987. *Manufacturing Matters: The Myth of the Post-Industrial Economy.* New York: Basic Books.

Cole, Robert E. 1989. *Strategies for Learning: Small-Group Activities in American, Japanese, and Swedish Industry.* Berkeley: University of California Press.

Commons, John R. 1934. *Institutional Economics: Its Place in Political Economy.* New York: Macmillan.

Consumer Reports. Various issues, 1980–1990.

Contini, Giovanni. 1986. "Politics, Law and Shop Floor Bargaining in Postwar Italy." In Tolliday and Zeitlin, eds., 1986, pp. 192–218.

Cornfield, Daniel B., ed. 1987. *Workers, Managers, and Technological Change: Emerging Patterns of Labor Relations.* New York: Plenum Press.

Crouch, Colin, ed. 1979. *State and Economy in Contemporary Capitalism.* New York: St. Martin's Press.

Crouch, Colin. 1990. "United Kingdom: The Rejection of Compromise." In Baglioni and Crouch, eds., 1990, pp. 326–55.

Crouch, Colin, and Alessandro Pizzorno, eds. 1978. *The Resurgence of Class Conflict in Western Europe since 1969.* Vols. 1 and 2. New York: Macmillan.

Crozier, Michel, Samuel P. Huntington, and Jogi Watanuke. 1975. *The Crisis of Democracy: Report on the Governability of Democracies to the Trilateral Commission.* New York: New York University Press.

Cusumano, Michael A. 1985. *The Japanese Automobile Industry: Technology and Management at Nissan and Toyota.* Cambridge, Mass.: Council on East Asian Studies, Harvard University.

CWA News (Communications Workers of America). Various issues.

Dabscheck, Braham. 1989. "A Survey of Theories of Industrial Relations." In Barbash and Barbash, eds., 1989, pp. 155–83.

Dahrendorf, Ralf. 1959. *Class and Class Conflict in Industrial Society.* Stanford: Stanford University Press.

Dalton, Russell J., Scott C. Flanagan, and Paul Allen Beck, eds. 1984. *Electoral Change in Advanced Industrial Democracies: Realignment or Dealignment?* Princeton: Princeton University Press.

Dankbaar, Ben, Ulrich Jürgens, and Thomas Malsch, eds. 1988. *Die Zukunft der Arbeit in der Automobilindustrie.* Berlin: Edition Sigma.

Deutsche Bundespost Geschäftsbericht. Various years.

Deutschmann, Christoph. 1987a. *Arbeitszeit in Japan: Organisatorische und organisationskulturelle Aspekte der "Rundumnutzung" der Arbeitskraft.* Frankfurt: Campus Verlag.

——. 1987b. "Economic Restructuring and Company Unionism: The Japanese Model." *Economic and Industrial Democracy* 8: 463–88.

Dickens, William T., and Jonathan S. Leonard. 1985. "Accounting for the Decline in Union Membership, 1950–1980.'' *Industrial and Labor Relations Review* 38, no. 3: 323–34.

Dogan, Mattei, and Dominique Pelassy. 1990. *How to Compare Nations: Strategies in Comparative Politics*. Chatham, N.J.: Chatham House.

Dohse, Knuth, Ulrich Jürgens, and Thomas Malsch. 1985. ''From 'Fordism' to 'Toyotism'? The Social Organisation of the Labor Process in the Japanese Automobile Industry.'' *Politics and Society* 14, no. 2: 115–46.

Dore, Ronald. 1973. *British Factory–Japanese Factory: The Origins of National Diversity in Industrial Relations*. Berkeley: University of California Press.

Dubinsky, David, and A. H. Raskin. 1977. *David Dubinsky: A Life with Labor*. New York: Simon and Schuster.

Dugger, William. 1990. ''The New Institutionalism: New But Not Institutionalist.'' *Journal of Economic Issues* 24 (June): 423–31.

Dunlop, John T. 1958. *Industrial Relations Systems*. New York: Holt and Company.

———. 1988. ''Have the 1980s Changed U.S. Industrial Relations?'' *Monthly Labor Review* 111 (May): 29–34.

Dyer, Davis, Malcolm S. Salter, and Alan M. Webber. 1987. *Changing Alliances*. Harvard Business School Project on the Auto Industry and the American Economy. Boston: Harvard Business School Press.

Eaton, Adrienne E., and Paula B. Voos. 1991. ''Unions and Contemporary Innovations in Work Organization, Compensation, and Employee Participation.'' In Mishel and Voos, eds., forthcoming.

Economist. Various issues.

Edinger, Lewis J. 1986. *West German Politics*. New York: Columbia University Press.

Edwards, Richard C. 1979. *Contested Terrain: The Transformation of the Workplace in the Twentieth Century*. New York: Basic Books.

Ehrenberg, Ronald G., and George H. Jakubson. 1990. ''Why WARN?'' *Regulation 13*, (Summer): 39–46.

Ellul, Jacques. 1964. *The Technological Society*. New York: Vintage Books.

Emerson, Charles. 1987. ''Building Assembly Automation.'' *American Machinist and Automated Manufacturing*, March, pp. 67–72.

EMF. 1988. ''EMF Calls for More Equitable Balance between European and Japanese Automobile Markets.'' Position Paper Adopted by the European Metalworkers' Federation Executive Committee on March 17, 1988, Brussels.

Enstrom, Peter, and Klas Levinson. 1982. *Industrial Relations in the Swedish Auto Industry*. Stockholm: Swedish Center for Working Life.

Express: Zeitung fü Betriebs- und sozialistische Gewerkschaftsarbeit. Various issues.

Ferman, Louis A., ed. 1984. *The Future of American Unionism. Annals of the American Academy of Political and Social Science*, vol. 473, May.

Financial Times. Various issues.

Fink, Gary, ed. 1977. *Labor Unions*. Westport, Conn.: Greenwood Press.

Flanagan, Robert J., David W. Soskice, and Lloyd Ulman. 1983. *Unionism, Economic Stabilization, and Incomes Policies: European Experience*. Washington D.C.: Brookings Institution.

Flynn, Michael S. 1984–85. ''U.S. and Japanese Automotive Productivity Comparisons: Strategic Implications.'' *National Productivity Review* 4 (Winter): 60–71.

Ford Annual Reports. Various years.

Ford-Werke AG Annual Reports. Various years.

Form, William H. 1973. "Field Problems in Comparative Research: The Politics of Distrust." In Armer and Grimshaw, eds., pp. 83–117.

Frankfurter Allgemeine Zeitung. Various issues.

Frankfurter Rundschau. Various issues.

Freeman, Richard B. 1989. "The Changing Status of Unionism around the World: Some Emerging Patterns." In Huang, ed., 1989, pp. 111–37.

Freeman, Richard B., and James L. Medoff. 1984. *What Do Unions Do?* New York: Basic Books.

Friedman, David. 1983. "Beyond the Age of Ford: The Strategic Basis of the Japanese Success in Automobiles." In Zysman and Tyson, eds., 1983, pp. 350–90.

Fujita, Eishi. 1988. "Labor Process and Labor Management: The Case of Toyota." Paper presented at an international symposium, The Micro Electronics Revolution and Regional Development, Labour Organization and the Future of Post-Industrializing Societies, University of Milan, April 11–13.

Galenson, Walter, ed. 1952. *Comparative Labor Movements*. New York: Prentice-Hall.

Garon, Sheldon. 1987. *The State and Labor in Modern Japan*. Berkeley: University of California Press.

General Motors Annual Reports. Various years.

George, Alexander L. 1979. "Case Studies and Theory Development: The Method of Structured, Focused Comparison." In Lauren, ed., 1979, pp. 43–68.

Der Gewerkschafter. Various issues.

Gilpin, Robert. 1987. *The Political Economy of International Relations*. Princeton: Princeton University Press.

Gnade, Albert, Karl Kehrmann, Wolfgang Schneider, Hermann Blanke, and Thomas Klebe. 1989. *Betriebsverfassungsgesetz: Basiskommentar*. Cologne: Bund-Verlag.

Golden, Miriam. 1988. *Labor Divided: Austerity and Working Class Politics in Contemporary Italy*. Ithaca: Cornell University Press.

Golden, Miriam, and Jonus Pontusson, eds. Forthcoming 1992. *Union Politics in Comparative Perspective: Economic Restructuring and Intra-Class Conflict*. Ithaca: Cornell University Press.

Goldfield, Michael. 1987. *The Decline of Organized Labor in the United States*. Chicago: University of Chicago Press.

Goldthorpe, John H., ed. 1984a. *Order and Conflict in Contemporary Capitalism*. Oxford: Oxford University Press.

———. 1984b. "The End of Convergence: Corporatist and Dualist Tendencies in Modern Western Societies." In Goldthorpe, ed., 1984a, pp. 315–43.

Gordon, David M., Richard Edwards, and Michael Reich. 1982. *Segmented Work, Divided Workers: The Historical Transformation of Labor in the U.S.* Cambridge: Cambridge University Press.

Gourevitch, Peter, Andrew Martin, George Ross, Chris Allen, Stephen Bornstein, and Andrei Markovits. 1984. *Unions and Economics Crisis: Britain, West Germany and Sweden*. London: Allen & Unwin.

Green, James R. 1980. *The World of the Worker: Labor in Twentieth-Century America*. New York: Hill and Wang.

Greenstone, J. David. 1977. *Labor in American Politics*. Chicago: University of Chicago Press.

Haber, William, ed. 1966. *Labor in a Changing America*. New York: Basic Books.

Halberstam, David. 1986. *The Reckoning*. New York: William Morrow.
Halfmann, Jost. 1989. "Social Change and Political Mobilization in West Germany." In Katzenstein, ed., 1989a, pp. 51–86.
Hammarström, Olle. 1987. "Swedish Industrial Relations." In Bamber and Lansbury, eds., 1987, pp. 187–207.
Hancock, M. Donald. 1989. *West Germany: The Politics of Democratic Corporatism*. Chatham, N.J.: Chatham House.
Handelsblatt. Various issues.
Harbison, Frederick H., and John R. Coleman. 1951. *Goals and Strategy in Collective Bargaining*. New York: Harper and Brothers.
Harbour, Jim. 1987. "The New UAW Contracts." *Automotive Industries*, December, p. 9.
Headey, Bruce. 1970. "Trade Unions and National Wages Policies." *Journal of Politics* 32: 407–39.
Heckscher, Charles C. 1988. *The New Unionism: Employee Involvement in the Changing Corporation*. New York: Basic Books.
Helstein, Ralph. 1966. "The Reaction of American Labor to Technological Change." In Haber, ed., 1966, pp. 68–81.
Herzenberg, Stephen. 1989. "Whither Social Unionism? Labor-Management Relations in the U.S. and Canadian Auto Industries." Paper Presented at the Conference on North American Labor Movements: Similarities and Differences, Center for International Affairs, Harvard University, February 3–5.
Hildebrandt, Eckart. 1981. "Der VW-Tarifvertrag zur Lohndifferenzierung." IIVG paper pre81–216, International Institute for Comparative Social Research, Wissenschaftszentrum Berlin, February.
———. 1988. "Work, Participation and Co-Determination in Computer-Based Manufacturing." In Knights and Willmot, eds., 1988, pp. 50–65.
Hinse, Ludger. 1989. "Offen streiten—gemeinsam handeln." *Metall: Zeitung für die Beschäftigten der Bochumer Opel-Werke*, no. 19, March, pp. 1–4.
Hirschhorn, Larry. 1984. *Beyond Mechanization: Work and Technology in a Post-Industrial Age*. Cambridge: MIT Press.
Hobsbawm, E. J. 1969. *Industry and Empire*. Harmondsworth, U.K.: Penguin Books.
Hoffmann, Jürgen. 1988. "Gewerkschaften in der Bundesrepublik: Zersetzungsprodukt oder strukturierender Faktor gesellschaftlicher Veränderungen?" In Müller-Jentsch, ed., 1988a, pp. 18–44.
Hohn, Hans-Willy. 1988. *Von der Einheitsgewerkschaft zum Betriebssyndikalismus: Soziale Schließung im dualen System der Interessenvertretung*. Edition Sigma, Wissenschaftszentrum Berlin.
Hölterhoff, H. 1988. *Funktion und Stellung des Meisters im Fertigungsbereich der Adam Opel AG*. Rüsselsheim: Opel, April 13.
Holusha, John. 1988. "Chrysler Keeps Acustar, But It Will Drop 4 Plants." *New York Times*, March 4, p. 29.
Howard, Robert. 1985. *Brave New Workplace*. New York: Viking Penguin.
Huang, Wei-Chiao, ed. 1989. *Organized Labor at the Crossroads*. Kalamazoo, Mich.: W. E. Upjohn Institute for Employment Research.
Huxley, Christopher, David Kettler, and James Struthers. 1986. "Is Canada's Experience 'Especially Instructive'?" In Lipset, ed., 1986a, pp. 113–32.
Hyman, Richard, and Wolfgang Streeck, eds. 1988. *New Technology and Industrial Relations*. Oxford: Basil Blackwell.

IG Metall. 1978; 1982; 1986; 1987. "Betriebliche Daten: Vergleichstabellen aus Werken der Automobil-Industrie." Frankfurt: IG Metall.

———. 1984a. *Aktionsprogramm: Arbeit und Technik.* Frankfurt: IG Metall.

———. 1984b. "Beschäftigungsrisiken in der Autoindustrie." Vorschläge der IG Metall zur Beschäftigungssicherung und zur Strukturpolitik in diesem Industriebereich. Frankfurt: IG Metall.

———. 1987. *Zukunft der Automobilindustrie: Symposium der IG Metall Wolfsburg in Zusammenarbeit mit dem Betriebsrat der Volkswagen AG Werk Wolfsburg.* IG Metall Verwaltungsstelle Wolfsburg.

Indergaard, Michael, and Michael Cushion. 1987. "Conflict, Cooperation, and the Global Auto Factory." In Cornfield, ed., 1987, pp. 203–28.

Inglehart, Ronald. 1984. "The Changing Structure of Political Cleavages in Western Society." In Dalton, Flanagan, and Beck, eds., 1984, pp. 25–69.

International Labour Organization. *Social and Labour Bulletins.* Various issues.

Ishikawa, Akihiro. 1984. "Japanese Trade-Unionism in a Changing Environment." *International Social Science Journal* 36, no. 2:271–83.

Jacobi, Otto, Bob Jessop, Hans Kastendiek, and Marina Regini, eds. 1986. *Technological Change, Rationalisation and Industrial Relations.* New York: St. Martin's Press.

Jacobi, Otto, and Walther Müller-Jentsch. 1990. "West Germany: Continuity and Structural Change." In Baglioni and Crouch, eds., 1990, pp. 127–53.

Jenkins, Peter. 1987. *Mrs. Thatcher's Revolution: The Ending of the Socialist Era.* Cambridge: Harvard University Press.

Johnson, Chalmers. 1982. *MITI and the Japanese Miracle: The Growth of Industrial Policy, 1925–1975.* Stanford: Stanford University Press.

Jones, Daniel. 1981. *Maturity and Crisis in the European Car Industry.* Brighton, U.K.: Sussex European Research Centre, University of Sussex.

———. 1987. "Analytic Notes for the BRIE Workshop on Production Reorganisation and Skills." Conference paper for meeting on Production Reorganization and Skills, Berkeley Roundtable on the International Economy, University of California, Berkeley, September 10–12.

Jürgens, Ulrich. 1987. "Gegenwärtige technisch- organisatorishce Wandlungsprozesse im Betrieb in arbeitspolitischer Perspektive." International Institute for Comparative Social Research/Labor Policy, Wissenschaftszentrum Berlin.

Jürgens, Ulrich, Knuth Dohse, and Thomas Malsch. 1986. "New Production Concepts in West German Car Plants." In Tolliday and Zeitlin, eds., 1986, pp.258–81.

Jürgens, Ulrich, Thomas Malsch, and Knuth Dohse. 1989. *Moderne Zeiten in der Automobilfabrik: Strategien der Produktionsmodernisierung im Länder- und Konzernvergleich.* Berlin: Springer-Verlag.

Juris, Hervey, Mark Thompson, and Wilbur Daniels, eds. 1985. *Industrial Relations in a Decade of Economic Change.* Madison, Wisc.: Industrial Relations Research Association.

Kamata, Satoshi. 1973. *Japan in the Passing Lane: An Insider's Account of Life in a Japanese Auto Factory.* New York: Pantheon Books.

Kassalow, Everett M. 1969. *Trade Unions and Industrial Relations: An International Comparison.* New York: Random House.

Katz, Harry. 1985. *Shifting Gears: Changing Labor Relations in the U.S. Automobile Industry.* Cambridge: MIT Press.

———. 1987. "The Industrial Relations Challenges Facing the World Auto Industry."

Briefing Paper for the First Policy Forum, International Motor Vehicle Program, May 5.

Katz, Harry C., Thomas A. Kochan, and Jeffrey Keefe. 1988. "Industrial Relations and Productivity in the U.S. Automobile Industry." *Brookings Papers on Economic Activity* 3:685–715.

Katz, Harry, and Charles F. Sabel. 1985. "Industrial Relations and Industrial Adjustment in the Car Industry." *Industrial Relations* 24, no. 3: 295–315.

Katzenstein, Peter J., ed. 1978. *Between Power and Plenty: Foreign Economic Policies of Advanced Industrial States*. Madison: University of Wisconsin Press.

——. 1985. *Small States in World Markets: Industrial Policy in Europe*. Ithaca: Cornell University Press.

——. 1987. *Policy and Politics in West Germany: The Growth of a Semisovereign State*. Philadelphia: Temple University Press.

——, ed. 1989a. *Industry and Politics in West Germany: Toward the Third Republic*. Ithaca: Cornell University Press.

——. 1989b. "Industry in a Changing West Germany." In Katzenstein, ed., 1989a, pp. 3–29.

——. 1989c. "Stability and Change in the Emerging Third Republic." In Katzenstein, ed., 1989a, pp. 307–53.

Keller, Maryann. 1988. "Japanese Cars Are Cheaper Than You Think." *Chilton's Automotive Industries* 168 (April): 15.

Kennedy, Donald, Charles Craypo, and Mary Lehman, eds. 1982. *Labor and Technology: Union Response to Changing Environments*. Department of Labor Studies, Pennsylvania State University.

Kenney, Martin, and Richard Florida. 1988. "Beyond Mass Production: Production and the Labor Process in Japan." *Politics and Society* 16: 121–58.

Kern, Horst, and Charles F. Sabel. 1990. "Gewerkschaften in offenen Arbeitsmärkten: Uberlegungen zur Rolle der Gewerkschaften in der industriellen Reorganisation." *Soziale Welt* 41, no. 2:144–66.

Kern, Horst, and Michael Schumann. 1984. *Das Ende der Arbeitsteilung?* Munich: C. H. Beck.

——. 1987. "Limits of the Division of Labour: New Production and Employment Concepts in West German Industry." *Economic and Industrial Democracy* 8 (May): 151–70.

——. 1989. "New Concepts of Production in West German Plants." In Katzenstein, ed., 1989a, pp. 87–110.

Kerr, Clark, John Dunlop, Frederick Harbison, and Charles Myers. 1960. *Industrialism and Industrial Man*. Cambridge: Harvard University Press.

Kittner, Michael, ed. 1988. *Gewerkschaftsjahrbuch 1988: Daten-Fakten-Analysen*. Cologne: Bund-Verlag.

Klebe, Thomas, and Siegfried Roth, eds. 1987. *Informationen ohne Grenzen: Computernetze und internationale Arbeitsteilung*. Hamburg: VSA-Verlag.

Kleiner, Morris M., Richard N. Block, Myron Roomkin, and Sidney W. Salsburg, eds. 1987. *Human Resources and the Performance of the Firm*. Madison, Wisc.: Industrial Relations Research Association.

Knights, David, and Hugh Willmott, eds. 1988. *New Technology and the Labour Process*. London: Macmillan.

Knights, David, Hugh Willmott, and David Collinson, eds. 1985. *Job Redesign: Critical Perspectives on the Labour Process*. Brookfield, Vt.: Gower.

Koch, Günther. 1987. *Arbeitnehmer steuern mit: Belegschaftsverstretung bei VW ab 1945*. Cologne Bund-Verlag.

Kochan, Thomas A., ed. 1985. *Challenges and Choices Facing American Labor*. Cambridge: MIT Press.

Kochan, Thomas A., Harry C. Katz, and Robert B. McKersie. 1986. *The Transformation of American Industrial Relations*. New York: Basic Books.

Kochan, Thomas A., and Michael J. Piore. 1984. "Will the New Industrial Relations Last? Implications for the American Labor Movement." In Ferman, ed. 1984, pp. 177–89.

Köhler, Christoph. 1981. *Betrieblicher Arbeitsmarkt und Gewerkschaftspolitik: Innerbetriebliche Mobilität und Arbeitsplatzrechte in der amerikanischen Automobilindustrie*. Munich: Campus.

Köhler, Christoph, and Hans Grüner. 1986. "Segmentation in Internal Labor Markets—the Case of the German Automobile Industry." Paper presented at the workshop Empirical Studies of Internal Labor Markets: Career Lines and Segmentation Processes in France and West Germany, University of Le Mans, September 11–12.

Köhler, Christoph, and Christoph Nuber. 1988. "Probleme und Strategien der Durchsetzung qualifizierter Gruppenarbeit." In Von Behr and Schultz-Wild, eds., 1988.

Korpi, Walter. 1980. "Industrial Relations and Industrial Conflict: The Case of Sweden." In Martin and Kassalow, eds., 1980, pp. 89–108.

Krafcik, John F. 1987. "Learning from NUMMI." Cambridge, Mass.: International Motor Vehicle Program, Massachusetts Institute of Technology, September.

——. 1988a. "Comparative Analysis of Performance Indicators at World Auto Assembly Plants." Master's thesis, Sloan School of Management, MIT, January.

——. 1988b. "Triumph of the Lean Production System." *Sloan Management Review* 30 (Fall): 41–52.

——. 1989. "A Diet for U.S. Manufacturers." *Technology Review* 92 (January): 28–36.

Kranzberg, Melvin, and Carroll W. Pursell, Jr., eds. 1967. *Technology in Western Civilization*. Vol. 2. New York: Oxford University Press.

Kuckelkorn, Wilfried. 1988. "Wege zur Gruppenarbeitsorganisation." In Roth and Kohl, eds., 1988, pp. 95–99.

Kurth, James R. 1979. "The Political Consequences of the Product Cycle: Industrial History and Political Outcomes." *International Organization* 33 (Winter): 1–34.

Kuwahara, Yasuo. 1987. "Japanese Industrial Relations." In Bamber and Lansbury, eds., 1987, pp. 211–31.

Labor Notes. Various issues.

Lange, Peter, George Ross, and Maurizio Vannicelli. 1982. *Unions, Change and Crisis*. London: George Allen & Unwin.

LaPalombara, Joseph. 1987. *Democracy Italian Style*. New Haven: Yale University Press.

Lash, Scott. 1985. "The End of Neo-corporatism?: The Breakdown of Centralised Bargaining in Sweden." *British Journal of Industrial Relations*. 23 (July): 215–39.

Lauren, Paul Gordon, ed. 1979. *Diplomacy: New Approaches in History, Theory and Policy*. New York: Free Press.

Lawrence, Paul R., and Davis Dyer. 1983. *Renewing American Industry*. New York: Free Press.

Lehmbruch, Gerhard, and Philippe Schmitter, eds. 1982. *Patterns of Corporatist Policy-Making*. Beverly Hills: Sage.

Levitan, Sar A., and Clifford M. Johnson. 1983. "Labor and Management: The Illusion of Cooperation." *Harvard Business Review* 83 (September-October): 8–16.

——. 1984. "The Changing Work Place." In Ferman, ed., 1984, pp. 116–27.

Lewin, David. 1987. "Industrial Relations as a Strategic Variable." In Kleiner et al., eds., 1987, pp. 1–41.

Lipset, Seymour Martin, ed. 1986a. *Unions in Transition: Entering the Second Century*. San Francisco: Institute of Contemporary Studies.

——. 1986b. "North American Labor Movements: A Comparative Perspective." In Lipset, ed. 1986a, pp. 421–52.

Lipset, Seymour Martin, and William Schneider. 1983. *The Confidence Gap: Business, Labor and Government in the Public Mind*. New York: Free Press.

Locke, Richard M. 1990a. "The Resurgence of the Local Union: Industrial Restructuring and Industrial Relations in Italy." *Politics and Society* 18, no. 3: 347–79.

——. 1990b. "In Search of Flexibility: Industrial Restructuring and Industrial Relations in the Italian Auto Industry." In Golden and Pontusson, eds., forthcoming.

Locke, Richard M., Thomas A. Kochan, and Chris R. Heye. 1988. "Industrial Restructuring and Industrial Relations in the U.S. and Itatian Automobile Industries." Paper presented at the Conference on Managing the Globalization of Business, Capri, Italy, October 28–29.

Lorwin, Val R. 1954. *The French Labor Movement*. Cambridge: Harvard University Press.

Los Angeles Times. Various issues.

Luebbert, Gregory M. 1987. "Social Foundations of Political Order in Interwar Europe." *World Politics* 39 (July): 449–78.

Luria, Daniel D. 1986. "New Labor-Management Models from Detroit?" *Harvard Business Review* 64 (September-October): 22–27.

——. 1987. "Technology, Work Organization, and Competitiveness: Automotive Subsystem Cost Reduction, 1986–1992." Ann Arbor: Center for Social and Economic Issues, Industrial Technology Institute, University of Michigan.

Lutz, Burkart. 1988. "Qualifizierte Gruppenarbeit—Überlegungen zu einem Orientierungskonzept technisch-organisatorischer Gestaltung." In Von Behr and Schultz-Wild, eds., 1988, pp. 99–112.

MacDuffie, John Paul, and Thomas A. Kochan. 1988. "Human Resources, Technology, and Economic Performance: Evidence from the Automobile Industry." *Industrial Relations Research Association Series: Proceedings of the Forty-first Annual Meeting*. Madison, Wisc.: Industrial Relations Research Association, pp. 159–71.

MacInnes, John. 1987. *Thatcherism at Work: Industrial Relations and Economic Change*. Milton Keynes, U.K.: Open University Press.

McKersie, Robert B. 1985. "Union Involvement in Entrepreneurial Decisions of Business." In Kochan, ed., 1985, pp. 149–66.

McLaughlin, Doris B. 1979. *The Impact of Labor Unions on the Rate and Direction of Technological Innovation*. Report prepared for the National Science Foundation, Grant PRA 77–15268. Institute of Labor and Industrial Relations, University of Michigan.

Mann, Eric. 1987a. "UAW Backs the Wrong Team." *Nation*, February 14, pp. 171–75.

——. 1987b. *Taking on General Motors: A Case Study of the UAW Campaign to Keep GM Van Nuys Open*. Los Angeles: Institute of Industrial Relations Publications, University of California at Los Angeles.

Markovits, Andrei S. 1986. *The Politics of the West German Trade Unions: Strategies of Class and Interest Representation in Growth and Crisis*. Cambridge: Cambridge University Press.

Markovits, Andrei S., and Christopher S. Allen. 1984. "Trade Unions and the Economic Crisis: The West German Case." In Gourevitch et al., 1984, pp. 89–188.

Marsden, David, Timothy Morris, Paul Willman, and Stephen Wood. 1985. *The Car Industry: Labour Relations and Industrial Adjustment*. London: Tavistock.

Marshall, Ray. 1987. *Unheard Voices: Labor and Economic Policy in a Competitive World*. New York: Basic Books.

Marshall, T. H. 1950. *Citizenship and Social Class*. Cambridge: Cambridge University Press.

Martin, Andrew. 1979. "The Dynamics of Change in a Keynesian Political Economy: The Swedish Case and Its Implications." In Crouch, ed., 1979, pp. 88–121.

——. 1984. "Trade Unions in Sweden: Strategic Responses to Change and Crisis." In Gourevitch et al., 1984, pp. 189–359.

Martin, Benjamin, and Everett M. Kassalow, eds. 1980. *Labor Relations in Advanced Industrial Societies: Issues and Problems*. Washington, D.C.: Carnegie.

Maurice, Marc, François Sellier and Jean-Jacques Silvestre. 1982. *Politique d'education et organisation industrielle en France et Allemagne*. Paris: Presses Universitaires de France.

——. 1986. *The Social Foundations of Industrial Power*. Cambridge: MIT Press.

Milkman, Ruth. 1982. "The Anti-Concessions Movement in the UAW." *Socialist Review* 12 (September–October): 19–42.

——. 1990. "Labor and Management in Uncertain Times: Renegotiating the Social Contract." Prepared for Wolfe, ed., forthcoming.

Milkman, Ruth, and Cydney Pullman. 1988. "Technological Change in an Auto Assembly Plant: A Case Study of GM-Linden." Final Report, Labor Institute for the United Automobile Workers and General Motors, New York, August.

Mishel, Larry, and Paula Voos, eds. 1991. *Unions and Economic Competitiveness*. Armonk, N.Y.: M. E. Sharpe.

Montgomery, David. 1979. *Workers' Control in America: Studies in the History of Work, Technology, and Labor Struggles*. Cambridge: Cambridge University Press.

Moody, Kim. 1988. *An Injury to All: The Decline of American Unionism*. London: Verso.

Müller-Jentsch, Walther, ed. 1988a. *Zukunft der Gewerkschaften: Ein internationaler Vergleich*. Frankfurt/Main: Campus Verlag.

——. 1988b. "Flexibler Kapitalismus und kollektive Interessenvertretung: Gewerkschaften in der dritten industriellen Revolution." In Müller-Jentsch, ed., 1988a, pp. 9–17.

——. 1988c. "Gewerkschaften im Umbruch: Ein qualitativer Vergleich." In Müller-Jentsch, ed., 1988a, pp. 265–88.

Muster, Manfred. 1988a. "Zum Stand der Gruppenarbeit in der Automobilindustrie in der Bundesrepublik." In Roth and Kohl, eds., 1988, pp. 259–81.

——. 1988b. "Neue Formen des Arbeitseinsatzes in hochautomatisierten Fertigungsbereichen der Automobilindustrie: Zur Problematik von Arbeitsteilung und Integration zwischen Anlagenüberwachung, Einlegearbeit und Instandhaltung." In Dankbaar, Jürgens, and Malsch, eds., 1988, pp. 95–113.

——. 1988c. "Das Doppelte Lottchen. Gruppenarbeit in der Automobilindustrie: Zwischen Managementstrategie und neuer Arbeitskultur." *Sozialismus*, no. 10, October–November, pp. 61–66.

Muster, Manfred, and Udo Richter, eds. 1990. *Mit Vollgas in den Stau: Automobilproduktion, Unternehmensstrategien und die Perspektiven eines ökologischen Verkehrssystems*. Hamburg: VSA-Verlag.

Muster, Manfred, and Manfred Wannöffel. 1989. *Gruppenarbeit in der Automobilindustrie*. Bochum: Joint publication of the IG Metall Verwaltungsstelle Bochum and the Gemeinsame Arbeitsstelle Ruhr-Universität Bochum.

National Academy of Engineering. Committee on Technology and International Economic and Trade Issues. Automobile Panel. 1982. *The Competitive Status of the U.S. Auto Industry*. Washington, D.C.: National Academy Press.

Negrelli, Serafino, and Ettore Santi. 1990. "Industrial Relations in Italy." In Baglioni and Crouch, eds., 1990, pp. 154–98.

New United Motor Manufacturing, Inc. 1985. "Agreement between New United Motor Manufacturing, Inc. and the UAW." July 1.

New York Times. Various issues.

Noble, David F. 1984. *Forces of Production: A Social History of Industrial Automation*. New York: Knopf.

Nohara, Hikari. 1988. "The Average Worker of a Large Japanese Company." Paper presented at an international symposium The Micro Electronics Revolution and Regional Development, Labour Organization and the Future of Post-Industrializing Societies, University of Milan, April 11–13.

Offe, Claus. 1981. "The Attribution of Public Status to Interest Groups: Observations on the West German Case." In Berger, ed., 1981, pp. 123–58.

Olson, Mancur. 1982. *The Rise and Decline of Nations: Economic Growth, Stagflation, and Social Rigidities*. New Haven: Yale University Press.

Ong, Paul Man. 1983. "Unions and Technological Efficiency in Auto and Steel." Ph.D. dissertation, University of California, Berkeley.

Oswald, Rudy. 1984. "New Directions for American Unionism." In Ferman, ed., 1984, pp. 141–48.

Pacific Telesis Annual Reports. Various years.

Parker, Mike. 1985. *Inside the Circle: A Union Guide to OWL*. Boston: Southend Press.

Parker, Mike, and Jane Slaughter. 1988. *Choosing Sides: Unions and the Team Concept*. Boston: South End Press.

Pellegrini, Claudio. 1987. "Italian Industrial Relations." In Bamber and Lansbury, eds., 1987, pp. 121–41.

Perlman, Selig. 1928. *A Theory of the Labor Movement*. New York: Macmillan.

Peterson, Richard B. 1986. "Research Design Issues in Comparative Industrial Relations." Paper presented at Industrial Relations Research Association Meeting, New Orleans, December 28–30.

——. 1987. "Swedish Collective Bargaining—A Changing Scene." *British Journal of Industrial Relations* 25 (March): 31–48.

Piore, Michael J. 1982. "American Labor and the Industrial Crisis." *Challenge* 25 (March-April): 5–11.

——. 1985. "Computer Technologies, Market Structure, and Strategic Union Choices." In Kochan, ed., 1985, pp. 193–204.

Piore, Michael J., and Charles F. Sabel. 1984. *The Second Industrial Divide: Possibilities for Prosperity*. New York: Basic Books.

Pontusson, Jonas. 1990. "The Politics of New Technology and Job Redesign: A

Comparison of Volvo and British Leyland." *Economic and Industrial Democracy* 11, no. 3, pp. 311–36.

Poole, Michael. 1984. *Theories of Trade Unionism: A Sociology of Industrial Relations*. London: Routledge & Kegan Paul.

Quinn, Dennis P. 1988. *Restructuring the Automobile Industry: A Study of Firms and States in Modern Capitalism*. New York: Columbia University Press.

———. 1989. "Dynamic Markets and Mutating Firms: The Changing Organization of Production in Automotive Firms." BRIE Research Paper 1, Berkeley Roundtable on the International Economy, University of California, Berkeley.

Raskin, A. H. 1986. "Labor: A Movement in Search of a Mission." In Lipset, ed., 1986a, pp. 3–38.

Rayback, Joseph. 1966. *A History of American Labor*. New York: Macmillan.

Regini, Marino. 1984. "The Conditions for Political Exchange: How Concertation Emerged and Collapsed in Italy and Great Britain." In Goldthorpe, ed., 1984a, pp. 124–42.

Rehmus, Charles M., Doris B. McLaughlin, and Frederick H. Nesbitt, eds. 1978. *Labor and American Politics*. Rev. ed. Ann Arbor: University of Michigan Press.

Rehn, Gösta. 1985. "Swedish Active Labor Market Policy: Retrospect and Prospect." *Industrial Relations* 24 (Winter): 62–89.

Rehn, Gösta, and Birger Viklund. 1990. "Changes in the Swedish Model." In Baglioni and Crouch, eds., 1990, pp. 300–325.

Reshef, Yonatan, and Alan I. Murray. 1988. "Toward a Neoinstitutionalist Approach in Industrial Relations." *British Journal of Industrial Relations* 26 (March): 85–97.

Reynolds, Morgan O. 1984. *Power and Privilege: Labor Unions in America*. New York: Universe Books.

Riffel, Michael, and Manfred Muster. 1989. *Bericht über das Planungsseminar "Neue Lackiererei Wolfsburg" vom 16.01–20.01.1989 in Hustedt/Celle*. Wolfsburg: Betriebsrat der Volkswagen AG, Wolfsburg.

Rose, Michael, and Bryan Jones. 1985. "Managerial Strategy and Trade Union Responses in Work Reorganisation Schemes at Establishment Level." In Knights, Willmott, and Collinson, eds., 1985, pp. 81–106.

Rosen, Sumner M. 1983. "The United States: American Industrial Relations System in Jeopardy?" In Barkin, ed., 1983, pp. 359–77.

Ross, Arthur, and Paul Hartman. 1960. *Changing Pattern of Industrial Conflict*. New York: John Wiley.

Ross, George, and Robert Fishman. 1989. "Changing Relationships between Labor and Intellectuals." *European Studies Newsletter*, Council for European Studies 19 (September–October): 1–5.

Roth, Siegfried. 1988. "Gruppenarbeit in deutschen Automobilbetrieben: Perspektiven aus gewerkschaftlicher Sicht." In Dankbaar, Jürgens, and Malsch, eds., 1988, pp. 185–210.

Roth, Siegfried, and Heribert Kohl, eds. 1988. *Perspektive: Gruppenarbeit*. Cologne: Bund-Verlag.

Roth, Siegfried, and Peter Königs. 1988. "Gruppenarbeit als Gestaltungsalternative bei CIM-Einsatz." In Roth and Kohl, eds., 1988, pp. 81–94.

Sabel, Charles F. 1981. "The Internal Politics of Trade Unions." In Berger, ed., 1981, pp. 209–44.

———. 1982. *Work and Politics: The Division of Labor in Industry.* Cambridge: Cambridge University Press.

Salisbury, Robert H. 1979. "Why No Corporatism in America?" In Schmitter and Lehmbruch, eds., 1979, pp. 213–30.

Salvati, Michele. 1981. "May 1968 and the Hot Autumn of 1969: The Responses of Two Ruling Classes." In Berger, ed., 1981, pp. 329–63.

Sandholtz, Wayne, and John Zysman. 1989. "1992: Recasting the European Bargain." *World Politics* 42: 95–128.

Sartori, Giovanni. 1970. "Concept Misformation in Comparative Politics." *American Political Science Review* 64 (December): 1033–53.

Scharpf, Fritz W. 1984. "Economic and Institutional Constraints of Full-Employment Strategies: Sweden, Austria, and West Germany, 1973–1982." In Goldthorpe, ed., 1984a, pp. 257–90.

Scherrer, Christoph. 1987. "The Conditions for Corporatist Interest Mediation in the United States." Paper presented at the ECPR Workshop on Meso-Corporatism, Amsterdam, April.

Schmidt, Manfred G. 1982. "Does Corporatism Matter? Economic Crisis, Politics and Rates of Unemployment in Capitalist Democracies in the 1970s." In Lehmbruch and Schmitter, eds., 1982, pp. 237–58.

Schmitter, Philippe C. 1974. "Still the Century of Corporatism?" In Schmitter and Lehmbruch, eds., 1979, pp. 7–52.

———. 1981. "Interest Intermediation and Regime Governability in Contemporary Western Europe and North America." In Berger, ed., 1981, pp. 285–330.

———. 1982. "Reflections on Where the Theory of Neo-Corporatism Has Gone and Where the Praxis of Neo-Corporatism May Be Going." In Lehmbruch and Schmitter, eds., 1982, pp. 259–79.

———. 1988. "Sectors in Modern Capitalism: Modes of Governance and Variations in Performance." Paper presented at the conference Markets, Institutions and Cooperation: Labour Relations and Economic Performance, sponsored by the International Economic Association and L'Associazione Italiana degli Economisti del Laboro, Venice, October 20–22.

Schmitter, Philippe C., and Gerhard Lehmbruch, eds. 1979. *Trends toward Corporatist Intermediation.* Beverly Hills: Sage.

Schneider, Volker. 1985. "Corporatist and Pluralist Patterns of Policy-Making for Chemicals Control: A Comparison between West Germany and the USA." In Cawson, ed., 1985, pp. 174–94.

Schultz-Wild, Rainer. 1988. "An der Schwelle zur Rechnerintegration—Zur Einführungsdynamik von CIM-Techniken in der Metallindustrie." In Von Behr and Schultz-Wild, eds., 1988, pp. 5–24.

Schultz-Wild, Rainer, and Christoph Köhler. 1985. "Introducing New Manufacturing Technology: Manpower Problems and Policies." *Human Systems Management* 5: 231–43.

Schumann, Michael, et al. 1988. "Trendreport über Rationisierungskonzepte und verläufe." SOFI working paper, Göttingen, April 29.

Scott, Bruce R. 1985. "National Strategies: Key to International Competition." In Scott and Lodge, eds., 1985, pp. 71–143.

Scott, Bruce R., and George C. Lodge, eds. 1985. *U.S. Competitiveness in the World Economy.* Boston: Harvard Business School Press.

Sengenberger, Werner, and Christoph Köhler. 1987. "Policies of Workforce Structure in the American and German Automobile Industry.'' In Tarling, ed., 1987, pp. 245–69.

Shaiken, Harley. 1985. *Work Transformed: Automation and Labor in the Computer Age*. New York: Holt, Rinehart and Winston.

Shimokawa, Koichi. 1986. ''Product and Labour Strategies in Japan.'' In Tolliday and Zeitlin, eds., 1986, pp. 224–43.

Siegel, Irving H., and Edgar Weinberg. 1982. *Labor-Management Cooperation: The American Experience*. Kalamazoo, Mich: W. E. Upjohn Insititute for Employment Research.

Silvia, Stephen J. 1987. ''Unions, Industrial Relations Systems and Crisis: The Impact of Sectoral Decline on West German and American Apparel Unions.'' Paper presented at the 1987 Annual Meeting of the American Political Science Association.
——. 1988. ''The West German Labor Law Controversy: A Struggle for the Factory of the Future.'' *Comparative Politics* 20 (January): 154–74.

Simmons, John, and William Mares. 1983. *Working Together*. New York: Knopf.

Slichter, Sumner H., James J. Healy, and E. Robert Livernash. 1960. *The Impact of Collective Bargaining on Management*. Washington, D. C.: Brookings Institution.

Social and Labour Bulletin. Various issues.

Solidarity (newspaper of the UAW). Various issues.

Sorge, Arndt, and Wolfgang Streeck. 1988. ''Industrial Relations and Technical Change: The Case for an Extended Perspective.'' In Hyman and Streeck, eds., 1988, pp. 19–47.

Sorge Arndt, and Malcolm Warner. 1987. *Comparative Factory Organisation: An Anglo-German Comparison of Management and Manpower in Manufacturing*. Aldershot, U.K.: Gower.

Der Spiegel. Various issues.

Spiro, Shimon E., and Ephraim Yuchtman-Yaar, eds. 1983. *Evaluating the Welfare State*. New York: Academic Press.

Stansbury, Jeff. 1985. ''NUMMI: A New Kind of Workplace.'' *Solidarity* 28 (August): 11–15.

Steinmo, Sven. 1989. ''Political Institutions and Tax Policy in the United States, Sweden, and Britain.'' *World Politics* 41 (July): 500–535.

Stephens, Evelyne Huber, and John D. Stephens. 1982. ''The Labor Movement, Political Power, and Workers' Participation in Western Europe.'' *Political Power and Social Theory* 3: 215–49.

Stieber, Jack, Robert B. McKersie, and D. Quinn Mills. 1981. *U.S. Industrial Relations, 1950–1980: A Critical Assessment*. Madison, Wisc.: Industrial Relations Research Association.

Strauss, George. 1982. ''Workers Participation in Management: An International Perspective.'' *Research in Organizational Behavior* 4: 173–265.

Straw, Ronnie J. 1984. ''The Effect of Divestiture on Collective Bargaining.'' Development and Research Department, Communications Workers of America. Paper presented at the annual meeting of the Industrial Relations Research Association, December.

Straw, Ronnie J., and Lorel E. Fogel. 1983. ''Technology and Employment in Telecommunications.'' *Annals of the American Academy of Political and Social Science*, vol. 470 (November): 163–70.

Streeck, Wolfgang. 1984a. *Industrial Relations in West Germany: A Case Study of the Car Industry*. New York: St. Martin's Press.

——. 1984b. "Neo-Corporatist Industrial Relations and the Economic Crisis in West Germany." In Goldthorpe, ed, 1984a, pp. 291–314.

——. 1985a. "Industrial Relations and Industrial Change in the Motor Industry: An International View." Public Lecture, University of Warwick, October 23.

——, ed. 1985b. "Industrial Relations and Technical Change in the British, Italian and German Automobile Industry: Three Case Studies." Discussion paper IIM/LMP 85–5. Wissenschaftszentrum Berlin, August.

——. 1987a. "Industrial Relations and Industrial Change: The Restructuring of the World Automobile Industry in the 1970s and 1980s." *Economic and Industrial Democracy* 8: 437–62.

——. 1987b. "Industrial Relations in West Germany: Agenda for Change." Discussion paper IIM/LMP 87–5. Wissenschaftszentrum Berlin, April.

——. 1989. "Successful Adjustment to Turbulent Markets: The Automobile Industry." In Katzenstein, ed., 1989a, pp. 113–56.

Streeck, Wolfgang, Josef Hilbert, Karl-Heinz van Kevelaer, Friederike Maier, and Hajo Weber. 1987. "The Role of the Social Partners in Vocational Training and Further Training in the Federal Republic of Germany." CEDEFOP Research Project No. 1236/1968, European Centre for the Promotion of Vocational Training.

Sturmthal, Adolf. 1983. *Left of Center: European Labor since World War II*. Urbana: University of Illinois Press.

Swenson, Peter. 1989. *Fair Shares: Unions, Pay, and Politics in Sweden and West Germany*. Ithaca: Cornell University Press.

——. 1990. "Employer Strategies, World Market Integration, and National Labor Movement Formation: Historical Lessons, Present Trends and Future Prospects." Paper presented at the Seventh International Conference of Europeanists, Washington, D.C., March 23–25.

Taira, Koji, and Solomon B. Levine. 1985. "Japan's Industrial Relations: A Social Compact Emerges." In Juris, Thompson, and Daniels, eds., 1985, pp. 247–300.

Tarling, Roger, ed. 1987. *Flexibility in Labour Markets*. London: Academic Press.

Tarrow, Sidney. 1989. *Democracy and Disorder: Protest and Politics in Italy, 1965–75*. Oxford: Oxford University Press.

——. 1990. *Struggle, Politics, and Reform: Collective Action, Social Movements, and Cycles of Protest*. Western Societies Program Occasional Paper 21, Center for International Studies, Cornell University.

Thelen, Kathleen. 1987a. "Union Structure and Strategies for the 1980s: Plant Mobilization in the IG Metall's Response to the Crisis." Paper presented at the Workshop Union Politics, Labor Militancy and Capital Accumulation, Cornell University, April 3–5; forthcoming as "The Politics of Flexibility in the German Metalworking Industries" in Golden and Pontusson, eds.

——. 1987b. "Continuity in Crisis: Labor Politics and Industrial Adjustment in West Germany, 1950–1987." Ph.D. dissertation, University of California, Berkeley.

Tolliday, Steven, and Jonathan Zeitlin, eds. 1986. *The Automobile Industry and Its Workers*. Cambridge, U.K.: Polity Press.

Towers, Brian. 1989. "Running the Gauntlet: British Trade Unions under Thatcher, 1979–1988." *Industrial and Labor Relations Review* 42, no. 2: 163–88.

Transnationals Information Exchange (TIE). 1987. *General Motors Counter Annual Report 1987*. Amsterdam: TIE.

Turner, Lowell. 1988a. "NUMMI in Context: A Comparative Perspective on the Politics of Work Reorganization in the U.S. Auto Industry." Paper presented at the annual meeting of the Western Political Science Association, San Francisco, March 10–12.

——. 1988b. "Are Labor-Management Partnerships for Competitiveness Possible in America? The U.S. Auto Industry Examined." BRIE Working Paper 36, Berkeley Roundtable on the International Economy, University of California, Berkeley, September.

Turner, Lowell, and Jana Gold. 1988. "Perceptions of Work Reorganization: Interviews with Business and Labor Leaders in Four Industries." BRIE Working Paper 34, Berkeley Roundtable on the International Economy, University of California, Berkeley, May.

Ulman, Lloyd. 1974. "Connective Bargaining and Competitive Bargaining." *Scottish Journal of Political Economy* 21 (June): 97–109.

——. 1987. "Who Wanted Collective Bargaining in the First Place?" *Industrial Relations Research Association Series: Proceedings of the Thirty-Ninth Annual Meeting.* Madison, Wisc.: Industrial Relations Research Association.

United Auto Workers. 1985. "UAW-NUMMI." Special Report to the Membership. June.

——. 1989. *Report of Owen Bieber, President, International United Union of Automobile, Aerospace and Agricultural Implement Workers of America (UAW). Part One: UAW in Action.* Submitted to the 29th Constitutional Convention. June 18–23, 1989, Anaheim, California.

U.S. Department of Labor, Bureau of Labor-Management Relations and Cooperative Programs. 1987. "New United Motor Manufacturing, Inc., and the United Automobile Workers: Partners in Training." No. 10, March.

U.S. Department of Labor, Bureau of Labor Statistics. 1968. *Manpower Planning for Technological Change: Case Studies of Telephone Operators.* Bulletin 1574. Washington, D.C.: U.S. Department of Labor.

Unterweger, Peter. 1986. "The Human Factor in the Factory of the Future." Remarks to the Engineering Society of Detroit, May 14.

——. 1990. "Group Work in West Germany: Union Guidelines." UAW Research Department. Overhead slides presented at the UAW-GM and UAW-Chrysler Paid Educational Leave program in Detroit.

Visser, Jelle. 1986. "Die Mitgliederentwicklung der westeuropäischen Gewerkschaften: Trends und Konjunkturen 1920–1983." *Journal für Sozialforschung* 26, no. 1: 3–34.

Volkswagen AG Annual Reports. Various issues.

Von Behr, Marhild, and Rainer Schultz-Wild, eds. 1988. *Arbeitsorganisation bei rechnerintegrierter Produktion: Zur einführung neuer Techniken in der Metallindustrie.* Munich: Institut für Sozialwissenschaftsliche Forschung.

Von Otter, Casten. 1983. "Labor Reformism Reshapes the System." In Barkin, ed., 1983, pp. 187–227.

Wallerstein, Michael. 1989. "Union Organization in Advanced Industrial Democracies." *American Political Science Review* 83 (June): 481–501.

Walton, John. 1973. "Standardized Case Comparison: Observations on Method in Comparative Sociology." In Armer and Grimshaw, eds., 1973, pp. 173–91.

Ward's Automotive Reports. Weekly. Various issues, 1983–89.

Wasserman, Wolfram. 1985. *Arbeitsgestaltung als Gegenstand gewerkschaftlicher Politik: Zur Soziologie der Arbeitsgestaltung am Beispiel der Textil- und Bekleidungsindustrie.* Bonn: Neue Gesellschaft.

Webber, Douglas. 1984. "German Social Democracy in the Economic Crisis: Un-employment and the Politics of Labour Market Policy in the Federal Republic of Germany from 1974 to 1982." Dissertation submitted to the School of Comparative Studies, Edinburgh, December.

———. 1987. "The Assault on the 'Fortress on the Rhine': The Politics of Telecom-munications Deregulation in the Federal Republic of Germany." Paper presented at the conference of the Council of European Studies, Washington, D.C., October 30-November 1.

Wiesenthal, Helmut. 1987. *Strategie und Illusion: Rationalitätsgrenzen kollektiver Akteure am Beispiel der Arbeitszeitpolitik 1980–1985*. Frankfurt am Main: Campus Verlag.

Wilensky, Harold L. 1976. *The "New Corporatism," Centralization, and the Welfare State*. London: Sage.

———. 1983. "Political Legitimacy and Consensus: Missing Variables in the Assess-ment of Social Policy." In Spiro and Yuchtman-Yaar, eds., 1983, pp. 51–74.

Wilensky, Harold L., and Lowell Turner. 1987. *Democratic Corporatism and Policy Linkages: The Interdependence of Industrial, Labor-Market, Incomes, and Social Policies in Eight Countries*. Institute of International Studies, Research Series 69, University of California, Berkeley.

Willman, Paul. 1988. "The Future of the Assembly Line in the U.K. Car Industry." In Dankbaar, Jürgens, and Malsch, eds., 1988, pp. 211–25.

Willman, Paul, and Graham Winch. 1985. *Innovation and Management Control: Labour Relations at BL Cars*. Cambridge: Cambridge University Press.

Wilson, Graham K. 1982. "Why Is There No Corporatism in the United States?" In Lehmbruch and Schmitter, eds., 1982, pp. 219–36.

Windmuller, John P., et al. 1987. *Collective Bargaining in Industrialized Market Economies: A Reappraisal*. Geneva: International Labour Organization.

Windolf, Paul. 1989. "Productivity Coalitions and the Future of Corporatism." *In-dustrial Relations* 28 (Winter): 1–20.

Windolf, Paul, and Hans-Willy Hohn. 1984. *Arbeitsmarktchancen in der Krise: Be-triebliche Rekrutierung und soziale Schließung*. Frankfurt: Campus Verlag.

Wolfe, Alan, ed. 1991. *The Recentering of America: American Society in Transition*. Berkeley: University of California Press, forthcoming.

Womack, James P., Daniel T. Jones, and Daniel Roos. 1990. "The Power of Lean Production." *New York Times Magazine, Part Two (The Business World)*, Septem-ber 23, pp. 20–23, 34–38.

Wood, Stephen. 1986. "The Cooperative Labour Strategy in the US Auto Industry." *Economic and Industrial Democracy* 7: 415–47.

———. 1988. "Some Observations on Industrial Relations in the British Car Industry, 1985–87." In Dankbaar, Jürgens, and Malsch, eds., 1988, pp. 229–48.

Zysman, John. 1977. *Political Strategies for Industrial Order: State, Market, and Industry in France*. Berkeley: University of California Press.

———. 1983. *Governments, Markets, and Growth: Financial Systems and the Politics of Industrial Change*. Ithaca: Cornell University Press.

Zysman, John, and Laura Tyson, eds. 1983. *American Industry in International Competition: Government Policies and Corporate Strategies*. Ithaca: Cornell Uni-versity Press.

Index

Abernathy, William J., 36–37
Adenauer, Konrad, 96
Administration Caucus (NUMMI), 56, 60, 69
AEU. *See* Amalgamated Engineering Union
AFG. *See* Work Promotion Act
AFL. *See* American Federation of Labor
AFL-CIO, xi, 37, 177. *See also* American Federation of Labor; Congress of Industrial Organizations
Agnelli, Giovanni, 207
Agreement on Efficiency and Participation (Sweden), 212–13
AGVs. *See* Automatic Guided Vehicles
Alli, Al, 80, 82
Altmann, Norbert, 109
Altshuler, Alan, 3, 42
Amalgamated Clothing and Textile Workers Union (ACTWU), 193, 195
Amalgamated Engineering Union (AEU), 201n.1, 202, 204
American Federation of Labor (AFL), 35–36. *See also* AFL-CIO
American Motors, 37
Ameritech, 182
Apparel industry, 24, 102, 175, 192–97
Apprenticeship system, 143, 144–45, 160, 164
Arbeitsforderungsgesetz (AFG). *See* Work Promotion Act
Arbitration, 36, 39, 40, 48, 99, 177
AT&T, 187, 236

and CWA, 117–18, 176–77, 178, 179–80, 182, 183
and Deutsche Bundespost compared, 184, 186, 190–92
divestiture of, 176, 178, 181, 190, 191
Audi, 95, 106
Auer, Peter, 213
Austria, 16, 26n.19, 165, 234
Automatic Guided Vehicles (AGVs), 70, 71, 75
Automation, 44, 46–47n.14, 70, 71, 75, 169
flexible, 107, 43
See also Technology
Automobile industry
in Great Britain, 24, 200–202, 204, 236
in Italy, 24, 206–8, 236
in Japan, 24, 25, 218–19, 220
methodology used in studying, 19–20
summary of findings regarding, 21–25
in Sweden, 213–14
Automobile industry (United States)
assessment of workers' interest representation in, 52–53, 86–90
combined adversarial and cooperative approaches in, 236
decline of, 33–34
explanations for industrial relations contrasts with West German automobile industry, 166–71
history of industrial relations in, 35–41
institutional factors affecting work reorganization in, 163–66

265

Library of Congress Cataloging-in-Publication Data

Turner, Lowell.
  Democracy at work : labor and the politics of new work
organization / Lowell Turner.
      p. cm.—(Cornell studies in political economy)
  Includes bibliographical references and index.
  ISBN 0-8014-2627-8 (alk. paper)
    1. Industrial relations.   2. Trade-unions.   3. Industrial management—Employee participa-
tion.   4. Industrial relations.   I. Title.   II. Series.
HD6483.T87   1991
331—dc20   91-55049

Cornell Studies in Political Economy

EDITED BY PETER J. KATZENSTEIN

Collapse of an Industry: Nuclear Power and the Contradictions of U.S. Policy, by John L. Campbell

Power, Purpose, and Collective Choice: Economic Strategy in Socialist States, edited by Ellen Comisso and Laura D'Andrea Tyson

The Political Economy of the New Asian Industrialism, edited by Frederic C. Deyo

Dislodging Multinationals: India's Strategy in Comparative Perspective, by Dennis J. Encarnation

Democracy and Markets: The Politics of Mixed Economies, by John R. Freeman

The Misunderstood Miracle: Industrial Development and Political Change in Japan, by David Friedman

Patchwork Protectionism: Textile Trade Policy in the United States, Japan, and West Germany, by H. Richard Friman

Politics in Hard Times: Comparative Responses to International Economic Crises, by Peter Gourevitch

Closing the Gold Window: Domestic Politics and the End of Bretton Woods, by Joanne Gowa

Cooperation among Nations: Europe, America, and Non-tariff Barriers to Trade, by Joseph M. Grieco

Pathways from the Periphery: The Politics of Growth in the Newly Industrializing Countries, by Stephan Haggard

The Philippine State and the Marcos Regime: The Politics of Export, by Gary Hawes

Reasons of State: Oil Politics and the Capacities of American Government, by G. John Ikenberry

The State and American Foreign Economic Policy, edited by G. John Ikenberry, David A. Lake, and Michael Mastanduno

Pipeline Politics: The Complex Political Economy of East-West Energy Trade, by Bruce W. Jentleson

The Politics of International Debt, edited by Miles Kahler

Corporatism and Change: Austria, Switzerland, and the Politics of Industry, by Peter J. Katzenstein